Georgie Lucas is a writer and  appeared in a wide variety of p *Telegraph, Stylist, Grazia, Po*

'This might be one of the mos you'll read ... Tender, heart-b quent, its pages flow with love, hope and sometimes even laughter' *Evening Standard*

'Extraordinary ... earth-shattering ... so full of love' **Anita Rani,** *Woman's Hour*

'Profoundly moving' *The Times*

'A heart-wrenching and hopeful book ... about the redeeming power of love ... A meditation on the meaning of life' *Sunday Post*

'Brave and unflinching' *The i*

'A testimony to empathy, care and humanity when life is at its hardest' *Stylist*

'[Lucas's] valuable story is important not just for its own sake; it could help us to speak more, and better, about an unfathomable experience that too many parents endure' *TLS*

'A message from one mother to another, reminding them they are not alone' *Mail on Sunday*

'Beautifully written, searingly honest and profoundly uplifting, this is a book to remind us what is most important in life; a book for anyone who has suffered a loss, or ever will ... In short, it is a book for everyone' **Katherine Webb**

'An extraordinary read ... This tender, exquisite memoir explores devastating loss and grief, yes, but most of all it is a book about the surpassing, redemptive power of love ... I cannot stop thinking about it' **Lucy Foley**

'Extraordinarily brave and tender ... A book that sings with love and hope' **Dr Rachel Clarke**

'The most beautiful thing I have ever read; a heart-breaking account of a tragic death that is also a profound, lyrical, sometimes funny and ultimately joyful meditation on the meaning of life. The book of the year, perhaps the decade' **Tom Bradby**

'Heart-breaking, beautiful, important, full of integrity, powerful and honest, inspiring and full of the wonder of women and love ... Georgie is a wonderful writer, clear and honest, but never sentimental. [It is] full of strength and hope and I've no doubt will both help many and also give comfort to other mothers and fathers who have lost a child' **Kate Mosse**

'The warmest, most beautiful book on love you'll read this year ... by turns funny, observant, deeply moving and always immensely readable ... an absolute must-read, whatever your experience of loss ... an extraordinary gift of a book by a truly brilliant writer' **Kat Brown**

'This quietly devastating account of birth, pain and loss is gripping ... Georgie Lucas portrays the world of the NICU in minute, often poetic detail, finding warmth and humour when life seems bleakest ... An unflinching and beautiful book, ending on a note of light and love in a way that should inspire us all' **Sophie Kinsella**

'Georgie Lucas writes superbly with her spare and unsentimental prose' **Miriam Stoppard**

'Heart-breaking and beautiful' **Sophie Ellis-Bextor**

'An amazing story, delicately but powerfully told ... Georgie's observations of people, places and events ring so true – they are so often searingly accurate and also so wonderfully compassionate' **Dr Richard Shepherd**

'Heart-breaking in the sense of loss and tragedy, but also uplifting in the way the love sings from each page ... Really quite extraordinary' **John Nichol**

'I was moved to tears and transported to a place no one ever wants to imagine, but it also reminded me about what really matters, it is a book filled with so much more than sadness, it wrapped me in warmth and so much love' **Izzy Judd**

'An amazing story of human kindness ... I've got huge admiration for Georgie for writing the book that no one would ever want to write, for having the courage to tell a difficult story and the talent to tell it beautifully' **Marina Fogle**

'I read this extraordinary book in a day and although a hugely emotional story, it is told with such love and humility that somehow it manages to create a feeling of hope amongst the heartbreak ... *If Not For You* is a reminder to appreciate the love we can find through experiences we never imagined would be part of our story' **Pippa Vosper**

'Incredibly moving and impeccably written ... The prose is understated and unsentimental, and all the more powerful for it ... It made me weep and yet somehow left me uplifted ... Above all, it made me think about what it truly means to be a parent and to love unselfishly' **Jennie Agg**

'The most beautiful book I've read this year ... Heart-wrenching, hopeful, brave and profound ... Georgie's words made me cry and laugh out loud' **Hannah Barrett**

'Georgie's story is filled with extraordinary details and observations, of all shapes and sizes, and amazing people. Profoundly sad and utterly affecting, it's full of love, unbelievable amounts of love, and it's a privilege to have been allowed to share it. As I did so, I just wanted to hug her, and at the same time tell her she is a completely brilliant writer' **Elizabeth Noble**

IF NOT FOR YOU

A MEMOIR

GEORGIE LUCAS

abacus
books

ABACUS

First published in Great Britain in 2022 by Little, Brown
This paperback edition published in Great Britain in 2023 by Abacus

1 3 5 7 9 10 8 6 4 2

A CIP catalogue record for this book
is available from the British Library.

Paperback ISBN 978-0-349-14483-2

Typeset in Bembo by M Rules
Printed and bound in Great Britain by Clays Ltd, Elcograf S.p.A.

Papers used by Abacus are from well-managed forests
and other responsible sources.

Abacus
An imprint of
Little, Brown Book Group
Carmelite House
50 Victoria Embankment
London EC4Y 0DZ

An Hachette UK Company
www.hachette.co.uk

www.littlebrown.co.uk

For my darling Grey.
*You will, for the rest of my days, be quietly
curled into my neck, fingers resting gently on my
chest, reminding me what matters most.*

The Uses of Sorrow

(In my sleep I dreamed this poem)

Someone I loved once gave me
a box full of darkness.

It took me years to understand
that this, too, was a gift.

Mary Oliver

PART ONE

THE HOUSE ON THE BEACH

1

17 November

Birth day

The anaesthetist slides the needle into my spine.

'Deep breaths, stay nice and still.'

Then I'm lying on my back, a blue curtain rising from somewhere around my chest, masking the lower half of my body.

'Knife to skin ...'

I feel nothing. The doctors talk in low voices. Jessica is explaining what she's doing to a student doctor. I catch the odd comment.

'I've done this by torchlight in Gambia ...'

I murmur a thank-you into thin air for this fully staffed, properly lit operating theatre in Kent.

I grip Mike's hand. Chest up, every part of me is shaking. My teeth chatter. Below the curtain I am still, except my insides, which are being carefully reshuffled. I remember the antenatal class description – 'like someone doing washing-up in your tummy'. The routine is familiar, it's the same process as seventeen months ago, but the circumstances are entirely alien. *Please let this baby be OK, please let this baby be OK, please let this baby be OK ...*

'It's almost here ...' Jessica looks over the curtain. 'Are you ready to meet your baby?'

When they first pull the tiny bundle out of my abdomen, it's so tightly curled that no one can see if it's a boy or girl.

There is no cry.

Then, 'It's a little boy. We have another son.' Mike's eyes are lined with tears.

A little brother for Finn. A head peeks briefly over the curtain and then he's whisked away.

Mike is ushered to the neonatal side room. As Jessica sews me up, he rushes back and forth, keeping up a commentary on the little boy who's been taken from me far too soon. The portable incubator is wheeled past me as our son is taken to the neonatal intensive care unit. It stops briefly by my head. I thank an upside-down consultant and several smiling nurses. I catch a glimpse of skin through the plastic, a transparent mask, a knitted hat, a striped blanket.

Double doors swing open and he's gone.

2

18 November

One day old

I've tried to rest. Shock, painkillers, the after-effects of anaes-
thesia – a potent cocktail. I ricochet between deep sleep and
being startlingly alert. I have my own room, and one of the
midwives has brought a camp bed for Mike. He's snoozing
under a blue hospital blanket. I look out of the window. We
are on one side of a courtyard. Fluorescent corridor lights
shine through half-closed blinds. We're in Kent, in a hospital
I didn't know existed until yesterday morning. Our baby is
here. No longer inside my tummy. In the world. But not our
world. Our world is at home, in London.

Mike has been with him, intermittently, sending me photos
from his cot-side. A different ward, a different section of the
hospital. I know it takes a few minutes to walk there because
of the gap between him leaving me and the first pictures. I
know he has to ring a buzzer. But I don't know where he
is. It's strange to think that if I needed to get to my baby, I
wouldn't know the way. He's doing well. On oxygen, but no
ventilator for now, which the midwives say is encouraging.
He's strong. I have to wait; I have to be well enough to go. The
doctors need to leave a certain amount of time post C-section
before I move around too much. I suppose they don't want
mothers passing out in the NICU.

This wasn't how it was supposed to be. He isn't a November
baby; he isn't a Kent baby.

Except, of course, he is.

*

Some time after midnight, Mike messages to say they're putting a tube into his lung.

'But they're laughing and joking, so I think it's OK.' That must be a good sign, but the frustration that I can't be beside him floods through me. I try to lull myself back to sleep. At some point the exhaustion takes over, because when I next wake the room feels different.

'Do you think he's Grey?' Mike asks suddenly.

It's the name that's somewhere near the top of our list.

'I love Grey,' I say. 'I think it suits him. Have you tried it?'

'Yes,' he says. 'I think it suits him too, but I want you to see him properly first, then we can decide.' He settles back in his fold-out bed at the end of mine. The room is L-shaped, so he's at right angles to me, his head by my feet.

'I really want him to have a name as soon as possible. In that cot in the NICU, without me beside him, he has no identity.'

It's four in the morning, eight long hours since I glimpsed my baby. Finally, Mike messages to say the NICU doctors are happy for me to come and see him.

'He looks like Finny now,' he writes, 'but there are a lot of wires, to prepare you.'

I wonder if I'll be scared.

The midwife on the ward has brought us an unwieldy old wheelchair and Mike is pushing me along the hallway to the neonatal unit. The wheels squeak on the linoleum. Two sets of double doors guard the entrance, manned via video security. The front desk is dark, silent. The lighting is clinical, the corridors eerily empty.

I look around. It's unfamiliar. Of course it is, we're in a different section from A&E, where I arrived yesterday. I know the hospital is all on one level, low to the ground; I remember thinking when I walked in from the car park yesterday morning how different it is from the London high-rise I'm used to. The building is bland, serviceable; sliding doors, PVC windows. A stark contrast to the blue skies and beach walks we'd planned for this trip.

Mike wheels me to the furthest room from the NICU entrance. Stuck-on letters above the door spell out 'Intensive Therapy Unit'. Scrubs-clad nurses walk purposefully to and fro. Hand-washing stations are dotted along the corridor, one right outside the ITU. Faded printouts demonstrate the in-house hand-washing technique. I lean awkwardly out of the wheelchair to follow their instructions. Mike passes me a paper towel, then squirts alcohol gel into my outstretched palms. I rub them together as he pushes open the door.

The room is divided in half, four incubators on each side. Full-length windows line the back wall, blinds down. There's quiet urgency here, the soft murmur of focused voices punctuated by low whirring and rhythmic bleeps. The lights are dim but I feel blinded. Our baby's incubator is on the right-hand side, furthest from the door. Mike wheels me over to him, navigating through the other incubators, past trolleys, monitors, wheelie doctors' stools, and parks me beside the rounded tank, the baby tank.

I peer through the plastic at our tiny son, plugged into numerous wires. Lines run from his translucent arms and miniature tummy. His face is hidden by the strapping of a ventilator, a tiny ski mask covers his eyes. He weighs three and a half pounds – a good size for a 'thirty-one-weeker', I'm told. Finn weighed twice that, and more. My eyes run over the lines of his bones, his lack of flesh.

My gaze rests on his hands. Exquisite, expressive fingers furl and unfurl, fluttering over the web of wires and tubes. His minuteness is otherworldly, amplified by the blue light of the jaundice lamp. Away from the intensity of theatre, the single snatched glance, I have time to look at him, so staggeringly unready for the world.

His head arches, as if he is looking around, but his eyes are covered. The blankets move as he stretches his legs, and the delicate hands flutter over the tube that's stuck to his mouth.

His lips move around it, as if forming words he can't say. He doesn't make a sound. There's something breathtakingly calm about this tiny boy. I am the only one of us who is distressed, I'm sure of it. Every part of him exudes a quiet serenity. As I watch him, I feel my breath slow, my shoulders lower almost imperceptibly. Somewhere inside me a knot of tension loosens, just a little.

'Grey is perfect,' I whisper. 'He's perfect, MG.'

'I'm Sofia, you are Georgina? I've met Mike already.' The nurse looks up from a giant clipboard at the end of Grey's incubator. As she smiles at me, deep dimples appear in her rounded cheeks. She is in pale blue scrubs with a silk scarf in a darker blue looped around her head. She makes the ensemble look very elegant.

'Yes – Georgie.' Three syllables make me feel like I'm in trouble.

'Congratulations,' she says. 'He's gorgeous.' She looks fondly into the incubator.

I smile a thank-you. The first congratulations; they feel strangely momentous. In the anxiety, the alien set-up, part of me has forgotten that I've given birth to my son. New life. Somewhere amongst the worry and fear, there must be room for celebration.

I ask if I can touch him, feeling absurd. Sofia wheels me back and adjusts the incubator so it's in line with my chair, then shows me how best to handle him.

'They like a firm grasp,' she explains. 'Your natural instinct is to stroke him gently, but doctors stroke the skin hunting for veins, and they quickly learn to associate it with pain.' She places one hand around his head, and with the other gathers up his spindly legs, holding them tightly into his body – 'Like this: we call it hand hugging.' She takes her hands away. My turn. I mimic her position and immediately his little feet push back. A wave of connection runs into my arms, a mild electric current. Our first meeting.

'See, he likes it.' She's smiling. 'They like authority – they want to feel like you know what you're doing.'

But I don't know what I'm doing. As she turns away to check his charts, tears come. I can feel the same love that flooded my being when Finn was born. But what use is it here? It bubbles away, then pours out, with my tears. I worry none of it finds its way to him. The incubator is a shield, my love washing off its sides, cocooning him from the good as well as the bad.

I can't make sense of it; I'm in a neonatal unit in a hospital in Kent, being taught how to touch my son. I can't even get to him properly, the incubator windows are obstacles; it's hard to find a position that feels natural, comfortable, to reach him. I give up and loop my hands through the side doors, my arms pressing awkwardly against their frames.

I grip Grey's fragile little body and let tears fall silently into my lap.

We'd escaped London for the seaside; a last weekend away as three before we became four. Before I became too unwieldy for beach walks, before baby prep got under way and the real countdown began. Finn and I packed up the car, leaving London later than I'd planned, just in time to catch the Friday rush hour. Mike was meeting us later, on the train. We sat in standstill traffic from the end of our road and barely made it to Greenwich Park by the time it was getting dark.

Then Finn was sick. As I stood in the drizzle, wet-wiping vomit from his sweatshirt in the bus lane by Blackheath, I'd considered giving up on the whole idea. It was only the queue of traffic heading back in the other direction that convinced me to press on. 'What an adventure,' I'd said brightly, as Finn's supper got later and later. I had no idea then how much of an adventure it would turn out to be.

Three hours later, we arrived in Seasalter and the journey was forgotten. Finny was wide-eyed; our little house was right on the beach, double doors tumbling out onto decking and sand.

I brought in his things while he pottered around, exploring each of the rooms. I lit the wood-burning stove, cooked him pasta – his favourite – then popped him on a pile of cushions and anchored him to the chair with a couple of tea towels.

He danced to Children in Need while we waited for Mike's train to arrive, remote control clutched in one hand, his little dungareed bottom bouncing up and down in time with the music. As I filmed him for his dada, laughing to myself, his sibling seemed to want to join in, wriggling energetically in my tummy. Suddenly Finn turned, wobbled purposefully towards me and took my hand, gesturing that I should dance with him. My rhythmic movement seemed to lull his brother or sister to sleep because the bladder-kicking subsided.

The sun was shining on Saturday morning; we'd picked a beautiful weekend. After a breakfast of eggs, croissants and orange juice we walked along the beach to Whitstable, amongst weekend dog-walkers and groups of runners. Finn had given walking his best shot, but decided Mike's shoulders offered a better vantage point for spotting trains on the branch line and approaching 'woof-woofs'. As we wandered the postcard cobbled streets, meandering in and out of shops and cafés, we fantasised about living there, giving up London for a cottage by the sea.

Mike bought a brushed cotton checked shirt – ready for the beachside life.

'How many weeks?' asked the shop-owner, a vibrant woman with bobbed hair, hoop earrings and a keen eye for Scandinavian designers, who'd moved from south-east London when her children were small.

'Thirty-one tomorrow,' I said.

'Do you know what you're having?'

'No – surprise baby.'

'Oh, that's lovely – I always had surprises – seems it's rare these days.'

'And how old is this little man?' She smiled down at Finn, who was riffling through the box of toys strategically placed by the changing room.

'He'll be one and a half in December.'

'You'll have your hands full,' she laughed. 'But it's a wonderful time – treasure every moment. Mine are all grown up now.' She paused, perhaps thinking back. 'I love babies.'

As she'd folded Mike's shirt, wrapping it in crisp tissue and slipping it into a canvas bag, I'd felt a shiver of excitement for what lay ahead.

We'd found a shack for lunch near the sea, with an open hatch and a scattering of wooden picnic tables. We'd chosen a table right next to the oyster-shucker, with only the harbour wall and a narrow path between us and the beach, both strewn with people making the most of the November sunshine.

Finn shovelled in fish, scampi and chips, his first real taste of salt, a look of ecstasy on his face. Mike had eaten an oyster for me, and we'd promised we'd be back in April to introduce the new baby to the seaside, so I could eat some myself. I'd looked at him, at our happy little boy, felt the baby wriggling in my tummy, thought how lucky I was, how content.

After lunch we'd wandered around the waterfront. Mike bought a fish pie and an enormous bag of clams for our supper from a place where the fishing boats docked. A suddenly over-tired Finny scuppered the walk back along the beach – we could always do that tomorrow – and we'd managed to track down an elusive Whitstable taxi.

'Kent born and bred, I am,' the cabbie told us, 'but I escape every summer to the Costa del Sol. It's not good here in the summer, too busy. Especially when the oyster festival is on ... Well, this is you.'

I realised we'd stopped opposite our little place on the beach. We piled out, Finny asleep in Mike's arms, and I paid the fare through the front window.

'Ta, love,' the cabbie said. 'Oh, and best of luck with the next one.' He pointed at my stomach and tipped the peak of his flat cap.

'Thank you.'

I'd waved as he deftly swivelled the wheel in a three-point turn.

While Finn had a late-afternoon nap, Mike revved up the wood-burning stove and pulled a pack of cards from his backpack.

'Shithead?'

'I'm kind of bored of shithead,' I said. 'Is there something else?'

'Knock poker?'

It was easy to learn, immediately addictive, and ate up the hour Finn slept. Then the two of them sat on the floor and played. Finny had quickly invented a new game: creeping as close to the stove as he dared before extending his hands, making an exaggerated 'hot' noise and racing back to Mike.

Darkness fell, and the lights from the opposite shore twinkled on the rippling waves as the tide crept up the beach, and only the occasional crunch of a late-afternoon dog-walker interrupted the rhythms of the sea. I lay back on the sofa and curled my feet beneath me, my book propped on my rounded tummy, while bath-time splashing and squealing drowned out the quiet of our waterside spot.

Freshly scrubbed, combed and dressed for bed, Finny climbed up next to me for stories and snuggles.

'Baby,' he said, looking mildly disgruntled, then prodded at my chunky knit with a pudgy forefinger, as if it was in his way. He managed to overcome the inconvenience of his unborn sibling for three readings of *Each Peach Pear Plum*, pushing away *You're All My Favourites* – one of the 'preparing for a sibling' books a friend had recommended.

We waved goodnight to the sea and I carried him into his bedroom, then realised I couldn't bend far enough to lower him into our travel cot. I kissed him goodnight and handed him to Mike, wondering how the next couple of months were going to work as I became too big to lift him.

He went silent almost immediately – a combination of fresh air and new surroundings. Mike hooked up his phone to the house speakers, so Cat Stevens could help him make linguine alle vongole for supper. It's only now, thinking back, that I remember it was what we'd eaten the night before Finn was born, at our favourite little Italian in Peckham.

I'd woken early that Sunday morning.

Something made me glance at my vegetable pregnancy app – I'd checked each week with Finn, counting down the days, but I barely remembered this time round.

'Jarl is the size of asparagus,' I'd told MG. We'd laughed at how arbitrary and unhelpful the comparison seemed. Our nickname for this bump arrived during the first trimester. Unlike the early days of my pregnancy with Finn, when I'd only been able to look at beige food, this time my only real craving was Jarlsberg cheese, by the bucketload.

Finn and I opened the blinds and looked out at the beach. The winter sun played on the millpond water as we ate breakfast.

Then I started bleeding.

I thought I'd managed to keep my voice steady as I asked Mike to find my maternity notes so I could call the midwife, but Finn had burst into tears and I knew I had to try to stay calmer.

In contrast to my panic, Mike was immediately business-like. 'Do we need an ambulance? How much blood?' It has always amazed me how measured he is in a crisis.

I called our London midwife, who sent us immediately to the nearest hospital. After a brief detour to a unit with no out of hours maternity services we were here.

*

13

It's not even twenty-four hours since we arrived at A&E and I was taken straight to the labour ward. I was ushered quickly into a private room, hooked up to monitors – for me, and for the baby.

The midwife quickly found the steady, reassuring *thump, thump, thump* of a heartbeat. 'Baby's doing fine – a nice strong heart trace. How's the bleeding?'

I released the breath I'd been holding since it started that morning.

'It's OK. It hasn't gone.'

'The consultant will be round soon to see you.'

She didn't leave my side. For most of that day there was barely a moment without a midwife right there with me.

The duty consultant was called Jessica. She suspected my placenta had abrupted. 'Sometimes, if it's only a little abruption and there's not too much bleeding, we can get it under control. Then we can get you back to London. It depends if it triggers labour. Either way, we'll need to monitor you for a few hours and might well need you to stay here overnight.'

Mike was in the car park with Finn asleep in his car seat; he wasn't expecting us to stay. I typed out a message: 'I'm on labour ward, will you come in when Finn wakes up? I think we'll be here for a bit.'

A few minutes later I heard muffled voices, 'Hi, I'm looking for Georgina ...', and then the door swung open.

Mike, carrying a grinning Finny. 'What's happening?' he asked. 'How are you doing? How's the Jarl?'

'We don't really know: they're trying to work it out. We might be able to get back to London, it all depends a bit on what happens in the next few hours. They don't know what's causing the bleeding.' I felt eerily calm.

Jessica was back.

'If it's OK, my love, I'm going to examine you,' she said. 'I want to work out where this bleeding is coming from.' She looked at me, then at Mike.

'I'll take Finn to get some lunch, I think. Probably better he isn't here for this part. Shall we go and find some food, Finny?'

'Uggs,' Finn replied, grinning and nodding.

'Well, we might not be able to find eggs. Let's see what they have.'

'Ah,' Jessica said as she started the examination. 'Your waters have broken. My love, you're not going anywhere. We'll have to keep monitoring you while we work out what we need to do.'

'What does that mean? Is the baby OK? What's going to happen?' I could hear the rising panic in my voice.

'Well, there are a few scenarios. Even with broken waters, if there's enough fluid around the baby, we can sometimes keep it inside for a while – sometimes weeks. There's a higher risk of infection so you need to be monitored very carefully, and you almost certainly won't make it to term. If you were under me, I'd aim for thirty-six weeks. I don't know if we'll be able to get you back to London today, but we'll certainly try in the next few days.' She paused. I knew there was another version coming. 'Or, sometimes, you'll go into labour.'

Labour. The word bounced around my brain. I can't go into labour.

'It says in your notes that you're booked for an elective C-section?'

'Yes,' I nodded.

'If this baby wants to arrive today, I'd suggest you labour naturally – it's better for their lungs, when they're this early.'

'I can't.' I explained that I had fibroid surgery two years ago. 'Is the baby going to arrive today?'

'It might. We'll prepare as if it is, then if it stays put for a bit that's a bonus. You need steroid injections as soon as possible for its lungs, and we'll get you on a magnesium sulphate drip for its brain.' The words, the terms, were alien, but she was so matter of fact part of me felt like I knew exactly what she was talking about.

*

15

I heard voices in the corridor: Mike and Finn were back.

'How are you?' Mike asked. 'Do we know what's going on?'

'Her waters have broken.' Jessica was smiling and straightforward.

'What? I don't understand ...' He's unusually rattled. 'Oh my God. I wasn't expecting you to say that. What does that mean? Is the baby OK?'

'The baby is fine, for now – we're monitoring it – and mum is doing OK too. We need to watch and see how things progress. It might be that this baby should be delivered today, in which case we need to be ready. It might be that it stays put a little longer. Either way, you're not going anywhere until at least tomorrow.'

Finn was pottering around the room, trying to open the bin, climbing on and off the chair, smearing banana along the floor.

'Did you find some lunch?' I asked when Jessica had left the room.

'In a manner of speaking,' Mike said as Finn climbed into the armchair next to my bed. 'I got him some pasta, which he rejected and then decided he wanted my sandwich instead. So then he very carefully opened it and took the cheese out and ate it, leaving me the bread – thanks, Finny. Then he had his third banana of the day, and some kind of yoghurt that he loved and you would probably hate. But he's eaten.'

I laughed.

'I think I'd better call my mum,' I said. 'Maybe she can come and get Finny, in case this baby decides to arrive.' A sticky-fingered, bin-crashing toddler is not delivery ward friendly.

I found my mum's number in my recently dialled list and hit call. It was the last thing she was expecting.

'Weird one, Mumma. The baby might be coming.'

She was immediately ready; she's always immediately ready. 'Right. What can I do?'

'It's a bit of a big favour ... Do you think you could come and get Finn?'

She said she'd set off from Somerset as soon as possible – a three-hour drive from where we were, where we are, in Kent. Ten minutes later a message popped through: 'Leaving now, satnav says three hours ten minutes. Love you x.'

I felt the sudden, spasming pain of the steroid injection to prepare the baby's lungs, and then the hot flushes and metallic taste of the magnesium sulphate drip for its brain. Dani, our midwife, had a soft voice and cold hands. She explained each shot to me before administering it. An expert, and not only in midwifery – she had been where I was. Except her babies were born at twenty-four and twenty-five weeks.

'Luckily,' she said, 'both were fine. We are really lucky.'

Her gentle presence was reassuring, steady.

Outwardly, I think I seemed calm. Inside, emotions surged and ebbed, tying my stomach and my head in knots. Guilt, that my body had failed my baby, that my placenta couldn't keep working like it should have done. Fear – thirty-one weeks is so early, too early. I had to squash that thought. Then a kind of relief, that what happened now was out of my hands – my waters had broken, it was up to the doctors. It mingled with excitement, that soon we'd meet our second child. I tried to quash it – the guilt told me I didn't deserve it.

Mike needed to go back to the Airbnb, to pack up and check out. He took Finn, hoping he might sleep in the car. A while later he sent a video of Finn cheerily waving 'bye-bye' to the sea through the double doors of the house. I'd realised I was stroking the screen. It was supposed to be his weekend; we should have all been by the sea together.

'You were staying in Whitstable, Mike was telling me.' Dani is adjusting my drip.

'Yes,' I reply. 'A little trip for Finn, before his new sibling arrived.'

'I live in Whitstable,' she says. 'It's lovely. Have you been before?'

17

'No, never. We all love the sea, but we normally go to Cornwall – my parents live in the West Country. But we're in south-east London, and Whitstable is so close, it felt like the perfect place. Except when you leave at rush hour on a Friday – but that's another story ...'

She chuckles. 'Where are you staying?'

'We're in a little house on the beach in Seasalter. It's so pretty.'

'Oh yes, lovely. A special place.'

'We didn't explore as much as we'd planned. But yesterday was great.'

My mum arrived while Mike and Finn were in Seasalter. She found her way to the labour ward and was shown to my room. Mike had suggested she meet him at the Airbnb and take Finn from there – it would save her an hour or so driving. I'd known before she replied what her answer would be.

Finn squealed when he spotted her. 'Nana, Nana,' he said, pointing and stamping his feet.

'Are you going on an adventure with Nana?' I asked.

'Yeah!'

'Say bye-bye to Mumma, Finny.' Mike lifted him up to hug me.

He wrapped his squidgy arms around my neck, pressing his open mouth to my cheek. I held on, determined not to cry.

MG scooped him up again.

My mum hugged me, kissed me on the cheek and squeezed my arm.

'Keep me updated, darling, and let me know if you need anything else at all.'

'We will,' I said. Then, 'I love you,' and they were gone.

We waited.

A line on the monitor next to me continually tracked my uterus movements – smooth, rhythmic loops.

The midwives kept calling it an 'irritable uterus'. The

expression made me smile, as if it has a mind of its own, as if I'd annoyed it in some way and it'd reached the end of its tether. I hoped my irritable uterus would calm down. I hoped we could go home. The midwives were reassuring: thirty-one weeks is early, there's no question, but it's better than it could be. Our baby should be fine, we were doing all the right things. A crash course in prematurity.

I was starving so Mike passed me a nutty snack bar he'd grabbed from the Airbnb. As I was chewing I suddenly remembered the C-section rules before Finny was born, the strict times I had to stop eating.

Dani was back. 'Am I allowed to eat?' I asked through a mouthful of caramelised Brazil nut.

'Yes.' She smiled reassuringly, then paused. 'In fact, let me check with Jessica.' She was back seconds later. 'Sorry, we think on balance better not, just in case.'

We waited. And waited. Time suspended. In the middle of the afternoon I saw the Instagram hashtag #WorldPrematurityDay. I knew our baby would arrive before midnight.

'Your cervix is one centimetre long.' The consultant who runs the labour ward, Dr King, had come to assess me. 'Even if your cervix is naturally short, that is very short – I think it's preparing for labour.'

I swallowed. This wasn't supposed to happen. 'My cervix isn't naturally short – at Finn's twenty-week scan the sonographer told me I had the longest cervix she'd ever seen.' It's a strange record to hold.

'This baby needs to arrive.'

'When?'

He glanced up at the clock. It was 6 p.m.

'Now.'

When Finn was delivered, he was holding on for dear life – I didn't ask to what – determined not to be removed. I'd always had a strange sense that, with this baby, unlike his or her big brother, I wouldn't get to my booking date, that he, or she, would arrive in their own time. But not at thirty-one weeks. It's too soon. Nine weeks early is far too soon.

'I'm sorry,' said Dr King, reading my face. 'But I don't want this baby to be delivered in an emergency at 3 a.m. I want Jessica and me to deliver your baby, calmly, carefully. With your fibroids, your previous scar tissue, we need to be able to take our time.'

After he'd gone, Jessica sat on my bed.

'This operation might be hard,' she said. 'But I can take it slowly. If I need to, I can slice you through here' – she traced a line above my tummy button – 'and pull the baby out that way.'

I searched her face.

'All you need to know . . .' she paused a beat '. . . is that I'm fucking good at my job.' She broke into a grin.

And did I imagine a wink?

I nodded. I liked Jessica.

The room swung into action.

3

18 November

One day old

It's later in the morning. Dr Sahu has come to our room on the postnatal ward to introduce himself. He explains that he'll be the consultant for the week. Every day, at around 9.30 a.m., he'll do a ward round, see every baby on the NICU, discuss the minutiae of each treatment plan, assess charts, files, notes. Every baby is meticulously tracked. Alongside the consultant rounds and regular doctor monitoring, our son will have a one-on-one nurse round the clock. He introduces the woman in scrubs standing next to him. She has shoulder-length curls and glasses. 'This is Nic,' he says, 'Baby's nurse for today. Nurses work twelve-hour shifts – roughly eight to eight – with a short overlap for handover. Nic took over this morning.'

Dr Sahu explains that overnight Grey has been put on a ventilator. This is pretty normal – sometimes early babies need a bit of help, and I'd only managed one shot of steroids before he arrived. Then his brow furrows. 'Amongst some of the checks we perform, we scan babies' brains by ultrasound – it's routine for babies born before thirty-two weeks. During Baby's scan, we saw an abnormality. His corpus callosum is not properly formed.'

'What does that mean?' I reach for Mike's hand. My brain has raced off at a million miles an hour.

'Please try not to worry.' He takes a piece of paper and a pen from his pocket, sketches out the brain, and points: 'The corpus callosum is the fibres which connect the left, logical

21

side of the brain with the right, emotional side.' He says that, on its own, the abnormality isn't necessarily a cause for concern. 'We don't know very much about the variations in corpus callosum as we don't routinely scan brains.' He gestures towards us. 'Probably none of us has had a brain scan ...'

We shake our heads.

'So we don't know how each corpus callosum is.'

'Is it because he's early? Could it grow as he gets bigger?' That must be the explanation.

'No, this is not linked to the prematurity. The corpus callosum starts to form before twelve weeks.'

'What could it mean?' I need more concrete information.

'I see perhaps seven or eight babies a year with the same thing – bearing in mind babies after thirty-two weeks aren't scanned. Half show no symptoms, half might have certain difficulties. Back in London they'll see how Baby grows and might consider an MRI further down the line.'

An MRI? This wasn't supposed to happen. Babies don't have MRIs. And Grey is so early, he has enough to deal with already.

'There is one other thing,' he says. 'Have you noticed Baby's ears are a little low?'

Mike says he did notice. I have barely seen his face.

'In my opinion, they are set a little lower than I might expect.' He holds his pen to the side of his head, drawing an invisible line from the edge of his eyes, around his head. 'I would expect the top of the ear to come at least up to this line. Baby's are lower.' He pauses. 'Though it is difficult to tell, especially with premature babies, as their heads might grow and alter the positioning entirely.'

'What could it mean?' I ask. 'If they are low, is it something bad?'

'It might be nothing,' he says carefully. 'In a week they might be higher, but considering the corpus callosum, his prematurity and these low ears' – he counts off the three points on his fingers – 'I think it is worth sending off some routine genetic tests.'

Genetic testing.

'You think there's something wrong with him?'

'It is very hard to tell at this stage.'

'But what would genetic testing be looking for?'

'As I say, it is hard to tell at this stage. But genetic testing will rule things out.'

'What kind of things?'

'Well, the three most common and well-known syndromes are called the trisomies: Down's—'

'The trisomies? That's what the Harmony test is for, isn't it? We had the Harmony test – it was low risk – the lowest risk that's possible ...' I've interrupted him. I take a deep breath. Let him do his job, Georgie. 'Sorry, go on,' I say quietly.

'Well that is certainly useful to know, but I still think it is worth us sending off the tests. Please, try not to worry too much about it.' He talks softly, gesturing in smooth, expressive movements, gently placating me.

'How long will it take for them to come back?'

'Usually they say five to six weeks. As we don't have a particular idea of what to look for.'

He pauses.

'If there is anything,' he says gently. 'They will scan all his chromosomes – this can take a little while.'

He pauses again.

'In each one of us, our genes are like a library. With books to cover every element – from eye colour, hair colour, to the more complex systems.'

He moves his hands as if to indicate a globe.

'No two libraries are the same. When we are examining genes in a microarray the scientists will look through every book, checking each line in every chapter. That's why it takes so long.'

He gestures in turn to Mike, me, Nic, himself. 'All of us will have lines that have not printed correctly – mini deletions, mini abnormalities – no set of genes is perfect. But in certain, rare, cases, an important chapter might be missing, or the single line which hasn't printed correctly might be more important than eye colour or hair texture. Once we've ruled out the trisomies – the triple chromosomes – the scientists are examining metres of DNA, reading through hundreds of books, and studying each line.

'Please try not to worry. I am letting you know what I think we should do. It does not mean they will find anything.'

His pager buzzes and he glances down.

'I'm sorry, I have to go. If you have any questions, please do come and find me. I will do my best to answer them. Nic ...' he nods at her '... will you help in the meantime?'

'Of course.' She turns to us as he shuts the door. 'I know this must be so scary, but we have to check everything. We just need to wait and see what comes back. Do you have any questions now?'

I look around dumbly. None that they can answer.

She presses her hands against the metal railing that runs along the end of my bed. 'I'll get back to Baby.'

I feel useless.

Our little boy is lying several rooms and sets of locked doors away from me. I can't even get to him without someone pushing me. There might be something wrong with him. And we have no idea what. Sitting cross-legged in my open-backed hospital gown and disposable pants, I sob.

Somewhere in my frazzled mind I remember it's Monday. A work day. I am self-employed – a writer-editor-marketing-journalist hybrid, mostly in fashion, sometimes interiors – so to some degree my time is flexible, but I should let my clients know that my work will come to an abrupt halt. I have one tight-deadline commission, due the day after tomorrow. I find my editor's email and scan our exchange – it's about 'mini-me dressing' – then draft a swift reply, explaining that Grey has arrived, that I won't be able to file. She's the first person outside our families to hear about his arrival. I wonder if she even knew I was pregnant. The brush with real life, the mundane normality of our previous correspondence, brings some semblance of balance – and then, almost immediately, I feel very far away.

How I wish I was waking this morning to spin out the fun, fuzzy piece on coordinating outfits with your children, sitting at our kitchen table, Grey safely in my tummy. I've been freelance for four years. I love being able to work with all sorts of different creative clients. I love the freedom of being my own boss. I love the control I have over my time, over my days. The control I once had. Typing the email seems to sap all the energy I've mustered, and I feel everything go wobbly.

I need to speak to Sama. My friend is on holiday in Miami with her husband Ed and daughter Agnes. Somehow, she manages to make sense of what's going through my mind a beat before I can. She knows baby fear. Last year her first child, a little boy named Blue, was stillborn. She was twenty-five weeks pregnant. She and Ed went through a post-mortem and a battery of tests, and still no one knows why. It's the worst thing that has ever happened to anyone I love. I still don't know how they managed to put one foot in front of the other and carry on. Her next pregnancy was nine months of terror.

I fire off a series of panic-stricken messages to her. She doesn't even know Grey has been born.

She rings immediately. 'I know how scary it is, G, I really do. But they have to test for everything; it doesn't mean they're going to find anything.'

I feel my shoulders loosen for the first time since Dr Sahu and Nic appeared in my room.

'G, you can do this,' Sama says. 'I know it's all so strange, so shocking, but you're strong, you can do this.' She pauses. 'Can you send me a picture? I bet he's so sweet, does he look like Finny?'

I smile. 'He's so sweet, Sama, teeny-tiny and perfect, with a big Lucas head.'

We laugh.

Seconds after I hang up, she messages. 'Blue's ears were really low, G, and all his genetic testing came back clear. Would you like to see pictures?'

Her kindness brings more tears – I know she's never shown anyone. I hold my breath as I study the photos. He is exquisite. Minute, perfect. It feels a little intrusive, me looking. The photographs feel sacred. I curse the cruelty that ended Blue's life before he ever had a chance to live it. That turned his miraculous journey towards the world into desperate tragedy for my friends.

Sama gives me back some balance. I take some deep breaths, try to stay calm.

At the perfect moment, my phone buzzes. A message from my mum – a video of Finn. He is sitting on a miniature rocking chair at my parents' house, moving purposefully back and forth, smiling. I stare at the screen, at his rounded cheeks, his huge eyes.

We start telling our close friends that Grey has arrived. Sending messages, pictures. The replies are so different from when Finn was born. It is a shock to everyone, and no one quite knows what to say. There is so much love. Some congratulations. Somehow many of the usual new-baby comments feel wrong. Is it exciting? I can sense the hesitation. It isn't how it's supposed to be. He looks strong, everyone says. He does look strong. He is strong. And for now, I'll hold on to that.

Mike showers quickly, then wheels me back to the incubator. I am still in my hospital gown. It gapes a little at the back. I don't have the energy to mind. My compression stockings are pulled up to my knees. I remember thinking minutes before Grey was delivered that I preferred this shade of forest green to the usual white ones, the ones I had with Finn.

Nic is remaking Grey's bed. She holds up gloved hands.

'He weed everywhere when I was changing him,' she says. 'Cheeky boy.'

'Oh no, little monkey.' I wish I could muster her enthusiasm.

She handles him with deft, practised movements. Completely natural. I sit a little back in the wheelchair, watching her change Grey's nappy – carefully avoiding the tubes and wires, securing the tabs around his tiny abdomen – a spectator in even the simplest parts of my newborn's care. As I sit next to the incubator, I notice a gentle rounding of her tummy – I'm sure it's a baby bump, the tell-tale solidity of the curve. I wonder how on earth she does her job while she's pregnant.

'Have you been given an octopus?' Nic says.

'An octopus?'

'Ah-ha, you haven't. A crocheted baby octopus – give me a second to finish off here and I'll go and find him one.' She snaps off her gloves, flicks open the bin with her foot and drops them in, then turns back to the incubator to shut the portholes. 'I'll be one minute.'

Mike's gone to get us water, so I'm left alone with Grey. I watch him, still bathed in the strange blue glow from the jaundice lamp. His mini mask covering his eyes. His long limbs move jerkily, a little puppet, still working out that he has control over them.

Nic's back, holding a small blue crocheted octopus. She hands it to me. 'The curly legs remind them of the umbilical cord – all babies love to hold the umbilical cord, early babies particularly,' she says. 'This is a good replacement – you can give it to him.'

'He can have it in the incubator?' What a silly question, I think, as I ask it.

'Yes – they're all washed and clean, ready for the incubators.'

I unwrap the tiny octopus and tuck it beside him.

'Give him one of the legs,' Nic says. 'Tuck it into his hand.'

I reach in and do as she suggests.

'That's right, like that.'

His fingers immediately close around it and he pulls it in to his chest.

'It should also stop him fiddling and pulling at any of his tubes and wires – or his ventilator. We really don't want him pulling that out.'

'Does that happen?' I ask.

'Oh yes – babies get fed up of them, and then, *whoosh*, out it comes.' She gestures with her hand, then rolls her eyes. 'They're stronger than you might think, these early ones ...'

Nic talks us through Grey's wires and lines. Two tubes run through his tummy button, giving him a cocktail of antibiotics – it's such early days, sepsis can't be ruled out. And nutritional supplementation – phosphate, sodium, magnesium – he would normally be getting from me; he should be getting from me. A millimetre-wide tube directs milk straight into his stomach.

'*Your* milk,' Nic says. 'You've got a lot of it, haven't you?'

A midwife has shown me how to hand-express colostrum – squeezing beads of sticky bright yellow liquid from my nipples and harvesting them into miniature syringes. I've been hand-expressing at least every three hours, to keep the colostrum coming. The tiny syringes are delivered straight to the NICU, where they're stored in the nursery fridge. My colostrum comes quickly and easily. I know I'm lucky: I've seen friends with full-term babies struggle, particularly in the early days of breastfeeding – low supply, engorged boobs, difficulty latching. And having a premature baby, I learn, makes you particularly vulnerable – often you just aren't ready, and then, starved of the oxytocin-releasing closeness which should define the early days of motherhood, milk can be slow to arrive and supplies low. A cruel double whammy.

A doctor in burgundy scrubs passes Grey's incubator in the middle of the morning. 'The genetic testing has been sent off,' he says to Nic. 'Please let the family know.' I am sitting on the window side, hidden behind the incubator, in my wheelchair. As he finishes speaking he catches sight of me and smiles. 'They have been sent off, the genetics.'

'Thank you,' I reply. 'How—'

'They say they can take up to six weeks,' he says, as though he's read my mind. 'But in my experience, some results come back faster. I will keep you up to date.'

I thank him again and he's off, skilfully navigating the incubators while studying the chart he holds in front of him.

That afternoon, one of the NICU nurses finds me at the incubator. 'Are you still hand-expressing?'

'Yes.'

'Have you ever used a breast pump? I think it might be worth you swapping over – it'll be quicker and easier with bottles than filling fiddly syringes by hand. I'll get someone to come and talk to you about it.'

A cheery Irish nurse brings over a large plastic case fixed to industrial-looking wheels. 'Have you expressed before?'

I say I have, with a little portable Medela.

'Hmm, this is a hospital-grade breast pump – it's going to be rather different.'

'I've heard they're terrifyingly efficient.'

She laughs and unclips the case. Inside are two dials and some transparent tubing. She points to each component of the pump, explaining how it works. 'As soon as you can, I'd get into double pumping – it saves a lot of time.'

'The idea of the single pump seems alarming enough, but I'll give it a go.'

She finds me a Colostrum Gold pack, explaining that the yellow cotton hearts are to keep in my bra and rotate next to Grey so he'll always smell me, and the small cool bag is for shuttling expressed milk to and from home, transforming me into a portable milk machine.

*

29

Somehow it's evening again. Mike is wheeling me down the corridor to the NICU. The process is slow and frustrating in the wobbly old chair. As we pass the postnatal ward I understand why we've been given a private room. A new father bounces rhythmically, up and down, a rounded baby on his shoulder – the most natural motion in the world. I smile at him, then tear my eyes away from the rolls of skin around the baby's wrists, the delightful fullness of its cheeks.

The gentle bleat of fresh newborn fills the air, both agonising and reassuring. I realise I have no idea what Grey's cry sounds like. Though the notes say he cried a little when he was first born, by that point he was no longer near enough for me to hear it, and now his voice is muffled by the ventilator. I could pick out Finn's cry from a roomful of babies, but I have never heard my second son's voice.

A midwife buzzes us through the double doors, to more double doors. This time, I notice the walls of the NICU. Every couple of metres there are framed stories; of babies who survived, who thrived. Triplets born at twenty-nine weeks weighing a kilo each, a twenty-three-weeker so tiny her dad's wedding ring fits around her upper arm. Stories of courage, triumph against the odds. Each one makes me sob. Each one gives me hope. Grey has weeks, and pounds, on so many of these babies. He'll get there, we'll get there.

'What if ... the genetic testing ...?' a voice whispers.

I push it away.

The unit is calm, quiet. The team are careful to preserve some level of normality in the clinical setting. The blinds are down against the dark of the night outside; nurses move around quietly, speaking in whispers, with the low thrum of the myriad machines keeping babies alive a constant bass line.

A small ticket on Grey's incubator lists his name – currently 'Baby' – both our names, our surname, his weight – 1.62kg – his gestation – 31+0 – and our booking hospital in London.

Two identity bracelets are taped next to it. Finn had one around his ankle. Grey is too small.

Sofia is beside Grey's incubator. Nic must have gone home. I glance at my phone and see it's nine o'clock. Today Sofia's headscarf is white, with metallic threads that catch the light when she moves. Her scrubs are pale blue again. I wonder what the colour of the scrubs means – whether burgundy or blue signifies anything.

'Hi.' She smiles broadly. 'How are you feeling?'

Her warmth is infectious, and I smile back. 'Better, I think. Fewer painkillers today.'

'Keep taking them when you need them, won't you?' She moves her hands as she talks. 'Remember, you had major surgery yesterday.'

Yesterday? It already feels like weeks ago.

'You weren't booked here, Mike was telling me.'

'No,' I say. 'We live in London.'

'I saw on Baby's label.'

'He has a name now.' She's the first person we tell aloud. 'His name is Grey.'

'Oh, that's lovely.' Her eyes twinkle. I like her so much.

'Yes, nice for him to have a name, important.' It feels so vital, in the circumstances, that we give him this piece of his identity.

'Yes, and Greg is lovely.' She is grinning as she reaches for a pen. I don't register the 'g' until she has crossed out 'Baby' and stood back to admire his new name. We'll work it out later.

'How did you end up here?'

I tell her about the Whitstable weekend and the abruption. 'And now he's here.' I look down at Grey. Something tells me to keep talking. A habitual need to make polite conversation? Or a resounding terror at the thoughts that come with silence? 'It's lucky it happened this weekend instead of last weekend – Mike was running the Athens marathon. Rather further from home ...'

'God, yes,' she says. 'Greek healthcare is good, but that is a long way.'

It was Mike's seventh marathon – he runs one a year with a friend of his, staking out a new European city each time. I get to go along as a cheerleader. I'd taken a midwife letter for our flight, thinking it was a little over the top – I was only thirty weeks pregnant, there was no chance the baby could arrive.

'He wanted to see the sea, didn't you, Greg?'

I should say something, tell her it's the wrong name, for goodness' sake.

'He did,' I say.

4

19 November

Two days old

My younger sister, Loula, is Grey's first visitor. An ex-nanny turned pre- and postnatal personal trainer and yoga teacher, she loves babies and children more than anyone I've ever met. Years ago, we nicknamed her the Baby Whisperer, for her astonishing ability to calm even the most fractious small person. Baby Whisperer was swiftly swapped to Baby Snatcher when our brother Nick's son, Sam, was born five years ago, based on the remarkable number of times he could be found in Lou's arms rather than anywhere else.

I don't realise how much I've been looking forward to seeing her until she arrives. We both cry as she hugs me tightly.

'Kimch met me in the car park,' she says. My family has a curious propensity to create bizarre nicknames. And both my sisters call Mike Kimchi. Ella, my youngest sister, once misheard me saying 'MG' – his initials – and the name stuck.

I look at her – it feels so long since I last saw her.

'I brought books,' she says as she straightens up. 'I've read that reading to them is good. Preemies, I mean; I've been doing lots of research. In between messaging Kimch about maternity pads.' She smiles. 'Probably one of the more surreal WhatsApp conversations we'll ever have. I brought these too.'

She holds out photos – one of Mike and me with Finn, and a Polaroid from Finn's christening. 'I don't know if he's allowed things in his incubator, but it says online sometimes they are, so thought these might be nice, if he can, so you can all watch over him all the time.'

It is such a lovely idea I suddenly want to cry. Why didn't I think of it? I need to crank my brain into gear. It's stuck, pinging between fear about the genetic testing and shock that Grey is here, that I'm not pregnant any more.

'That would be so lovely,' I say. 'We'll ask his nurses.'

'Did you know Grey is a Scorpio – strong-willed and spirited?'

'Strong-willed is right ... Mr I'll-arrive-when-I-want-thank-you-very-much.' Things feel the most normal they have since before breakfast on Sunday morning.

I've given up on the wheelchair, the navigation was frustrating me, and I need to be able to get to Grey without a chaperone. So I'm shuffling along the hospital corridor in mismatching slippers. I guide Lou through the incubators to Grey's cot-side.

She gazes at him through the reinforced plastic, her head on one side. 'He's bigger than I was expecting, I think,' she says, 'not scarily small,' then quickly adds, 'I mean, I know it's so scary, I wasn't saying it wasn't, just I think he looks quite a good size – I expected to be more shocked. He's long and lanky, like Sam.'

My brother Nick is six foot five, so it's no surprise that his son is heading in the same direction.

'Can I touch him?' Loula asks.

I show her how to cup her hands around him. She gets the hang of it instantly, her slim fingers holding him with author-ity. I hear Sofia's voice in my head: '... like you know what you're doing ...' How does Lou know? I watch her. Yoga-toned legs clad in black leggings, an oversized grey sweatshirt over the top. She pushes her long dark hair behind one ear as she smiles down at her nephew. She is so together; she's processing all this much more efficiently than I am, already researching preemies, bringing all the right things, saying all the right things. The Baby Whisperer.

*

34

Loula has been sitting with Grey and Mike while I pump. Suddenly, she appears in the family room. 'Mike went to get us lunch and then when I went back in they said they had to do something with Grey and I should wait outside.'

'Is he OK?' I'm moving towards the door; things can change so fast in here.

'I think so. They seemed very calm, they just said they needed to do something.'

'We'll go back in.'

In the nursery, four nurses are stationed around Grey's incubator.

'Come on, little man, we need more breathing than that.' It's Anna, a Great Ormond Street-trained NICU nurse who moved from London to the Kent countryside when she had children. She exudes an air of quiet authority, absolute capability.

'Is he OK?'

She looks up.

'I said, please can you wait outside . . .' she trails off, seeing Loula beside me. Her glance flicks from Lou to me, momentarily confused. Then, softer, 'He's OK, he really is, but we need to focus, so please, wait outside for a few minutes and I will come and get you. He's fine.' She looks me straight in the eye.

Loula and I wait outside; I pace by the hand-washing sink.

'I think she thought I was you,' Loula says. 'When she told me to wait outside earlier.'

'I think so too.'

We're often told we look alike, Lou and I. I find it hard to see, but occasionally in photos I do a double take at the arch of her eyebrows, and can sometimes recognise mannerisms I thought were exclusively mine. We look a little as if I was Mother Nature's practice run; with Lou she has honed her craft.

She is quiet for a bit, then, 'I got ticked off.' She looks sheepish.

35

'Ticked off?'

'I was looking at the other babies—'

'Loula! You aren't supposed to look at the other babies.' I'm half laughing.

'I didn't know,' she says. 'They're all so sweet and tiny.' Her huge eyes are full of love. 'I hope I didn't get you into trouble.'

I smile. 'You won't have done.'

Anna emerges from the nursery a few minutes later. 'You can come back in now.'

She leads us back to Grey's incubator.

'Sorry you had to wait outside. Grey seemed to be doing well with his breathing, so we tried to extubate him. But he didn't like it.'

I feel my throat tighten.

'He didn't manage for very long before we had to put the tube back in.'

'Is that bad?' I ask.

'Hard to say. We might expect a thirty-one-weeker to last a little longer, but it's still really early days. He might need some more time, a bit of weight. Sometimes babies do come on and off them. It's rarely a straight line.' We're back at his cot-side. 'I'm going to take some blood and then I'll leave you guys.' As she pricks Grey's tiny heel I tuck my finger into his curled hand.

Mike is back with our lunch. 'They tried to extubate him, MG. It didn't work. He had to go back on it straight away.'

'G, they warned us that might happen. It's not unusual.'

'Anna said he didn't last long at all. It makes me worried.'

'Give him a chance. He's doing so well, he's still only two days old.'

I nod, wishing I had his confidence.

One of the midwives has brought me the stack of paperwork that signals I'm free to leave my room on the postnatal ward.

I'm being discharged. When Finn was born, we were packed and waiting by the time the midwife brought my forms. Dressed, ready – Finn in his car seat, hat on, wrapped in a blanket my mum knitted for him, looking at us through narrowed, slightly disdainful navy blue eyes. Today, everything is different. Grey isn't coming with us. And we aren't going home.

I take off my hospital gown for the first time in forty-eight hours and stand hunched under the jets of the hospital shower, clinging to the mobility rail. I pat myself dry with a crunchy hospital towel and pull on leggings and an oversized shirt. I feel more together dressed in proper clothes, on a more even keel now that I've cast aside the standard-issue patterned cotton wrap and mismatching slippers.

'Ready?' Mike asks.

To leave this room? To leave the postnatal ward? To leave Grey? I feel my brief steadiness tip sideways again.

'To see Finn,' I say to myself. 'Ready to see Finn.'

In Grey's nursery, there's more paperwork. Gaby, one of the nurses Mike has already befriended, talks us through everything, explaining the locker room – no coats, scarves or bags are allowed in the unit. I have a sudden image of the NICU reception in London where we'd taken Finn for a jaundice check when he was three weeks old. I remember couples coming and going, carrying tiny nappies, dark circles under their eyes. Mike and I had noticed the panel of lockers, seen people loading and unloading bags and coats, wondered what they were doing. I remember turning Finn away, my bouncing chubby baby, willing the doctor to arrive quickly.

Gaby is telling us about the family room – it's a space for visitors, for siblings, to minimise crowding around the incubators. Then she runs through the NICU rules and guidelines: phones on airplane mode, the afternoon quiet time hours reserved solely for parents. She's one of those miraculous people who makes me feel that my whole existence is entirely self-serving. When she isn't being a senior neonatal nurse, she works in child protection and adopts rescue dogs. She seems quietly sure of herself, is incredibly funny, and not even thirty. We put down a deposit for our locker padlock, and for the breast pump I can borrow while Grey is on the unit.

'We have to take a deposit.' She rolls her eyes.

'Surely this little man is the best deposit,' Mike says, pointing at Grey.

'Well exactly.'

'And if those things are as brilliant and precious as we keep being told, I don't think twenty quid would stop someone from walking off with one!'

'We'll hold your baby hostage.' She gives us a sparkling smile. Even her teeth are pearly white.

'One other thing – you've probably noticed those?' Gaby points to what look like several pairs of cordless DJ headphones looped over the machines behind Grey's incubator.

'Oh yes,' Mike says. 'GDPR, right?'

I look blank. To me, GDPR is pesky legislation that affects the way my clients launch new collections to their email marketing list. A word from another world.

'Gaby can explain.'

'Thank you, Mike,' she says. 'So, each morning there's a ward round. The doctors come round and talk about each baby, with all the registrars and sometimes some students.'

I nod.

'You aren't allowed to hear about other babies – not that you'd be interested. GDPR says we have to have headphones, so we can make sure you aren't listening . . .' Of course, data protection plays a far more significant role here. 'You should wear them for the whole ward round – just take them off when the doctors come to Grey.'

Rules are reassuring, procedure is reassuring. Something to follow, some semblance of routine. One foot in front of the other.

*

The milk room is sandwiched between the milk kitchen and the laundry. The distinct, hypnotic scent of newborns drifts over the clinical hospital smell. In spite of the rigour of the NICU's regular cleaning and disinfecting routine, milk wins the day; a small triumph.

I don't yet feel brave enough to pump next to Grey's incubator, so I wash my hands in the milk kitchen and gather my apparatus – two sterilised bottles, the breast shields, the suction tubing.

Outside the milk room, I knock gently as I open the door. Inside, a standard lamp throws a soft glow over two armchairs facing one another, so the fluorescent strip lights can be kept switched off. It makes the room feel instantly cosier, like stepping out of the hospital for a few minutes. The walls are painted a soft putty colour. Framed photos capture early motherhood in the NICU – a gallery of women who have been where I am now. Three electric candles sit alongside a small vase of fabric flowers. Another mother, with a cloud of dark hair and a broad grin, is sitting on the chair facing the entrance.

'Do you mind if I . . .' I gesture at my pumping equipment.

'Of course not,' she says. 'Come on in.'

I sit down and set myself up.

She looks well practised.

'How are you?' I ask. 'Do you have a little girl? Little boy?'

'Boy.' She adjusts her pump. 'Benjamin. You?'

'Boy too. Grey.' I busy myself with the apparatus. 'How early was Benjamin?'

'He was born at term, but has some problems with his heart and lungs so he's been in SCBU. Was Grey early?'

'Thirty-one weeks. He's on the NICU. How's Benjamin doing?'

'He's doing *so* well now. He has Down's syndrome.' Her smile seems to brighten the gentle glow of the standard lamp.

'I'm so pleased he's doing well,' I say.

'We're hoping to take him home soon.'

'That's great. I've been discharged today.' I pause. 'It feels strange to leave without a baby, doesn't it?'

She nods. 'All wrong.'

'I hope you get to go home with Benjamin soon.'

We should be tucking Grey into his car seat, pulling a little hat down over his forehead against the November wind, turning round a thousand times to check he's OK. Instead, I kiss my fingers, place them on his head, tell him I love him and walk away from his incubator. As the winding lanes take us further and further away from him, they take us towards Finn. It shouldn't be like this. I always expected a division of my attention, my time, with a second child, it's inevitable – I remember my mum saying many times as I grew up, the oldest of four children, that it would be useful if she could clone herself. But I never imagined a physical divide, this constant forced separation from one of my babies.

The radio plays the opening bars of 'Bring Him Home' from *Les Misérables*. Incongruous, after the usual string of singalong classics, and then bizarrely familiar. It's one of my favourite musicals, but I've heard these notes recently. I turn up the volume and try to place the memory.

'This was playing in the theatre, MG. This is the *Les Mis* song that was playing just before Grey arrived.'

'What music would you like?' Jessica had asked as they wheeled me to theatre.

'If you're happy, I'm happy. You choose.'

'No one lets me choose, because I like drum and bass.' Jessica grinned. 'Don't worry, we'll put on the radio.'

I quite liked the idea of my baby being delivered to Andy C, but *Les Misérables* had come on between burbled bulletins about the local weather.

I turn up the volume now and we listen to the words. '*He is young, he's afraid. Let him rest, heaven blessed. Bring him home . . .*'

We aren't going home, not yet. South-east London is too far

from the NICU. Mike has found an Airbnb fifteen minutes from the hospital. We stop at Tesco on the way. I wait in the car while Mike does a speedy supermarket sweep, pinging me photos and questions as he flings anything and everything we might need into a trolley and then into the back of the car.

While I wait, a message comes through from an old friend. Our parents were next-door neighbours before I was born and we spent every summer holiday in Cornwall together until our late teens, but I haven't seen her for years. My mum must have told hers about Grey. Her first baby was born at twenty-five weeks and they'd spent months on the NICU in London. It's reassuring to speak to someone who understands, who has already navigated this strange path, or one like it. Before Sunday, my only knowledge of the NICU was via a couple of people I follow on Instagram.

We arrive in the dark, at the annexe of an old mill house. Built right on the river, it has a weeping willow by the front door and a soundtrack of running water. The ceilings are low, with beams that catch the very top of your head even if you remember to duck.

Finn is waiting for us with my mum, his nana. I bury my face in his neck and cling to him. He humours me for a few seconds, tucking his soft head into the crook of mine, arms and legs wrapped around me. I grasp his little body as I might a lifebelt.

'Mama,' he says, pushing me away with chubby hands. 'Chitchin.'

'Oh yes,' says my mum, 'that's in here, isn't it, Finny?'

He takes her hand and bustles into the hallway, moving with the unique combination of confidence and unsteadiness of a toddler who hasn't been toddling long. I follow, stooping a little from the C-section, moving slowly as my insides feel like they might fall out.

It's a higgledy-piggledy house – the walls and ceilings all run at odd angles – cosy, in a ramshackle way. Along a small corridor from the kitchen is the sitting room. Inside, there's a mixed selection of furniture. An enormous dining table currently operating as a food overspill area, a sofa perched on a threadbare Moroccan rug and in the corner a grand piano combine to create a feeling of faded grandeur.

Finn points proudly at his kitchen, an early Christmas present from my mum. Then he takes her phone from the side table, holds it to his ear and wobbles around the sitting room. 'Hallo, hallo, ya … ya …' he says, picking things up and putting them down as he goes – the perfect imitation of an adult phone conversation.

'Who is it, Finny?' his nana asks.

'Dada,' he says with authority, although Mike is right in front of him. It's only been three days, but he seems to have grown up so much.

I lower myself into the sofa. Most of the springs have lost their energy, but the odd one stands resolute, so I shuffle awkwardly to find a spot that avoids them. Finn is busy tottering to and fro, bringing me food from his kitchen, chattering on my mum's phone. I watch him for a while, then lie back and close my eyes. The pause seems to slide back the bolt on a gate I've managed to keep locked for all of about an hour, and tears run down my face.

I feel a hand on my arm.

'Mumma?' Finn is looking up at me intently, his tiny brow furrowed, his eyes wide.

'I'm OK, Finny,' I say. 'Mumma's OK. I'm just a bit worried about your brother and everything feels a bit strange. But I'm OK, I promise.' I wonder if it's the first time he's seen me cry.

My mum fills the table next to me with snacks – crisps, dips, bread, olives.

'You need to keep your energy up,' she says.

'Feeder,' I reply, smiling weakly.

'It's very pretty in daylight.' My mum gestures to the thick brocade curtains hanging in front of French windows that look out on the dark. 'Fields all around on this side, beyond the river. And a little sort of island with a meadow and sheep. You'll see in the morning.'

I close my eyes again. When I open them, Mike is standing over me with a plastic tube in his hand. 'Injection time ...' he says. I'd forgotten. The anticoagulant. A grim C-section follow-up; I detest needles. Mike has to do them for me while I hold my hands over my face. I feel him pinch a bit of my tummy between his thumb and forefinger; there's a click and a sharp ache as he presses the plunger.

Mike gives Finn a bath. I perch on the loo seat, watching, useless to Finn as well as Grey. I can't pick him up, I won't be able to for a while, and he can't even sit on my lap, the stitches are still too tender. After the bath, I manoeuvre myself into an armchair and listen to Mike reading to him from the stack of books my mum has gathered from Somerset. I look around the room – she seems to have brought everything, reconstructed his nursery. It's lovely, so cosy with all his things lined up.

'Will you come here and give me a hug goodnight, Finny?' I ask.

He shakes his head. 'No. Nana.' He heads out of the room and down the corridor. 'Nana, Nana?'

I hear footsteps on the stairs, and then '*Nana!*'

It's understandable, I tell myself. Our Athens trip had been the first time we'd left him for longer than a night, so he's really spent most of the last couple of weeks with my mum. It's good that he's happy with her, maybe happier with her than with me. Leaving him would be even more gut-wrenching if it were any different.

When Finn is in bed, I sit at the kitchen table while Mike unloads the shopping. My mum grins as endless things emerge from endless bags. 'We won't be running out of oats, or Hellmann's, any time soon.' She points at matching packs on the side.

'It doesn't look like we'll be running out of *anything* any time soon,' Mike laughs as he squeezes stuff into the already packed fridge.

After a quick supper with my mum and a waved-aside attempt to help her clear up, we drive to the hospital. The NICU is quietest in the late evening. Calm, like yesterday. A nurse called Jackie is looking after Grey. She's solid, old school; she's looked after countless babies, seen it all, knows exactly what she's doing. I can't decide if that is comforting or terrifying. No-nonsense, with a heart of gold, she's wonderfully caring and brilliant company.

Mike and I sit next to the incubator. It is so different from the way I expected our first evenings to be, from how they were with Finn. Everything is misaligned; I feel redundant in this new and alien set-up. Left alone with me, Grey wouldn't survive. It's a strange thought.

I watch the feeding tubes and countless monitor wires keeping this little boy alive. It's amazing really, that it takes a team of highly trained nurses and doctors and thousands of pounds of machinery to do what my body was doing for him, should be doing for him. What women's bodies do for babies every day, all round the world, while they get on with their lives. What I wish my body was still doing for Grey. It brings the miracle of pregnancy into sharp relief, watching what happens when it ends too early.

The NICU is looking after Grey. My mum is looking after Finn. And here I am, suspended between them, torn between them. Brain scrambled, body broken.

'It's strange, I'm not doing anything for him, am I? You are all looking after him, keeping him alive.'

Jackie looks at me over the top of her glasses, puts down her pen and runs a hand over her hair. 'The things you are doing are so important – talking to him, being with him. And, the vital thing: milk. All that milk, Georgie, none of us can do that.'

'It's so ... frustrating ...'

'I know. But give yourself a break. It's been a hell of a couple of days for you.'

It really doesn't feel like I'm doing enough. But then, perhaps the NICU merely acts as an amplifier. Since Finn was born, my mum has warned me not to strive for perfection. 'There's no such thing as a perfect mother,' she often says. 'A good-enough mother is all any of us can hope for.' But am I being a good-enough mother, to either of my boys?

I read to Grey. One of the books Lou gave him. '*You're here for a reason ...*'

I'm crying before I reach the end of the first page.

'I've got to stop doing that, Greyman, haven't I, crying all the time. It's no good to you, no good to anyone. I need to be braver.'

It's been a theme of my whole life. The need to be braver. I've lost count of how often my mum has told the tale of the time I climbed all the way to the top of the spiral slide in Battersea Park, aged four. Only to freeze, petrified by the steepness of the slope below me. The queue had reached the bottom of the steps, so the story goes, by the time I'd steeled myself for the launch. A little older, during summers in Cornwall, my siblings and friends had unthinkingly flung themselves from the top of a jagged rock that was a popular sea-jumping spot. I'd wait, watching as person after person plopped into the deep blue water, every once in a while plucking up the courage to take a few steps forward, glimpsing the drop. My dad, Nick, friends, would all call up to me, promising the first ice cream, extra milkshakes, first choice of Saturday cartoons, if only I'd take the leap. Eventually I would, but it took every shred of nerve I possessed.

I take a deep breath and try again. This time I manage to read most of it, getting to the final lines before dissolving. '*I just can't imagine a world without you ...*'

'I can't, little man,' I whisper to him. He's changed my world. Finn changed my world, but I felt prepared in some way for how he altered me, altered us. Grey's arrival has shifted my axis. He is so delicate. He has stamped onto my heart the fragility of life, stamped me with the things that matter.

I lean forward. He's still bathed in the blue light from the phototherapy lamp. And the blinds haven't yet been rolled down, so the dark and the street lamps are reflected in the Perspex incubator panels. As a car starts outside the window behind me, headlamps momentarily spotlight the fractured reflections. I see a ghostly image of myself, superimposed over my son. Limp, dark hair framing my face, eyes wide. The light exaggerating the shadows beneath them.

As the headlamp beams sweep across the car park, for a split second everything is distorted. My eyes seem to bulge, out of nowhere my cheeks look hollow, my pale, twisted features loom over Grey's tiny body. Then the car moves off and my view clears. He is sleeping, peaceful.

As I close the book on my lap I notice two footprints alongside the dedication inside the front cover – to the author's granddaughter. They are tiny. I wonder if she was premature.

It's time to go. This time for the whole night. I feel an invisible tie holding me to Grey. It feels wrong to tear myself away.

'Do you have our number?' Jackie asks.

'The hospital number?'

'The NICU direct line. You can call it any time you want, any time of day or night. If you are away from him and just want to check he's OK.'

'Oh no, I don't have that.'

'I have it, G.' Mike looks up from Grey's files, which Jackie's told him we're allowed to read.

'Call any time you want,' Jackie repeats. 'I guess you'll be pumping in the night – sometimes mums like to call then. Apart from anything else, it's nice to know someone else is up when the other half is snoring away next to you.' She gives Mike a dig with her elbow.

'Hey, hey, I was up at five this morning, Jackie, I'll have you know. And I'll see you at six tomorrow ...'

She laughs, a deep, infectious chortle. I take a breath and think of Finn as we walk out of the nursery, away from Grey.

'I'll come back first thing, on my own. I like an early morning,' Mike says.

We're on our way home, driving the already familiar roads. 'And I don't have to wake in the night to pump.'

'True, that would be weird.'

'Then I can be back for Finny's morning milk and to make his breakfast while you pump.'

The beginnings of a plan.

My alarm buzzes at three. I drag myself from dreamless sleep. I haven't dreamt since Grey was born. I lower myself down the stairs to collect my sterilised pump pieces. When I am set up, I call the NICU.

'Hi, is that Jackie? It's Georgie, Grey's mum.'

'It is, Georgie. Are you pumping?'

'I am. Can you hear the milking machine?'

She laughs softly.

'How's he doing?'

'He's being a good boy, he's sleeping, his oxygen is good, nothing much to report.'

'Good, we like that.'

'We do. Now you go and get some sleep. I'll see Mike in the morning.'

'Thanks, Jackie.'

I hang up.

I look around the room as the milk level on the small bottles rises. I am sitting in an armchair in the corner of a stranger's bedroom, next to a window that looks out onto a river. I can hear the mill race living up to its name beneath me. It must be all the rain. I noticed when we drove back earlier that the fields on either side of the river are becoming submerged.

Mike is asleep on the other side of the bed. Finn is asleep next door. There is a portable breast pump where the Moses basket should be. I am listening to a rhythmic, mechanical slurp, feeling the intense suction of plastic machinery rather than the gentle suckling of a newborn. Grey is a fifteen-minute drive away.

I finish pumping, stow the precious bottles safely into the fridge, then tuck myself in beside Mike and let the sound of the river lull me back to sleep.

5

20 November

Three days old

I'm suddenly aware that an alarm is going. It's getting light.
The space next to me is empty. My brain feels foggy, confused. As I drag it awake, I hear a crunch on the gravel, the
front door opening, Mike's voice, the sound of a tap running,
then feet on the stairs.

'The little man's doing well,' he says coming into our
room, carrying the sterilised pieces of my pump. 'I thought
you'd need these.' He carefully lines up the pieces inside the
casing. 'It's a good time to go, just before the night nurse
hands over to the day nurse. I had a good chat with Jackie
about how he's doing. I think it makes sense for me to try
and always go at that time. It's nice and quiet, calm. Good
for us to hang out. Father-son time. We checked BBC Sport
together. I told him that the autumn internationals would
usually be on around now, but they aren't this year because
the World Cup just finished. We discussed how the three of
us would be going to Twickenham together, and who'd be
buying the beer.'

'Three?!'

'I meant four, of course ... but those tickets are like
gold dust, G!'

'And I'm not exactly a rugby fan ... Fair. But when it's
cricket, I'm coming.'

'Deal.'

*

After breakfast, Mike helps me into the car.

My mum lifts up Finn and he presses his nose against the kitchen window, waving enthusiastically and calling 'Bu-bye, bu-bye.'

While Mike shuts the gate to the mill house, I look back. Finn is still waving, beaming, his arm wrapped around my mum's neck. I smile to myself, for her, for him, for how happy he is to be with her, how happy they are together.

The road winds back through the village, and then out into the countryside, re-joining the main artery just outside the town. As we meet a series of roundabouts I have a strange sense of déjà vu. This is part of the route we drove on Sunday. As Spotify's baby lullaby playlist soothed Finn to sleep, I remember feeling the reassuring flutters of movement in my tummy – the baby was OK, Grey was OK. Safely inside me. I look down at my stomach now, baggy, tender, empty. So empty.

I relish the methodical ritual of the hospital hand-washing, NICU hand-washing. Lathering every part of each hand, sweeping one over the other, covering every inch of skin. Pulling a single paper towel from the dispenser on the wall, drying each hand, then switching off the tap with the towel, lifting the lid of the bin with the pedal, dropping it in, hearing the bin clang shut, coating my palms with the powerful alcohol rub.

Today a slight girl with poker-straight dark hair is in front of me at the sink; a small boy with a shock of curls stands next to her. She holds up her hands. 'Red raw! This hand-washing ruins them, doesn't it?'

'Mine are the same.' I show her, but resist telling her that the intense sting of the alcohol rub on my parched skin brings me a curious satisfaction.

'I need to remember to get some hand cream,' she chuckles.

'So do I – apparently lanolin is the best – it's supposed to be nipple balm, but it's really greasy and protects your hands from drying as well, I think.'

'Lanolin? I'll try and get some – I'm not sure when, though.'
She gestures at the small boy next to her. Then, 'But I'll try.
Come on, Caleb, let's go and see Cora.' She turns back to me.
'See you soon,' she says.

'See you,' I reply.

We are greeted with good news. Grey's jaundice levels have
fallen to within a normal range. A small but significant victory
that means his phototherapy lamp has been put away – he is
no longer bathed in blue light and doesn't need a mask, so we
can see his eyes. They flicker open and look around. He looks
so suspicious, I want to laugh. It reminds me of Finn's eyes as
we got him ready to leave the hospital, trying ineffectually to
buckle him into his car seat.

A nurse called Melia is looking after Grey today. She speaks
softly, is quietly businesslike, and has dainty, precise hands
with graceful fingers that catch my attention as she talks.
They look like an artist's hands, the way she moves them. She
finds us a NICU pack. 'I think this is a girl's one.' She looks
apologetic. 'But I looked through them all and it's the one
that's most OK for a boy. Is it OK?'

I can see she is concerned.

Inside is a laundry bag printed with colourful clouds and
a cotton quilt covered in cheery little aeroplanes. My own
style veers towards the minimalist – white shirts, jeans, black
sweaters, navy, occasional stripes, the uniform of a decade
in fashion – and I've been determined to keep Finn's wardrobe chic, understated. His boldest tones are mustard and
burgundy. I laugh at myself, at how seriously I've taken my
not-yet-two-year-old's look.

'It's perfect,' I say.

'Have you seen this?' Mike holds up a small book. A kite
has been collaged onto the front, with 'G-R-E-Y' in sparkly
letters down one side. 'The nurses made it for him,' he says.
'They keep it like a diary.'

I trace the letters with my forefinger. Grey's diary. I open it and read the first entry, alongside a photo of him sleeping next to his octopus.

My name is Grey.

I was born on 17th November 2019 @ 18.54hrs.

I weighed 1.62kg.

Mummy and Daddy and my brother were having such a lovely time at the seaside that I felt I wanted to see the sea too. I was born early, and initially I needed some help with my breathing. You can see that from the picture opposite.

I am having lots of Mummy's breast milk and it's making me feel stronger every day. Last night I got a lovely goodnight kiss from Mummy and Daddy, which made us all feel better about things.

Let's see what today brings ... xxx

'How beautiful,' I whisper. Let's see, indeed.

The registrar who told us the genetic tests had been sent off returns to Grey's incubator in the same burgundy scrubs to tell us that there's no news. We weren't expecting results this early, but it's nice to know that someone is keeping track. Mike discusses the missing corpus callosum with one of the other registrars. The condition is rare enough, and so variable, that no one can tell us much more than we already know. At this stage we have to wait, see if other symptoms emerge, or disappear. There's a query about a sacral dimple, but Grey is moving his legs well. Every symptom seems to be the same story: might be something, could be nothing. Grey is too small, too early, for anyone to really get a handle on anything.

Back in the milk room, I've worked out how to wedge the pumps into my bra so I am hands-free. It's a good time to try to reply to messages, to keep our family and friends up to date with what's happening, how Grey's doing, how we're doing. I haven't told many people about the concerns that the doctors have. There are more questions than answers. And I can't face more questions.

At least once a day friends send hopeful stories of people they know who were born prematurely and are now thriving.

'Born at twenty-five weeks, he's now twenty-one ...'

'Born at thirty-one weeks, she's thirty-three and fine ...'

'Twins born at twenty-eight weeks, now twenty-seven ...'

The power of hope.

For Finn, I expressed enough milk for a daily bottle – Mike got home after he'd gone to bed so it gave him a chance to feed him, to see him late in the evening, and because someone told me it was worth getting him used to it. NICU pumping is a different ball game. Conventional wisdom dictates I should pump at least every three hours, and never leave it longer than five hours, clocking up eight to twelve sessions in twenty-four hours. Night-time pumping is particularly important for supply.

Every three hours during the day, four-hour gaps during the night, creates a neat structure. At the end of each session I clean the pump rigorously with the disinfectant wipes that sit in bright green packets in every corner of the NICU. I scrub and then rinse the parts, submerging them in a sterilising bucket marked with Grey's name. I carefully label the full bottles of milk, storing them in the fridge. I rejoice in every second of the ritual. Control in a world that has spun away beyond my own.

During the first few days my nipples become sore and chapped, ringed with tiny blood blisters where the hard plastic rubs delicate skin. But I won't let up. I smother on lanolin and keep pumping. Perhaps, I think, I deserve some of the pain. Grey is plugged in to a million wires; he has blood tests, X-rays, scans, heel pricks and suctioning throughout the day. I can cope with a couple of tiny blisters. They heal fast and my nipples harden themselves against the relentless slurp of the plastic sucker.

The process is surreal. Feeding two plastic cups, looking up at pictures of other people's babies, at other people's motherhood. Some days I sit with the pumps plugged to my front, tears streaming down my face, my poor confused uterus rippling with the contractions that will eventually shrink it down to its original size. But it gives me purpose. Filling each little sterilised bottle with milk is a small victory, something I can do for Grey, a tangible way to love him.

I'm about to start pumping when there's a knock. A curly-haired woman pokes her head around the door; we've smiled at each other in the corridor.

She sees me and starts to retreat.

'It's OK, come in, there's another chair, I don't need it all to myself.'

She does so, and settles herself. When we are both pumping, she turns to me. 'How are you doing?'

I'm quickly realising that when someone asks how you are in the NICU, it isn't just politeness, they really want to know. We're in this together.

'I'm OK. I'm doing OK today,' I say. 'How are you?'

'It's tough, isn't it?'

'It is.'

Her phone rings.

'Sorry ...' She winces at me.

'No, no: go ahead.'

After a brief conversation, she hangs up. 'My parents, they're on their way in to visit. It's a ten-minute drive and my mum says they'll be here in half an hour.'

I smile. 'My mum's the same. Safety first.' I pause. 'To be honest, it's probably sensible. None of us need any more stress right now.'

'Yeah,' she says. 'Well, especially with cars. My waters broke when we switched off my friend's life support. She was in an accident.'

I inhale.

'I'm Lisa, by the way.'

'I'm Georgie. Lisa, I ... I don't know what to say. I'm

so sorry, that's so ... awful ...' My words are completely inadequate.

'I know. I was here, in NICU, a couple of years ago with her. Supporting her through all this.' She gestures around at the room. 'I'd just told her I was pregnant, a few days before her accident. Then a month later they told us there was nothing they could do, we had to switch off her life support.'

I am speechless.

Lisa keeps talking. 'And now my daughter is in an incubator. I'm a nice person, I do nice things, I think I deserve a break.' She takes a breath. 'Well, karma can fuck off.'

It really can, I think.

Lisa and I pump in silence for a while, each deep in our own thoughts. The things people go through. The NICU has opened my eyes to realities that my cosseted existence has shielded me from. And here's Lisa, still smiling, still pumping. If she can do it, then so can I.

'How's your daughter doing now?' I ask. 'What's her name?'

'She's called Scarlett. She's OK, still on a ventilator.'

'How many weeks was she?'

'Twenty-eight. How about you? Boy? Girl?'

'A little boy,' I say. 'Grey, thirty-one weeks.' I pause. 'My placenta abrupted, no one knows why.'

'How's he doing?'

'He's on a ventilator. We're hoping they might try and take it out in the next few days. I guess we'll see ...' I trail off. 'This place is pretty surreal, isn't it?'

'It is,' she says. 'It is, Georgie.'

I've finished. I screw the lids onto my milk bottles and gather up my apparatus.

'Bye, Lisa,' I say. 'It was nice to meet you. I'll see you soon.'

'Bye,' she says, still smiling.

As I approach Grey's cot-side, Melia is showing Mike how to change his nappy.

'Ah!' They both jump back, then Mike starts laughing.

'Buddy, really? Just as I take off your nappy?' Then, turning to me, 'He's weed everywhere!'

'Mum, would you like to change his bed? We need to change everything.'

I nod. 'Of course.'

'Will you go and get one of these preemie covers and a padded cocoon, size medium. I think this small one is getting a little tight for him.'

'He's growing . . .'

She smiles and directs me down the corridor to the linen store. I gather the bits and pieces we need with great care. It is the most involved I've been in looking after Grey since he was born. As I walk back I realise I've chosen blankets and covers in colours that match the new heart-covered cocoon.

Melia shows me how to change his bed. With gloved hands, she gently undoes his heart rate electrodes, oxygen probe and temperature sensor. Then explains that she will lift him while I swap the mattress. The process needs to be fast, and as careful as possible. He can't be unplugged for too long and too many movements are likely to unsettle him. I follow her instructions to the letter. It feels vitally important that I carry out this task perfectly. I force my hands not to shake as Melia lowers Grey once more, plugs him in and then shows me how to roll him back into his little nook. My pulse is racing, my heart is pounding. I think it's the scariest thing I've ever done.

The bubble of early motherhood, early parenthood, is a curious, wonderful, terrifying melding of senses, impossible to untangle. NICU parenting is another story – touch is limited and smell tends to be clinical, so voice becomes vital to bonding. Here, no matter how discreet and respectful each member of NICU staff is, true alone time with your baby is impossible. And as soon as you know someone might be listening, the dynamic changes: it's hard to voice thoughts, or even form them, without reservation.

Reading is my lifeline. With the possibility of many hours

ahead of us, I start to revisit *Harry Potter.* I remember reading the magical stories for the first time, devouring each in a single sitting, staying up long into the night to finish them. Mike never read them – I tell him it's because he's too old – so it's perfect. We make a pact with Grey that we'll be home before it's finished. As I shake his little hand with the pad of my finger, I don't specify if we mean the book, or the full series. It gives us a little leeway – useful, since every time I start reading Mike falls asleep and I have to repeat the chapter.

Finn is finishing his supper when we get back to the mill house.

'Doctor, doctor,' he repeats.

My mum took Finn to the GP today, while we were at the hospital. He has a cough lingering after a cold and I want to check he doesn't need antibiotics. 'What did they say?'

'Nothing to worry about,' she replies. 'Just a cough, fine as far as she's concerned – simply a case of sitting it out. But she said to ask the NICU; she felt maybe they might not be happy for him to visit until it's gone.'

'I don't think I'm happy for him to visit with a cough. It's not worth the risk for Grey's little lungs, and for the other babies, is it?'

I expect Mike to protest, to tell me it's fine.

'They have a lifetime to hang out,' Mike says. 'There's no need to rush it.'

'This arrived for you.' My mum points at a package on the kitchen table. Mol's writing. One of my closest and oldest friends, I've known her since we were about eleven and used to chat for hours on our home phones, winding the coiled wire round our fingers as we discussed every detail of the latest episode of *EastEnders.* Over the years we've dissected everything – jobs, boyfriends, heartache, weddings, babies, dreams, life. She's married to one of Mike's best mates; they introduced us one chilly Sunday evening, almost exactly four years ago. She'd been gently asking for our address, said she had a few things to send. I smile; the box is huge. 'A few things', to the most generous person I know. I slice open the brown paper and look inside. It is stuffed. Preemie babygrows and little hats, a canvas bag with a beautiful cashmere eye mask and socks, snacks, treats.

Mike is peering over my shoulder and starts laughing.

'I think this might be for you,' I say, handing him the beef jerky.

'So Mol,' he says.

'Oh look: two tubes of lanolin. I must have mentioned Cora's mum – you know, the dark-haired girl whose daughter is opposite Grey. We were comparing dry hands. That's so kind of her.'

I grab one of the balms and a handful of the snacks to take to the hospital.

'She's a genius.'

Jackie is on nights, looking into Grey's incubator when we arrive. I like it when she's on duty. I like our matter-of-fact 3 a.m. chats, her telling me Grey is fine, to go back to sleep.

'Jackie, which is the best pub around here?' Mike asks.

We have a vague plan to mark the end of the week with a pub supper – give my mum a break from cooking.

'Straight in with the important questions.' She thinks for a moment. 'I like the one just behind the hospital – they do a good pint. I'm not sure I've eaten in many pubs round where you are recently, but the Queen's Arms is usually a good bet.' She searches her memory. 'And the Fisherman's Rest is supposed to do good food.'

The Fisherman's Rest is right opposite our Airbnb. Perfect.

6

21 November

Four days old

There's a busy level crossing to the left of the house, on the other side of the river. Mike pulls out of the drive and turns right, the back route – he's already Kent's answer to a black-cab driver, with an encyclopaedic knowledge of ways to beat the myriad roadworks, floods and level-crossing queues that might delay our arrival with Grey.

I look down at the same leggings and oversized shirt I've been wearing for the last three days. I don't have the energy to care.

When I was twenty-one, during my year out from uni, I'd got on a plane to New York on New Year's Eve. I'd travelled light, very light, hoping to find a design internship, and then to shop for a whole new fashion-ready wardrobe. The first part of my plan had gone smoothly – I'd managed to wangle my way into a slot at Zac Posen.

'Can you start on Monday?' his studio manager had asked.

'Of course,' I said.

It was 10 a.m. on the Saturday. I had half a day to find an apartment, open a bank account and get a phone. The wardrobe would have to wait.

I rotated the same few outfits for seven weeks of non-stop work before their Fashion Week show. I thought I'd managed to get away with it until I reappeared after a short trip back to the UK with a full suitcase. 'Oh,' said an incredibly chic workmate who'd studied at Rhode Island School of Design and already completed internships with Marc Jacobs and Ralph Lauren, 'you *are* kind of a cute dresser.' She'd wrinkled her nose. 'I always wondered why you wore those same funny leggings every day before the show.'

The memory makes me smile.

Jackie is still there when we arrive. 'I see his bed had to be changed – I'd made it all coordinating for you, Georgie, and then I hear that Dad let Grey wee everywhere.' She widens her eyes dramatically and shoots a look at Mike. 'But then I had to change it all again anyway because in the night your young man pooed and it all came out of his nappy.'

'So whose fault was that, Jackie?' Mike is grinning.

Jackie is sorting out Grey's bed, gently turning him onto his side, untucking his covers, rearranging him. 'Well, I checked the notes and it would seem that the last nappy was changed by ...' she looks up and raises an eyebrow '... Dad, so ...'

'Ah ...' Mike says.

'It takes a bit of time to get the nappies right. You'll get it, with a bit of practice.' She winks at me. It hasn't taken her long to get the exact measure of my competitive husband. 'So, come on, are you going to get some practice?' She gestures towards the waiting nappy apparatus.

'George hasn't done one yet.' He looks towards me. 'So she needs more practice than I do.'

'I'm on milk duty!' I pause. 'No, of course I will. I'm just a bit scared, I don't know what to do.' The truth is, I'm terrified. I'm not good at not doing things well, and the idea of changing Grey's nappy for the first time in front of this NICU veteran fills me with dread.

'OK, I'll do it and you can watch,' Mike says.

Jackie turns to walk away.

'Aren't you going to stay and check my technique?' Mike asks. 'We don't want any more leakage.'

Jackie laughs. 'Oh, I'm supervising, am I?'

'Well, we don't want to have to change his bed again, do we? And I'm still getting the hang of this NICU changing.'

I can tell he wants Jackie's reassuring presence. So can she.

'We might run out of bedding,' she says, and stays. 'I'll give you my special tip – use your little finger to hold a cotton ball against his willy. It stops any unexpected accidents.'

She watches while Mike carefully changes Grey's nappy, giving him other handy NICU pointers as he goes. 'I fold the tabs in on themselves so they don't get in your way ... You can lift his legs a bit higher ... I like to wind the wires together into a little loop ... Fold the nappy in on itself, so the wee gets collected inside, that's right ... Now just tuck the wires under one of the tabs, to keep them neat ...

'And you're done. Beautiful job, Mike.' She pats him on the back.

'Have I made up for the leakage?'

'Time will tell,' she says, 'won't it?'

'Who makes the blankets, Jackie?' I ask.

'Ah-ha,' she says. 'We have a troupe of miraculous grannies, knitting away, day and night.' She mimes clacking needles. 'I'm joshing, but it's probably not far off the truth – they appear on the doorstep every few months with bags of blankets for the babies.'

While we chat, Mike flicks through Grey's charts, looking up at the monitors around his incubator. He has become an expert in different ventilation methods and the meaning of the multiple green bars and lists of numbers that run across the screens. Coloured lines and numbers on a monitor above Grey's head constantly record his oxygen saturation, CO_2, heart rate and blood pressure. I can suddenly picture him on his Atlantic crossing, scrutinising the charts, determined to understand every detail of the sailing variables.

A month after we met, Mike announced that he was going to race from the Canary Islands to St Lucia the following year, with three friends.

'I didn't know you could sail,' I'd said.

'I can't,' he replied. 'But I'll learn.'

The exchange taught me so much about the man who is now my husband.

He's doing the ward round alone today. Talking to the doctors, hearing about what has happened over the last twenty-four hours, what it might mean. We know much of it already, of course, we spend most of the day with Grey's nurses. But the consultants make the treatment decisions. They're accompanied by a bevy of registrars. Kind as the doctors are, the medical terminology and detailed discussion, over the incubator, peering in at our tiny helpless baby, activates deep-rooted protective instincts that make me want to scream at them to leave him, to stop finding things that need to be checked, to let him be.

Mike finds intricate knowledge empowering: listening, absorbing, rationally processing the possibilities, the risks. I don't fear the medical information; I'm better with facts than uncertainty. But I can't help watching each face, each gesture, each expression as they deliver that information. Does that extra shuffle of the papers mean you think this is a certainty rather than the possibility you're voicing? Does that pause mean you know more than you're saying? The influx of precarious details paralyses me; I hear the worst in every word.

This way, Mike digests it, feeding it back to me in manageable chunks, free of the apparent nuances that I can't help attempting to decipher. He doesn't keep anything from me, that's not what I want, but somehow hearing the same things from him makes them easier for me to process. I'm torn between guilt that I can't face the conversations and the knowledge that panic is no good for Grey.

So I'm in the family room. The brunette girl is here, with her small dark-haired son, Caleb, who's racing round the room with giant plastic stacking blocks, and a man with longish hair pushed back from his face.

'How are you doing?' I say. 'I'm Georgie, by the way.'

'Carla,' she says. 'And this is Dom.' She gestures to the guy, who smiles and holds up a hand.

'How is your baby?' I ask. 'Cora . . .?'

Carla nods. 'I think OK for now, but it goes up and down a lot in here. She's a twenty-five-weeker, so it's early days.'

'Wow,' I say dumbly.

'Caleb was a twenty-three-weeker,' she says, gesturing at her son.

'Wow,' I say again. 'How old is he now?'

'Three.'

'He looks pretty tall, for his age.'

'Yeah, he's doing well,' Carla says fondly. 'Do you live near here?'

I explain how we ended up at the hospital. 'And so Grey – our little boy – is in the NICU, and we're in an Airbnb.'

'Grey – cool name,' Dom says. 'Really cool, I like it.'

'Thank you.' I feel myself smiling. 'Do you guys live near here?'

'No, well, an hour away – out by the coast,' Carla says. 'So we drive in every day.'

'That's full on.'

'I hate leaving her,' Carla says, 'but we have other kids, they're at school, so we have to.'

'How many kids do you guys have?'

'I have two other girls,' Carla says.

'And I have two girls,' Dom echoes.

'I can't imagine how on earth you juggle that.'

'We make it work,' Carla says. 'School run, then here, spend as much time as we can with Cora – that can be hard as Caleb gets a bit bored, bless him – then back to pick the girls up from school, then I call loads when I'm not here, to check she's OK. At the weekend we'll try and bring them all.'

I instantly feel feeble for finding this hard. My mum has dropped everything to look after us. We've rented an Airbnb

63

without a second thought. We're doing this NICU thing with 24/7 childcare, a full-time housekeeper and cook, and a fifteen-minute commute. And neither of us has to worry about work. As a director in a creative ad agency, Mike is close to his boss, who has immediately told him to focus on Grey, to put work out of his mind. My handful of fashion and interiors clients have said the same. We have it very easy.

Cora is in the middle of the bank of incubators opposite Grey. Closer to the door are girl twins, thirty-two-weekers, born the day after him. 'Phil and Grant, we call them,' their dad tells one of the nurses. 'We bumped into Ross Kemp the day we found out we were having twins.'

'That's brilliant,' says Mike, overhearing.

'We didn't change the names when we found out they were girls. Phil and Grant stuck.'

I think of these babies as Grey's dorm-mates. When he was first born a little girl called Lily was opposite him, but she's already moved into the high-dependency unit, one rung down from the NICU. Things can change fast here, for good as well as bad.

When the ward round is finished, Mike comes to find me. I'm in the milk room, and feel my heart racing the moment he opens the door.

'It's fine, it's OK, G,' he says as soon as he sees my face. 'Milk up, lines out, normal heart, no more anti-bs. It's all fine. Nothing bad.'

He pauses.

'What?' I ask.

'Nothing, just they think the trisomy results will come back maybe today, maybe tomorrow.'

'Is that bad?'

'It's not good or bad, it's simply when they think the results might come. Honestly, Dr Sahu seemed pretty positive. Grey was the last baby on our side to be seen.' He smiles. Babies are usually seen in ascending gestations, but this order is trumped by medical priority. At thirty-one weeks, Grey is the latest gestation on our side, but for the last week he's been first on the list.

Back in the nursery, I open Grey's book. There's a new entry, in Mike's writing. I smile – Kipling's 'If—'. Mike has the word tattooed on his ankle. His grandfather was a prisoner of war during the Second World War, and kept a diary. To try to preserve his sanity he wrote things down – a list of FA Cup winners, of Grand National winners, and every line of the poem. It's always been one of my favourites – I once planned to have it inked onto my ribs. I think the moment I spotted Mike's tattoo was when I knew I'd marry him. I read it now, and my finger hovers over the last words: *'you'll be a man, my son!'*

I look down at my tiny boy. And such a strong one, I think, after all this.

Visiting the NICU is strictly monitored. To control infection, and to ensure the unit isn't overrun, alongside parents and siblings each baby has a guest list of six. Maximum. The list is set for the duration of a NICU stay. In our immediate family there are three on Mike's side, five on mine. Eight. However we play this, someone – two people – won't be able to visit.

Mike's mum, Sally, has bronchitis, and though she is champing at the bit to be in Kent with us, it's not worth the risk. My mum's at the tail-end of a cold that's holding on to most of her voice. Though they can't visit yet, we agree they'll each take a special pass, leaving four slots. My dad's winter cough means Mike's dad is the only grandparent fit enough to meet the NICU's (and my) rigorous health standards, so my father-in-law drives down from London when Grey is four days old to meet his fourth grandchild, his third grandson.

Malcolm is charming, with mischievous blue eyes and a roguish edge. Mike has inherited his charisma – hence the friendships he's already made with a decent proportion of the NICU (here, when I'm not Grey's mum, I'm Mike's wife). Malcolm has a tendency to make jokes, or at least light, of most situations and does have a rather loud voice, so Mike wants to brief him ahead of time on the delicate, highly charged atmosphere of the unit. We meet in Costa for a quick coffee and one of the white chocolate and cranberry slices we've become curiously addicted to. 'Now, this is a really sensitive environment, Malcolm. Don't talk too loudly, don't look at other babies and for God's sake don't say anything inappropriate!'

Malcolm is bemused. 'Why on earth would I look at any other babies?'

'I had to mention it. Lou's already been ticked off.'

We needn't have worried about inappropriate comments. My father-in-law is stunned into silence by the NICU. A man who always knows what to say, speechless. Through his eyes, I remember how alien the environment is – I realise I've quickly learnt to see past the clinical set-up, the anxiety-inducing sounds. I try to focus on the deep care, the overwhelming love. He draws a quiet breath as we approach the incubator, looking at Grey in silence for several minutes. I watch tears collect in the corners of his eyes. When he speaks, it is in a low, sober tone. 'Photos don't prepare you for how small he is.'

'I'll leave you for a bit,' I say to Mike. 'I need to pump anyway.'

Carla is already in the milk room when I knock; she gestures for me to come inside.

'How are you doing?' I say as I sit down. 'How are your hands?'

'Pretty raw.' She holds out her spare one to show me – the skin is red and dried, like mine.

'NICU hands . . .' I say.

'It's my tummy that's really bothering me, though,' she says. 'I haven't had a C-section before, it has made me feel so floppy, urgh, it's horrible. And I can't look at my stitches.'

'I've had two. I found it heals faster than you expect. Early on with Finn I thought I might never recover – everything feels like it might fall out – but it does get better.'

'It's horrible. The midwife keeps telling me to eat and drink more, but I just can't. I'm really bad at it, I just focus on the children.'

There's no point me telling her she must eat.

'How's Cora?'

'She's all right, she's doing OK. Better than with Caleb; you see how every week inside makes a difference. Caleb was only here for a few days and then was sent to the NICU in London. He had to have emergency surgery when he was three days old. He was in the NICU there for months; we nearly lost him so many times. It was horrible.'

'That must have been so scary.' Not for the first time, I have no idea what to say.

'All my babies, except my first, have been in this NICU,' she says. 'Chloe, my first, was born at term, then Carmen was twenty-eight weeks, Caleb twenty-three weeks . . .' She pauses. 'I had a little girl, Carabelle, who was born at twenty-three weeks, but she died when she was eleven days old.'

'Oh my God, Carla, I am so, so sorry.' My words continue to feel pitifully inadequate.

'It was horrible. Did you see Dr King?' she asks, changing the subject.

'Yes, he was there when Grey was delivered.'

'He's amazing, I've seen him through all my pregnancies. My body reacts to pregnancy and so my immune system gets really low and I get sepsis every time. No one knows why.' Her tone is so matter of fact, so practical about a situation so terrifying.

'But Cora is here, and we just have to take it day by day. It can be really up and down in NICU.'

'I really feel that. Grey is thirty-one weeks, but he's on a ventilator and he couldn't cope when they took him off it.'

She nods. 'One day he'll just get it. Sometimes they have

to come on and off a bit; sometimes they even pull them out themselves, and that's it.'

'Yes, I've heard – how on earth do they do that?'

'Just grab it and pull. They start annoying them.'

I've finished pumping, but don't want to stop talking to Carla. Her experience, her knowledge, is helping make sense of this alien world.

As I wash up the pieces of my pump, I think about Carla and her babies, about everything she has been through, is going through. About tiny little Carabelle who died, about how you would ever begin to deal with that. How you'd be brave enough to try to have another baby. The NICU is a steep learning curve all right, emotionally as well as intellectually. And if I could have even one ounce of these women's strength, Grey would be proud.

'Would you like to give Grey his milk?' Melia asks. I'm by myself at Grey's cot-side; Mike and his dad have gone to the pub for a sandwich. It's clear the visit has shaken Malcolm more than he expected it to, so I sent them off for some father-son time. Melia's holding out a syringe, connected to Grey's tiny feeding tube. 'Have you done it before?'

'I haven't, but I'd love to.'

'OK, you take it like this—' She hands it to me. 'You don't need to push it through, it drips into his tummy with gravity. If it's not going down you can hold it a little higher and it will go faster. Let me know when it's finished.'

I hold up the syringe as she walks away.

'It's just you and me, Greyman, while you have your milk.' I put my spare hand on his tummy and watch as the measured breast milk trickles out of the syringe. 'I'm feeding you,' I whisper. In a manner of speaking, at least. I remember the first time I fed Finn, in the recovery room after my C-section, this wriggling creature naturally zeroing in on my nipple. I wonder when I'll be able to breastfeed Grey, if I'll ever be able to. I try to stop myself from thinking too far into the future. I need to take each day as it comes.

When the syringe has emptied, Melia brings a sterilised cotton bud on an extra-long stick, and an almost empty bottle of milk. 'Now he can taste it too,' she says. She shows me how to swirl the cotton bud in the breast milk, then hands it over. 'You can give it to him. Put it gently into his mouth, let him taste it, and then you can use it to clean around his mouth, around the ventilator.'

I glance at her anxiously as I aim the bud towards his tiny lips, then gently slide it between his bottom lip and the breathing tube. I laugh as I feel the cotton bud being tugged away from me, his little mouth sucking with all its strength.

'He likes that, doesn't he?' Melia says. 'Do you like Mummy's milk, Grey?'

Joy floods through me. He does like it. His eyes are open, his hands furling and unfurling with pleasure as I move the bud to clean around his mouth. His lips are like a homing device, immediately slurping it back in.

'You can give him another one.' Melia hands me the bottle of milk. This time I scoop the layer of fat from the top and watch his whole body wriggle in ecstasy as he sucks on the bud.

'Nena! You're back.' Mike greets the nurse at Grey's cot-side like a long-lost friend, wrapping an arm around her shoulders.

'I am,' she says quietly.

He turns to me. 'G, do you remember Nena? She was on duty when Greyman was born; she stayed really late after her shift to make sure he was settled. She's brilliant.'

'Hi Georgie.' She smiles gently, shyly at me.

'Hi Nena – I'm sorry, I don't remember. I don't remember much of the evening he was born. It's nice to meet you.'

She squeezes my arm. 'He's been a good boy, I hear.'

'He has,' I say.

'He's grown.' She's squinting at him through the incubator.

I watch Nena go about her business. She is special. I can tell. There is something in the careful way she moves around the cot, the way she handles Grey, deftly, but so tenderly. The way she looks at him.

'I'm really pleased that Nena's back,' Mike tells me on the way home. 'She was so great on the night he was born – a really measured, calm presence. And she stayed so late checking absolutely everything, even though the overnight nurse had taken over and kept telling her to go home.'

I look out into the dark. It's turning colder. The headlights brush against the threads of mist drifting past the car.

7

22 November

Five days old

It's Friday. Finn and my mum stand in their usual place at the window. It's become a little morning ritual, the two figures waving until Mike closes the gate, climbs back into the car and we turn onto the road. We follow the now familiar route, snaking our back way to the hospital.

Dr Sahu is on duty. Grey is putting on weight, stable numbers. He increases his milk, he's 'tolerating' it well. Dr Sahu turns to one of the registrars to ask for news on the genetics. The same doctor who told us the genetic tests had been sent off, who'd been at the ward round every day, dressed in burgundy scrubs, shakes his head, then smiles sympathetically at me. 'I called the lab this morning,' he says. 'No news yet, I'm afraid.'

As Dr Sahu continues with his checks, he tells us that Grey's nurses have noticed he doesn't have much of a gag reflex, and has a lot of fluid secretions on his lungs.

'What does that mean?' I ask, for what feels like the thousandth time. I curse my lack of knowledge, my inability to help. Why did I study art? Why did I focus on the particular quality of light in Van Gogh's canvases? Why did I spend my degree learning how to tailor a jacket? This is all so far outside my field. I can never catch up.

'Sometimes they can be slower to develop, but we'd really expect a thirty-one-weeker to have a better one than Grey has. The nurses are suctioning him, and he really isn't gagging at all with a tube stuck into his throat.'

'Could that be just a characteristic, though?' I ask. 'I don't have a gag reflex.'

He smiles, slightly awkwardly.

'I think you would, if someone pushed a tube far down your throat.'

'No, I really don't, nothing ever makes me gag.'

He shifts his weight from one foot to the other as I stare at him, silently imploring him to tell me this might be OK.

'We'll keep monitoring it,' he says finally.

As Dr Sahu moves on to the next baby and we put on our headphones, I realise Mike is laughing. 'I can't believe you told Grey's doctor you have no gag reflex!'

My hand shoots up to my mouth. In my desperation not to add this to the growing list of 'might be wrong's, the subtext hadn't even crossed my mind.

'"I really don't have a gag reflex,"' Mike says, smiling brightly, imitating me. 'As every registrar and nurse is looking away and poor Dr Sahu is wanting the ground to swallow him up.'

'I wasn't talking about that. I didn't mean, oh my God, he's going to think I was making myself out to be some sort of porn star. I just want Grey to be OK ...'

'I know, I know ...' Mike wraps an arm around me. 'It was funny, G. Don't stress.'

Dr Sahu has reduced Grey's ventilation pressure a little. He's 'in air', which Mike explains means he doesn't need any more oxygen than the 21 per cent in regular air. It's a good sign. I sit with him, talking to him, thinking. Loula is coming back today. I'm so looking forward to seeing her. I wonder if I knew before, really knew, how much I need my family, how much I love them, how unbelievably lucky I am to have them. I think about the message Lou sent me this morning – 'My mind has become the most clear it's ever been in what matters and what doesn't since Grey has been born.' I feel the same. Along with the worry and angst and moments of sheer, blinding, head-spinning panic, this small boy has delivered me perspective. So many tiny things I might normally worry about day to day have paled into insignificance. They fell away the day he arrived.

'I'm learning a lot here,' say Mike, out of the blue. 'It's quite satisfying – I rarely learn things these days.'

'So much.' I nod. 'It's crazy, isn't it? It makes me realise I pass most of the days of my adult life not learning anything very much at all. I'm sure it's a terrible reflection on my character.'

'Like, did you know beef doesn't actually have as bad a carbon footprint as we all think?'

'Excuse me?'

'Beef: it's not as bad as we all think – if it's UK beef. Our climate naturally grows a lot of grass and we have a lot of rain so it's a perfect environment for cows,' he says with authority.

I'm puzzled. 'What are you talking about? Have you been chatting to Nic?' What do beef carbon footprints have to do with Grey?

'No, I've been listening to farm radio.'

'*Farm* radio?'

'It's on at five in the morning, when I drive in. It's really interesting.'

'You're mad.'

'But you love me.'

'I do,' I say, looking at my husband. He's dressed in the brushed cotton checked shirt he bought in Whitstable over a T-shirt, with jeans and brown leather lace-up boots – his holiday outfit turned NICU uniform. His palest green-blue eyes twinkle the way they always do when he's smiling. His ever-so-slightly receding hair is swept up and to the side, until he next runs a hand through it. It's that kind of mid-brown colour that hair often goes when small boys grow out of a bleached mop, no longer blond but not as dark as mine, or Grey's. He gets better-looking as he gets older. Lucky man.

And he once told me he looked more like Jude Law than 99 per cent of the population, so he's modest as well.

Carla is washing her breast shields in the milk kitchen sink when I go to collect my bits and pieces for pumping. Unlike the cosy milk room, it's resolutely functional in here – strip lighting, lino floor, clinical smell. Two enormous freezers run along one wall. Steam sterilisers are lined up like toy soldiers beside the double sink.

'How often do you pump?' Carla asks.

'I think roughly every three or four hours.'

'I need to pump more.' She looks deflated. 'It's hard to fit it in, and by the time I have a moment, it's late and I'm quite tired.' She stands away from the sink, turning to face me as she dries the shields.

'God, Carla, I'm not surprised. You have all your other kids to take care of; I don't know how you ever find the time.'

I'm in the doorway, clutching my empty bottles. She's dressed in pristine blue tracksuit bottoms and a pale pink sweatshirt. Her shiny dark hair is perfectly clipped back from her face. I put down my bottles to flick my matted ponytail over my shoulder.

'I'm not very good at other people doing things for me,' she says. 'Or for them. I like to pick them up from school, give them their tea, put them to bed.'

She taps the bin pedal with her toe and drops in the paper towels, then stretches an arm up for one of the jars of Milton steriliser on the shelf over the sink. She's on tiptoe and straining a little, so I reach across to help her.

'You're superwoman,' I say. 'The only reason I can pump this often is that I only have one other child and my mum looks after him all the time.'

'My mum offers to help ... but she works ...'

'Carla, you're doing so amazingly, you really are. Just pump when you can; it's a wonder you're pumping at all – I'm sure I wouldn't be, in your position.'

'Thanks,' she says.

'How's your tummy feeling?'

'It's OK. I saw the midwife today. It's healing OK.' She pauses. 'She said again I need to drink more water and eat more. I just find it really *hard* ... really hard to look after myself.' She shrugs.

'You have *so* many other people to look after.'

Mike has been chatting to Dom in the hall while Carla and I put away our pumps. We wave them goodbye, off with Caleb for the hour's drive, school pick-up, tea, bed. I hope Carla manages to have some food, drink some water, get some rest.

'He's a good bloke,' says Mike as I fill my water bottle.

'Dom?'

'Yeah. He offered to do our washing.'

'Our washing?'

'He said he and Carla had been talking about us, about how tough it must be being away from home. They were wondering if we even had a washing machine, so he was saying they could do our washing for us.'

'God, that's kind. As if they don't already have enough on their plates.'

'I know.'

'Do you think it's a comment on my NICU look?' I give him a sideways glance as we walk back to the nursery. I'm wearing the checked version of my oversized shirt, paired today with holey maternity leggings.

'Chic wife,' Mike chuckles.

The milk-room door says 'free', but it's shut, so I knock.

'Come in.' Lisa is sitting in the back chair, facing the door. 'Join my pump party.'

I smile and put down my kit by the chair. 'How are you doing?'

'I'm OK, Georgie,' she says. 'Yup, OK. How are you?'

'I'm OK too.' I hesitate. 'Except I just had a funny conversation with a woman in the midwife waiting room. And by funny, I mean annoying.'

'Oh God,' she says. 'Tell me . . .?'

'We got talking, she asked about my baby so I told her he was early, didn't go into details. And it turned out she was due around the same time I was due. Maybe a bit earlier – late December. About thirty-three weeks pregnant. And then she told me she is "so done" with this stage of pregnancy.'

'NO!' Lisa says. 'God, some people. I'll swap any time love, because I can tell you I'm pretty done with seeing my daughter fight for her life in an incubator. I'm pretty done with not being able to hold her. I'm pretty done with . . . this.' She gestures down at the pump, the plastic cone encasing her nipple, skin whitening against the suction.

Then she laughs.

I laugh too. 'I know she didn't mean anything by it really.'

'People don't know what to say, though, do they?' Lisa sighs. 'I had a colleague say, "At least she'll be home for Christmas." I thought, *no she won't, she'll be in the NICU at Christmas, it's still seven weeks before her due date.*'

'Oh God . . .' I keep thinking about Christmas in the NICU. 'Seriously?'

'Another told me I was lucky to have an emergency C-section because my bits are intact. I felt like telling her I'd sacrifice all my "bits" – my whole fanny, and my bum, while we're on the subject, and all sex, for ever, if it meant having a chunky, bouncing full-term baby.'

Her frankness makes me laugh out loud.

'But you can't get it, can you?' I say. 'Unless you've been here. My first son was full term and I had absolutely no idea what this was like, what the NICU was like, no idea at all. I took it all – not exactly for granted, I don't think, I hope, but I certainly never expected anything else.' I adjust the pump – I still can't quite bring myself to invest in one of the ugly, industrial double-pumping bras. 'How's Scarlett?'

'She's OK. She came off the ventilator for a bit. She had to go back on again, but she was off it for longer this time – progress, eh? How's Grey?'

'He's all right,' I hear myself saying. 'Hanging in there.'

'They say the small ones are the toughest,' Lisa says.

I'm sure, whoever *they* are, that they're right.

'U-N-I-T-E-D, United are the team for me, with a knick, knack, paddy whack ...'

Mike is singing his favourite football chants into Grey's incubator. He used to sing them to Finny. I've had to explain several times that 'Why don't City eff off home?' isn't totally appropriate for babies.

Grey's little eyes are flickering open at the sound. I wonder if he'll share his father's love of sport. Ten years ago, a junior account exec at a big ad firm, Mike was one of only three people chosen to work on the London 2012 Olympics account, which was down to his encyclopaedic knowledge of every single sport. He's a regular at Twickenham, the Euros dictate summer holidays, we watch the Tour de France, every Open, Test matches, boxing, even the darts world championship. When we chose our C-section date, his willingness to agree with my wanting Finn to be delivered on 14 June made sense when I found out the World Cup kicked off that very night – England's first game was the Sunday. I think we watched every match. Perfectly timed paternity leave. I remember him telling a days-old Finn about the first football match he watched with his dad. Apparently the second son, with a close age gap, is statistically more likely to play sport at championship level. Niche knowledge ...

He changes tack before the last line.

I recognise the words instantly. *Do you hear the people sing ...?*

The rallying cry feels curiously fitting. 'How do you know that?' I ask. Mike isn't big on musicals.

'Morning listening,' he says. 'I play "Bring Him Home"

every morning – it's become Grey's little morning mantra – and then other ones from *Les Mis* quite often follow.'

'In between farm radio?'

'Of course.' He squeezes my hand.

Loula arrives on the NICU around midday, clutching a miniature drawing of a G intertwined with a giraffe. 'For his incubator,' she says.

'It's beautiful, Lou. Lucky boy.'

We stick it to the outside of his incubator, next to his name label.

'I've been looking at pictures of myself when I was little,' Lou says. 'I had really low ears and they're still pretty low.' She holds out her phone, flicking through photos of herself as a baby and then a toddler. She pauses on one, from when she's about four. 'Look,' she says, 'low little elf ears. I don't think the ears mean anything. I really think we have every reason to be positive.'

'I hope so, Loula,' I say. 'I hope so, so very much.'

We sit for a while in companionable silence, next to Grey.

'I've promised him that no matter what happens, I will make sure his life is amazing. Even if things get really tough, I will do everything I can to make it wonderful,' I tell her.

We're both looking straight ahead, looking at Grey.

'We will,' she says. 'We all will. It's not just you. We will all help; we all love him so much. We'll deal with anything, anything at all.'

Tears slide down our cheeks, splashing into our laps. I've given up trying to push them away, or stop them. There's a sign in the milk room, 'The Ten Commandments of the NICU'. 'Thou shalt cry' is number one.

'What if there's something really bad, Loula? And then we die before him. What happens then? Who will look after him?' I voice one of the fears that play on a constant loop inside my head. I speak softly; the words terrify me.

Loula lays a reassuring hand on my arm. 'If, IF, that happens, then he has Finn, his big brother, and he has his cousins – Sam, and Elsie and Wilf.' Mike's sister Zoë's kids are four and one. 'They would, they *will* take care of him.' She pauses. 'He is always, always, going to be taken care of. I promise.'

'I'm scared,' I say.

'I know. I wish I could take that away.'

We look through the portholes at Grey. Soft, warm, peaceful, his little chest rising and falling as the ventilator pumps air into his lungs, his hands curling around his octopus, his little nose turned up above the strapping, his blanket tucked around him. He knows nothing of this worry. It's my job to make sure it stays that way.

Alessia is looking after Grey today. While I hold up his syringe of milk, she flicks through his charts. 'I want to see if he's had his caffeine today,' she says.

Preemie babies are given caffeine to help remind them to breathe. Grey has been on it for a couple of days to hopefully help boost his lung power before they try to extubate him again.

She stops flicking. 'No, he's due caffeine.'

She reaches into a drawer, extracts a little plastic syringe and records the details carefully in the thick stack of A3 pages clipped to Grey's trolley. 'I'll add it to his milk,' she says.

'A little afternoon cappuccino.'

'Exactly. Or a latte. No chocolate for you, Mister Grey.' She smiles as she squeezes the clear liquid into his syringe.

We sit with Grey, reading, talking and then chatting to Alessia. She is Spanish, flamboyant, exuberant, bubbling with optimism. When she laughs it seems to come from deep in her tummy. It's infectious.

'I need to eat more healthy food,' she announces while Lou helps Mike change Grey's nappy. 'But I get to the end of a shift and then all I want is pizza.' She raises her palms. 'Too much pizza.'

'I'd love a pizza,' Mike says. 'A Four Hundred Rabs.' He smiles at me. Four Hundred Rabbits is the pizza place near home.

'Maybe we can have a pizza on Friday night. I think they do them in the pub in the village.'

'The Walnut Tree must be just up the road from you,' Alessia says. 'I like it there. It makes me feel fancy. It's the kind of place where they take your coat when you arrive. I love having my coat taken.'

We all laugh. I look around at the four of us, hanging out around Grey's incubator, and for a brief moment it feels almost normal.

It's the daily pre-supper drive home from the hospital. I'm in the passenger seat, as usual. Neither of us talk. We are both thinking.

'At least I know I've married the right person,' I say suddenly. 'I mean, I knew it before, but then this happens and sometimes all I can think is, thank God I'm going through it with you. There's no one else I could do this with.'

He's quiet for another couple of moments. When he speaks I can hear the smile. 'Well that's lucky, isn't it, George?'

He pauses.

'Imagine if you were sitting there thinking *shit*. It would be unfortunate timing . . .'

I laugh.

He glances sideways and squeezes my hand.

The Baby Whisperer opens the door. She's holding Finn.

'Bol, bol, bol!' he shouts as soon as we're in the kitchen, pointing out into the hallway. Loula puts him down and he totters with all the resolute purpose of a one-year-old, still a little unsteady on his legs, towards a fluorescent fabric ball pond packed full of shiny new balls.

My mum and Lou look slightly sheepish.

'He loves it,' Lou says.

Finn dives into the sea of brightly coloured plastic, squealing in delight.

Later we cross the road to the Fisherman's Rest. Inside, it's suddenly Friday night; prickling with the anticipation of a December weekend – a warm, festive buzz that's completely at odds with my mindset, my mood. I swallow my dread as we're shown to a table in the bar. Next to us, two small boys, brothers, one blond, one dark, are playing – they must be close in age. Finn is fascinated. I wonder if Finn and Grey will one day be playing like that, in the pub. I don't know. I know I need to be positive, but now my vision of the future is blurred by uncertainty. By Grey's tests. What if we never get there?

The landlord comes to our table to say hello. 'I've got two,' he says proudly, ruffling Finn's hair.

So have I, I think, but just give him a smile. Too complicated.

We order. The pretty waitress brings Finn a colouring book and a cup full of crayons, cooing at him as she puts them down. He grins back at her, batting his eyelashes.

'You really are an outrageous flirt, Finn Grumbridge,' Mike says from across the table. Finn's deep chortle is more knowing than his seventeen months should ever allow. The waitress flashes him a broad smile.

As soon as I've finished eating, I feel fidgety. It feels wrong to be here. Out and about, without Grey, as though everything is OK, everything is normal, when it isn't. I feel unsteady, outside the bubble of the hospital and our temporary home.

8

23 November

Six days old

Mike returns for breakfast with a card – Grey's footprints overlaid on a collage of a butterfly. On the back it says '*To Mummy, Daddy and Finn, I love you very much, love and kisses, Grey.*'

'Nena was on overnight, she made it for us,' he says. 'There's another one in his book.'

I run a finger over the tiny footprints, imagining Nena's midnight craftwork. I wonder if it's therapeutic. There in the hushed nursery, night after night, focused on keeping those tiny humans alive. I imagine her methodically arranging the papers, the inks, carefully printing Grey's tiny feet, creating the miniature collage.

'So kind.'

'I love Nena,' Mike says. 'She's so great.'

'MG, what are we going to do about painting Finny's new room?'

We're having breakfast before heading back to the NICU. Granola, yoghurt and stewed apple for me. The insatiable breastfeeding hunger has been curbed a little by the circumstances, but I find it hard to function without a decent breakfast. Toast in one hand for Mike, the other trying unsuccessfully to encourage Finn to eat his porridge. His wide eyes tell me he knows that as soon as we get in the car my mum will make herself scrambled eggs and he'll eat most of it. I know it's become one of their own little rituals, in spite of Mike repeatedly asking her not to let Finn have any unless he's eaten his porridge.

'I suddenly remembered when I was pumping in the night. We need to try and get it sorted for him, don't we?'

We're in the middle of redecorating our spare room so Finn can move in there and the new baby can have Finn's room.

'It needs to be painted so the carpet can be laid. I know he won't be in there for a while, but we need to think about it—'

'It's done,' my mum says.

I look at her blankly. 'What's done?'

'The painting,' she says. 'It's done. Sama and Ed have done it.'

'What? How?'

'Sama knew the paint you wanted – she ordered it for you, didn't she? So they've been over there in the evenings and now it's done.'

I'm speechless.

Our friends are saints.

'They did it as a surprise, but she said to tell you if you were panicking about it. She also said Ed did his very best cutting in and she really hopes it's up to your standards.' My mum smiles at me. 'She knows you so well ...'

I laugh. So does Mike. 'She really does,' he says.

Sama and I went to Leeds Uni together. We went into town one morning, soon after freshers' week, to go to Topshop before lunch. At 4 a.m. the next day we crawled into our beds in halls. Shopping had turned into lunch which had turned into afternoon drinks, then evening drinks, dinner I don't know where (if we ate it, I'm not sure we could have named a place the next day, let alone fifteen years later) and then dancing somewhere else. We'd lived together then, syncing every outfit for every fancy-dress party (it was the early noughties, there was a lot of fancy dress) and in London as twentysomethings, where we'd swapped student haunts for London pubs and clubs. I've crawled into her bed with a hangover more times than I can count; she's been by my side for most of the defining moments of my adult life. The thought of her and Ed spending their evenings painting our house when they have a five-month-old baby of their own moves me deeply.

'I think his chin has grown.' I'm squinting sideways at Grey through the incubator plastic.

Jackie is beside me. 'I agree. I thought that this morning. His face is looking older, filling out a little.'

'Bones moving into place?' I ask.

'It happens remarkably quickly,' she says.

'Any news on the genetics?'

'Not so far, Georgie. I'm sorry. But Dr Kumar will be around in a little while. There's no official ward round at the weekend, but the doctor still comes round and checks on all the babies, so we can ask him.'

Dr Kumar is small and balding, with animated eyes and a permanent sense that the corners of his mouth are about to lift into a smile. His visit is brief, and positive. There's no news on the trisomies – the first round of genetic tests we're expecting. He notices Grey is very active, which is a good sign, his blood gas is brilliant, and all his electrolyte levels are normal. He suggests increasing his caffeine dosage to help with his breathing ahead of a Monday extubation.

I bump into Lisa in the milk kitchen. Her eyes are red and puffy, and she's not as smiley as usual. She tells me they tried to extubate Scarlett and it didn't work.

'But, I guess, she isn't supposed to even be in the world for ages,' she says.

'What was your due date?' I ask.

'The fourteenth of February,' she says. 'Valentine's Day. It feels months away. She was supposed to be our little love baby – my partner's surname is Heart. When we found out our due date he said to me, "Don't start getting ideas about a shotgun wedding so you can have a Heart baby on Valentine's Day.'"

We both laugh.

'Now I wonder if we'll even get her home by then.' She's plunging the pump pieces back into the water. There is no point me telling her they will; none of us knows what will happen. I put a hand on her shoulder. 'One step at a time.'

She nods. 'Day by day.'

We have a parcel to collect and I need some breast pads, so after I've pumped at the hospital, I venture out into the 'real' world. Beyond the enveloping, all-consuming bubble of the NICU, everything looks bigger, sounds louder, feels busier. After the post office, I go to John Lewis with my mum and sister. Trees, lights, tinsel at every turn signal that Christmas is here. It has crept in while Grey's been in his incubator. I wander the aisles aimlessly, rudderless without a pram or sling. Anyone looking at me would have no idea Grey existed, no idea I gave birth less than a week ago.

Finn is pottering around in the toy section. 'Oooh,' he says, pointing things out. He is crouching to rummage through a crate of plastic food. Pressing any buttons he can reach.

Suddenly he stops.

'Octa, octa,' he calls, attempting to jump up and down without his feet actually leaving the floor. He's pointing at a giant stuffed beige octopus.

'We showed him a pic of Grey's,' Loula says. 'I think he needs one too.'

She scoops it up, then hoists Finn into her other arm. She is making her way to the till before I have a chance to protest that he really doesn't need any more toys. I follow them to the Advent calendars lined up in front of the tills. I should buy some for our godchildren. Each one I flick past is too bright, too modern, too covered in glitter. I wish there was something simple, minimal. Classic, though not necessarily old-fashioned. 'You're so fussy!' I hear Mike's voice in my ear and smile to myself. I'm not fussy, I'm particular. And so is he.

Finally I choose little cut-out nativity scenes. A note tells me they're designed to stand on their own with a tea-light illuminating the figures around the manger.

My mum, Lou and Finn have reached the front of the queue and are unloading things onto the counter.

'Is this a present?' the sales assistant is asking cheerily.

'No. Well, yes. But it doesn't need wrapping,' my mum says. 'It's for Finn.' She turns to him. 'It's to match your brother's, isn't it, Finny?'

'Oh *sweet*. And where's your brother?'

'He's in the NICU,' my mum says. 'He was born early.'

She stops dead. Her eyes are filling with tears as I arrive at the desk.

'Here's his mummy.'

'Oh darling, my son was in the NICU,' she tells me. 'You'll get through it, you take it one day at a time.'

I glance down at her badge. Her name is Donna.

'Thank you,' I say. 'It's odd, isn't it? Like a secret world.'

'I just got the shivers when you said that,' she replies. 'That's exactly what I always used to say; it's a strange, secret world. Horrendous. Amazing. My son was born at term, with an undiagnosed heart defect. He was transferred to the NICU in London, we spent five weeks there; it was touch and go.'

She goes silent, reliving the memories.

'He turns twenty in January. You'll get through this.'

She pauses.

'Can I give you a hug?'

I lean across the desk and she wraps her arms around me. 'You can do this,' she whispers.

I am hugging a perfect stranger, at the Christmas counter in John Lewis, as a queue builds up behind us. She holds on. So do I. I can feel the strength of her experience enveloping me.

86

Finally, she pulls away and clasps my arms below my shoulders, looking me in the eye. 'You *will* be OK. You *can* do this. I'll be thinking of you.'

As we walk back to the car, I feel lifted.

It's Saturday afternoon, our first weekend in the NICU. My sister-in-law arrives to meet her tiny nephew. Zoë's driven down from south-east London, leaving her husband, Jon, and two children, Elsie and Wilf, at home. I leave Mike to introduce her to Grey while I head to the milk room. The little nursery is busier than it has been all week.

Over vegetable curry in the hospital canteen, we tell her his middle names, speaking them aloud for the first time. Atticus Fox. Grey Atticus Fox. Atticus, as in Finch, forever the champion of the underdog, and Fox, because they're scrappy, survivors.

I text Sama, along with a drumroll emoji.

'And ... we have a full name ... Grey Atticus Fox ... slightly eccentric, but I think he pulls it off.'

'Eccentric?! Don't forget, you're talking to the mother of Agnes Napier Janet Carmichael ... It's the BEST name!'

When Sama and Ed added Janet to Agnes's name in honour of their wonderful bereavement midwife, word across the hospital was that it was the first time in her thirty-plus-year career that anyone on the maternity ward had seen her cry.

Seconds later, my phone buzzes again.

'To clarify – Grey's is the best, not Agnes – that would be an odd response to your telling me your baby's name.'

'By the way, I gave Carla the cream,' MG says through a mouthful of curry. He puts down his fork. 'It was slightly awkward – I thought it was nipple cream.'

'It is,' I laugh. 'But it's also brilliant for really dry skin. A make-up artist told me about it once on a shoot – works as lip balm and intensive hand cream too.'

'Well, I thought I was giving her nipple balm while she was waiting outside the midwife's office with Dom, so thanks for that little mission.'

It's quiet time when we get back to the NICU. Two hours when the blinds are down and the lights are dimmed. Only parents are allowed by the incubators and doctors avoid scheduling tests or X-rays.

'So ...' Jackie looks up from measuring milk into syringes '... are you ready to hold your young man?'

It is so utterly unexpected, my mind is slow to register the question.

Hold.

Grey.

'Yes ... I mean ... can I, am I allowed to?'

I've waited for six days. Six days that in one sense have disappeared – a haze of tests, checks, meetings, doctors. And in another have seemed an eternity, each minute so taut with emotion that it stretches out to fill a lifetime. Every time I look at Grey I imagine how it will feel when I can at last tuck him into my chest and properly breathe him in. I can be patient, I've been telling myself.

In any case, up until now it hasn't mattered much whether I can or can't. I didn't have a choice.

I can't imagine how mothers cope with prematurity in first babies. I held Finn within minutes, perhaps seconds, of him being delivered, his fresh wriggling form laid instantly onto my chest, covered in a crisp white towel. As my abdomen was sewn shut, his dark navy eyes looked straight up at me, wary of this strange new world.

I've told myself I can wait. Repeated it to myself each evening as I clasp Finn tightly, wrapping my arms around his sturdy seventeen-month-old frame, squeezing his soft flesh, kissing his head, breathing into his hair.

'I think it's time.'

'Can I do a wee first?'

'Of course,' Jackie says. 'Nothing happens in a rush here.'

She calls Kerry over to help, explaining that it's a bit of a performance with the ventilator and other wires and tubes. She warns me that there's a chance his stats will drop and he'll have to go straight back in.

'If he's happy, when he's settled, we don't like moving them again too quickly. So have your wee, fill up your water, get comfy, and with any luck you'll be here a while.'

Prepped and ready, we position a faux leather chair in a curious shade of purple next to Grey's incubator and prop me in a semi-lying position. I unbutton my shirt.

'Ready?'

On a count of three, Kerry transfers Grey's ventilator, taping it to my arm, while Jackie lifts his little tadpole body and places him on my chest. 'There you go, little chap, a nice cuddle with Mummy.'

I barely register his weight on me, but his gossamer skin is the softest thing I have ever felt. His tiny arms reach sideways, tickling the skin of my chest. One hand clasps the button of my shirt and his eyes blink open, looking at me. Here, with the reassuring thrum of his heart beating next to mine, machines, bleeps, lights melt away.

I expected to sob, to unsettle him with my emotion and then chill him with fat, wet tears. Or worse, that I might feel stilted and awkward, that, frozen in the moment, amongst the lines and wires and under the watchful eye of the nurses, I might forget how to hold him. I'm convinced he'll have to be snatched away and tucked safely back into his incubator for me to wait days before I can try again.

Instead, I feel a deep calm. I wrap my shirt around his back and scrunch my neck to kiss the top of his head. His milky newborn scent mingles with the plastic of the ventilator. Grey's smell. His oxygen levels rise, his heart rate regulates, his breathing steadies.

'He's happy.' Jackie checks his machinery. 'Really settled;

you can see in his numbers.' She nods to me and turns back to the charts.

I look at Mike; he's pulled up a smaller chair next to us. 'If only Finny was here,' he whispers.

'He will be, soon,' I say.

From the trolley behind her, Jackie scoops up a digital camera. Holding it slightly awkwardly, the way my dad holds his iPhone, she lifts it, as if to her eye, and holds it very close to her face as she takes a picture. Then, peering at the camera over her glasses, she hunts for the picture review.

'All this technology,' she says, jabbing at buttons on the screen, 'gives me a bit of a headache. It's like our bloody garage door.' She's still fiddling with the buttons on the camera. 'My husband is a real petrolhead, he's got all these precious bikes, so now we have this very jazzy new electric garage door, with all these alarms. Great. Except it's a nightmare. The alarm's always going off and locking things inside.' She's still prodding the camera. 'I like things simple.'

The irony isn't lost on me – that a NICU nurse, who operates sophisticated baby-lifesaving equipment every day, could be flummoxed by a digital camera, or a garage door.

Finally she finds the photo, and, satisfied, takes it over to the printer at the desk.

It's funny, at first, having some level of surveillance during every interaction. It brings a strange intensity. I feel like a dressage horse, carefully picking up my hooves, anxious to do well, knowing I have an audience. It takes a little while to settle into it, to forget the environment. To remember the nurses aren't testing me; they aren't here to catch us out. Mike leans back against his chair, head on one side so he can look at us, and we sit, Grey nestling on the body that should still be housing him, me holding the back of the little wise man I shouldn't be meeting for two more months. Wrong, but right.

*

I rarely let Finn sleep on me as a baby: as I had left the operating theatre after he was born, an older midwife – not one who'd helped deliver him – barked, 'Never let him fall asleep on you.' It stayed with me. With permission, encouragement, to hold Grey now as long as I can, I drink in every second. It's only when the gradually increasing tingle in my boobs makes me look at the clock that I realise we've been sitting for two hours – pumping is an hour overdue. Reluctantly I tell Jackie I need to go.

'Shall we transfer him to you, Mike? His numbers are so regular, I think he'll be OK out for a bit longer.'

As Jackie lifts Grey, I shimmy out from underneath him and Mike neatly slides in while Kerry re-tapes the ventilator to his arm. Seamless. Two of my three boys are together. I wish Finn was here.

'He's amazing,' Mike says. 'So amazing, G.'

My milk is never in short supply, but today my body has finally flooded with unlocked oxytocin. I could pump for hours and it wouldn't run out.

The same doctor has been in the NICU every day since Grey arrived. He's updated us each morning on the lab, with a reassuring smile. He's a constant presence in the nursery, checking gases, scheduling X-rays, looking at charts. He's here today. He finds us at Grey's bedside and says he's called the lab for the genetic results; they need a little more time, he'll keep chasing, he's sorry the answer is always the same – no news. He pauses by Grey's cot a second longer. 'I can't promise anything, of course, but in my experience, positive results tend to come back quickly. If a baby has a trisomy, they usually call me within a day or two. So keep your faith; let's hope the delay is good news.'

Mike asks him his name.

'Isa,' he says. He's a quiet, thoughtful bear of a man, with a hint of an accent I can't quite place.

'When are you going to get a day off, Isa?' Mike asks.

'You're always here. Surely it's time for a break?' He puts on a mock stern voice. 'Who do I need to speak to?'

'I know, my friend – complain to my boss.' He gives a theatrical wink and claps Mike on the back.

Later, when the NICU is quiet, Isa comes to tell us he's called the lab again. The results still aren't ready.

He hesitates, weighing up whether he'll say more.

'You must keep smiling. You must keep the faith. You must never let him see your worry; he will feel it. You must surround him with positivity, always.' He gestures gently towards Grey. 'He is brave. You can be brave too.' His face lights up. 'He needs you. He needs you, and he needs your positivity. You are all that he needs.'

9

24 November

One week old

Grey is lying on his side. Kerry explains that his lungs sounded wet in the early morning and a swift chest X-ray showed one has collapsed. She quickly reassures me that it isn't uncommon with ventilation, and his level of fluid secretion. They'll lie him on the opposite side to help the fluid drain and let the lung inflate.

'Does it hurt?' I ask.

They don't think so, but will keep an eye on him.

The doctors are on the other side when we arrive. When it's Grey's turn we run through the various tests we're waiting for. Waiting and waiting. As Mike and the doctors update each other, I look at Grey's serene little form and will him to transfer some of his calm to me. Will him to teach me how to be patient.

'I don't think he has a trisomy.' Dr Kumar looks up at Grey as he goes through his notes. 'No.' He shakes his head emphatically. I feel my heart give a little leap.

Kerry agrees. 'I don't think so either.' She shakes her head too, tutting a little.

'We'll wait for the results, of course, but he has strong movements; he doesn't look how I'd expect if this were to be the diagnosis,' Dr Kumar continues.

This *has* to be good news. Surely a doctor wouldn't say this if there was even a shred of doubt in his mind?

As Dr Kumar examines Grey, he notices the size of his head and asks his student to add that to his notes. He looks up at me. 'Has the size of his head been noted before?'

'No. Well, not really. Is it bad? Could it be something bad?' Most of Mike's Googling seems to suggest chromosome abnormalities are connected to small heads.

Dr Kumar shakes his head. 'He does have a big one, but then ...' He's still looking intently at me.

'So do I?'

He nods, and looks from me to Mike. 'You both have large heads ... very large heads.' He is looking pointedly at me. 'I think perhaps this is hereditary. Do you mind if I measure ...?'

He pulls a paper tape from a drawer and I bend a little as he wraps it around my forehead.

'No!' He double-checks the result, aghast. 'You really do have a *very* large head.' He's now shaking his own average-sized head in disbelief. 'Especially for a girl.'

He peers at me, half impressed, half astounded, then turns to Mike – also large, apparently, though not as outrageously enormous as mine. 'Add that to the notes,' he says, still looking at me in amazement.

The student is momentarily confused.

'Please write it on the notes that the mother has an abnormally large head.'

'So that's not bad? For Grey, I mean, it doesn't mean anything bad? The size of his head ...'

'I don't think so. I think he is from a big-head family.'

Our big-head family. I decide it's time to change the subject.

'Did you know that Winston Churchill was born at thirty-one weeks?'

'No – I don't believe it.'

'It's true, honestly. And Isaac Newton, and Charles Darwin – he wasn't expected to survive. Pablo Picasso, Mark Twain ...' I reel off my list of newly discovered world-famous preemies.

'I like this,' says Dr Kumar. 'Could you please print me the list?'

'Aren't there any sportsmen?' Mike asks.

'One.' I pause. 'But I don't know how good he is ... Wayde van Niekerk.'

Mike looks at me, aghast. 'How *good*?! He's an Olympic champion, George. He won gold in Rio. He holds the world record for the four hundred metres.'

So quite good then.

Now I do most of my pumping by Grey's incubator, singing to him or chatting as the whirring machine extracts every drop of precious milk. As I finish my mid-afternoon session, I shift a little in my chair and feel my phone start to slide out of my pocket. I have a split-second choice: milk or phone? There's a sharp crack as it lands screen down on the blue floor. I dismantle the pump and screw the lids tightly onto the bottles before gingerly turning my phone over. I register a flash of irritation as I see what I already know – the screen has shattered. I run a finger across it; nothing happens. Dead. I expect to feel a flood of annoyance, upset, anger even. It doesn't come. My mind leaps immediately to the practicalities of this inconvenience: I can't remember how many people I owe messages to; it's lucky I took out insurance; I wonder how long a replacement will take to arrive. As long as the hospital know my number is out of action, I don't suppose it matters very much.

Sofia is tucking Grey in when we arrive for bedtime stories. The NICU is quiet. A kind of Sunday-evening hush.

'I was near where you're staying all day yesterday,' she tells me, 'watching my sons play football. It was freeeeeeeezing. I spend so much time watching football in the freezing cold.' She is smiling at me.

'Two boys,' I say.

'Two boys,' she echoes.

10

25 November

Eight days old

Monday morning. A week in the NICU and a new COW –
consultant of the week, an acronym Mike has discovered, to
his delight, chatting to one of the registrars.

Excitement mingles with nerves.

A second extubation attempt.

A week of developing, bigger feeds, a little more weight.

Please be ready, little man.

Dr Stewart introduces herself at the ward round in a soft
Scottish brogue. She's telling one of the registrars about a
Georgian house she's doing up on the coast that is being perpetually delayed. 'I don't know why I ever started the project,'
she says. 'It's taking twice as long as anyone expected.'

'Ours is a Victorian terrace,' I say, 'and Grey's bedroom
floor currently has several missing boards. Hopefully it'll be
ready for when he comes home.' I have plans to source recla-
mation boards, sand and paint them, then get a big rug to go
over the top.

She laughs. 'The lesson is – never buy an old house.' She
turns her attention to Grey. 'Hello, little man. Let's have a
look at you.' She gently lifts off his covers and examines him,
feeling his limbs, checking his heart, cupping his head.

We tell her that we're waiting for a transfer back to London
and that Dr Sahu has mentioned we would try to extubate
him today.

She nods, checking his charts, discussing him with his

nurses. 'Over the weekend, Grey's started needing a little more support from his ventilator.'

I try to read her expression.

'He's gone from being in air to needing a little more oxygen.'

She tells us she thinks Grey might have a floppy airway. His chest is a little bit narrow, he has quite a small jaw for his age and the size and shape of his head might mean his tubes don't line up to let him breathe on his own.

'What does a floppy airway mean?'

'Some babies have them and they gradually get a bit better; it might mean he needs support for a while.' She pauses. 'I think we need to wait for the chromosome results, they might tell us more.'

She thinks there's something wrong with him.

'What are they looking for?' I ask. 'With the chromosomes, I mean.'

'Honestly, it is difficult to tell.'

'Will it be something that makes his life very hard?'

'It might.' The registrars are scribbling away in Grey's book while we talk. 'I'm afraid we just don't know for now. I wish I could give you more answers.' She turns back to Grey, feeling his tummy, bending his legs, examining his spine. 'The other thing is going back to London. It's easier to transfer a ventilated baby; when babies come off the ventilator they need a bit of time to settle before being loaded into an ambulance to be jiggled about on a big journey, all right?'

Transfer relies on a bed and an ambulance both being available at the same time, and Grey being well and stable enough to make the journey. If an extubation was successful, it might be a few days, or even a week or more, before he could make the journey.

'While he's ventilated, we can move fast,' she says. She looks from Mike to me. 'I'm sorry, I don't think today is the day.' She smiles sympathetically. 'It's a marathon, not a sprint. Let's give him a bit more time.'

We agree. But it's frustrating, the waiting. The not knowing.

'Surely we can't keep waiting for these chromosome results, which could take five or six weeks,' Mike says. 'Chromosome results on their own aren't necessarily a diagnosis, are they? Shouldn't we still be trying to work out what, if anything, is wrong?'

'I agree,' Dr Stewart says. 'First, let's see what the situation is in London.' She tilts her head towards Grey's nurse for today, Rebekah. 'Please could you call?'

While Mike continues to discuss how to manage the tests Grey needs before the transfer with Dr Stewart, I watch Rebekah across the room, her bobbed hair and blunt fringe swinging as she shakes her head, the phone in one hand. She looks over slim wire-framed glasses as she scribbles something on a piece of paper.

'No cots, I'm afraid.' She's back beside us. 'They're five beds over. They understand the situation, they know they're your booking hospital and the closest to home, but they don't anticipate having a cot for Grey any time soon. We need to keep calling. They have a bed meeting at eleven every morning. If Grey's nurse calls just before that, then he'll be at the front of their mind.'

I realise I am relieved. With each day that goes by I feel some security, some safety, being here in Kent. Shuttling between the hospital and our Airbnb. Our bubble. I'm not sure about starting again, even at a hospital we know; everything will be new – the set-up, the protocol, doctors and nurses who don't know Grey, don't know us.

'I'm so sorry, we'll keep calling,' Dr Stewart says. 'Given transfer is not looking likely to happen soon, I think we should give Grey an MRI. Ultrasound can only see so much – we'll have a clearer idea of what we're dealing with if we have a more detailed picture.' She looks at each of us, smiling her reassuring smile. 'As you say, Mike, we need to start ruling things out. We'll keep chasing for the genetic results, but while they are on their way we can start running some other tests. Once we've done the MRI, we can think about some metabolic tests, look at acids in his body.' Her face is full of sympathy. 'I know it's hard, but putting together a picture can take time.'

We snap on our headphones as she turns to check the next baby. Floppy airways, narrow chest, under-developed chin. More symptoms. I dig my nails into my palms in frustration and stare straight ahead. I am not going to cry. I understand, I really do, why we have to wait, why we have to be patient. Anything that can be done quickly is being done, I can see that – blood tests, X-rays, scans, a doctor snaps their fingers and there they are. An MRI will give us more answers. We *are* moving forward, though it feels like painfully slow progress.

I go to fill up my bottle. As I hold down the button on the water cooler in the corridor, I try to force the negative thoughts swirling through my brain away. I'm vaguely aware of someone walking past me with a stack of papers. Stopping, retracing his steps. It's Isa.

'Why are you not smiling? You are always smiling.'

'Sorry, Isa,' I say. 'Tough day.'

'I want to see that smile.'

Somehow, I muster a smile.

'That's better,' he says. 'You keep positive. That little boy needs you to be positive.' He holds up crossed fingers, then pats me on the shoulder.

He's right. We don't know what's going on, and while we don't know, it's better for everyone to expect the best. I'll try. I really will.

'What does it all mean, MG?'

It's dark and foggy. We're driving home to put Finn to bed.

'Look, G, they have to tell us all the things they see. They're doctors, and he's being monitored all the time. They're bound to spot things, bound to notice every little thing. It really doesn't mean anything is wrong.'

I nod. It's not the first time we've had this conversation, and I know it's unlikely to be the last. 'But what if something is really wrong, what if his life is really hard? I couldn't bear that for him.' The thoughts that tie my head in knots come tumbling out.

'Then we'll work that out, G. But for now, what are we looking at? He has slightly lower than average ears. So do you, so does Finny. He's having trouble breathing – he was born nine weeks early, maybe ten weeks early, we don't know the exact dates; every scan said he was due at a different time. He has narrow shoulders – so do you. He has a smaller corpus callosum, but they have only used one of those crappy portable ultrasounds, and said they can't really see properly. And that didn't show up on the London scans – the best machinery and best sonographers in the world.'

This is our trump card, our real source of reassurance. But in the back of my mind I remember all the in-utero scan warnings: it's impossible to see everything, the scans might miss things, not everything is guaranteed. I push the thought out of my mind.

'And even if his corpus callosum is missing,' Mike goes on, 'we don't know that you, or I, aren't also missing one. And from the reading I've done, it could manifest as something like being less aware of danger.'

'Well, we've all seen you on a ski slope ...'

I manage a weak smile. It all sounds so rational, of course he's right. But I can't shift a feeling that maybe we're being too optimistic.

11

26 November

Nine days old

On the way back from the shower, I see Finn wandering around our room, chattering to himself. He spins when he hears me. 'Bubs,' he says, grinning proudly. He's holding the plastic pump pieces against his chest, cupped into the arch between his thumb and forefinger, exactly mimicking my pumping position. 'Bubs. Mulk.'

My mum hears my laughter and appears in the doorway. Finn turns to her.

'Bubs,' he repeats.

We look at each other and dissolve into laughter once more. Finn laughs too, hysterically, chanting 'Bubs, bubs' over and over as he dances across the carpet, the pump still in place.

Dr Stewart comes to Grey's cot-side during the ward round. Mike has gone to fill up our water bottles.

'How are you doing?' she asks.

'I'm scared,' I say. 'I'm scared that there is something badly wrong with Grey that might mean he can't live any kind of life. I'm scared of that for my baby. Do you think that is what's going to happen?'

'It is a possibility,' she says. 'But we *really* don't know. The difficult thing with chromosome testing is it is such a new science. That's why the results take so long. And even when the microarray – that's the wider testing, when they look at every single gene – comes back, some things are so rare there might be one lab in the world that knows about them – the bloods might need to go to Australia, or somewhere in Europe. Sometimes it can be months, for very rare things.'

'I see.' I'm coming across as calm and rational, but I'm not, not at all.

'What's happened?' Mike is back, and he's seen the panic in my eyes.

'We were just talking about the different possibilities from the chromosome results,' I say. 'Some things are really rare, and more tests have to go to different places.'

'But nothing has come back yet?'

'No, nothing yet,' Dr Stewart says. 'And as I said to Mum, it's a case of ruling things out. We don't know what's going to come back; the frustrating thing is the waiting. We're ruling things out at the moment. So it's one step at a time.'

Over her shoulder I see Isa heading towards the nursery door. He's come to find us every day to update us on the genetic testing, and to share his lyrical words of wisdom. He catches my eye and spins on his heel. 'Georgie, I called again this morning.' He nods at Dr Stewart. 'There are still no results yet. They are processing as fast as they can. They have promised they will let me know as soon as they have them.'

He and Dr Stewart look at Mike and me.

'I know the wait is frustrating,' Dr Stewart says. 'I really do. I wish there was some way for me to speed up this process. We'll keep chasing, all right?'

She reaches out and lays a hand on my arm. I can feel the gentle pressure of her cool fingers through the cotton of my shirt. There's some shred of reassurance in the connection. 'I'm around later, so please, any questions – come and find me, or ask Jackie to find me.'

Jackie is looking after Grey. Kerry is on our side too. She wears oversized, dark-framed glasses and manages to keep her thick, straight hair in a pristine ponytail all shift long, I don't know how. And there's a nurse called Caroline with cropped, bleached hair, who I haven't met before.

It's quiet, so Jackie and I are chatting.

'What do you do, Georgie?' she asks.

'You mean in life? When I'm not in a NICU, pumping?'

'Your job, yes,' she laughs.

'I don't want to tell you,' I say. 'It is so insignificant. I do something which really doesn't matter at all. Mike and I keep talking about that on our way home. We feel so embarrassed about our jobs when you are all here keeping babies alive.'

'But that's life, Georgie. This is my job. I probably couldn't do what you do.'

'I write about clothes.' Saying the words aloud makes it sound even more trivial, ridiculous really, here in this room with these amazing women, these tiny precious babies.

'Fashion – I don't know much about that world,' Jackie says, without reflecting any of my own disdain.

'I'm a sort of editor, consultant, writer, sometimes a journalist. I mostly write about luxury fashion – expensive clothes.' I glance down at my outfit – still rotating the two old oversized shirts I took to Whitstable with maternity leggings. 'Feels quite far away right now,' I laugh. 'It's fun. I like it, I do. I'm lucky I get to do something I love. But then you're suddenly catapulted in here and it doesn't feel like it matters very much.'

I do love what I do. I always wanted to be a fashion designer. I studied it at university, after an idyllic art foundation course at Falmouth in Cornwall. A variety of lucky internships blended design, editorial, styling, journalism. In the early days, I resisted anything to do with writing. That was my dad's world. I wanted to make it on my own. The irony, of course, was that I would never have been able to find my way in the fashion industry without the support of my parents. I was determined and I worked hard – in New York that meant seven days a week – and sometimes, before a show, through the night. It took me a few years to realise I would never be a designer. I wasn't good enough. And really, I love words too much. Words are where I feel at home. I moved sideways into editorial, and when I'd gathered enough clients, decided to go it alone.

'How long have you been in the NICU for?' I ask.

Caroline and Kerry look up from what they're doing.

'Too long, Georgie,' Jackie says.

'We're the old-timers,' Caroline says.

'I've worked here since before the NICU was even here,' Jackie continues. 'It used to be the other side of town, then it moved. And it moved thirty-something years ago.'

'I started the week it did so,' Caroline says.

'I started on the same day,' Kerry chimes in.

'Longer ago than any of us would care to mention.' Jackie laughs, and turns to Caroline. 'Do you remember when the one ventilator we had was in that old leather suitcase?'

'And we had no incubators in this unit – just heat shields,' Kerry says.

'How early was early then?' I ask. 'It must be quite different now?'

'I think we got quite excited if we had a twenty-eight-weeker in those days. It's very different now.'

'It must have changed so much; all the scientific advances ...'

'Yes.' Jackie pauses. 'It *is* amazing. I just don't know how far it can go.'

'Viability, you mean?'

Jackie nods.

'I was talking to Dani, on the labour ward, about that. She said it can give people false hope. But she had two real preemies, who were both fine.'

'The very early ones have a real time of it,' Jackie says.

'And they're talking about lowering the viability gestation, aren't they?'

Jackie sighs. 'I think if the limit goes down, it'll be time for me to retire. I've seen twenty-two-weekers: the pain, the

104

intrusive treatments, it's really not humane.' She shakes her head. 'They have to go through so much, and they have so little chance. Let's just say, if I went into labour at twenty-two weeks, I know what I'd do. And it wouldn't be come to hospital.'

Kerry and Caroline are shaking their heads.

'A long walk along the beach . . .'

Her words hang in the air.

Nena is back this evening. I slip Grey's octopus in beside him and watch him reach out to grasp a tentacle and pull it towards him, tucking it under his chin. 'I'm pleased he can have a little toy to cuddle. It's nice.' I pause. 'Finny has a rabbit, Rab; he sleeps with him every night.'

'My son has a Mickey Mouse,' Nena says. 'He's fourteen, but he still has him – although I find it hidden in his cupboard when his friends stay the night.'

'That's so sweet,' I say, 'but I cannot believe you have a fourteen-year-old son.' I stare at her. Straight, dark hair, cut in a sharp line and worn in a ponytail; gleaming skin, huge eyes. Nena looks in her late twenties, at a push. 'You really don't look old enough.'

'I am old.' She gives a wry smile. 'Look at these.' She points at non-existent greys along her glossy hairline.

12

27 November

Ten days old

Finn's lingering cough has finally disappeared.

'Do you want to meet your brother today, Finny?' I ask at breakfast.

'Uggs,' he replies, pointing at my mum's scrambled eggs.

'Can you say "brother"?' Mike says.

'Uggs,' Finn repeats, still pointing.

Possibly the wrong moment to bring it up.

Back at the hospital, I open Grey's book. A new butterfly print has been hole-punched and interleaved. Of course, Nena was on duty overnight. *'Ten little fingers, ten perfect toes, two beautiful eyes, one button nose xxx'*

I run my finger over the tiny footprints. These overnight additions to Grey's book remind me of Finn's childcare diary, and the little projects Lorraine, his childminder, undertakes with her charges. They provide me with capsule moments of calm, a roundabout sense of normality.

At the morning ward round, Dr Stewart tells us that Grey's pH levels have been a bit unstable. She's wondering if perhaps there's a mechanical problem that might be linked to his other symptoms.

I fix my gaze on his face to try to stop my heart from sinking.

She tells us she's requested an MRI, which should be able to happen as early as the weekend. He will be gently sedated, she explains, to ensure he stays completely still. It might make him very drowsy for six to eight hours, but it's the best way of ensuring a clear picture.

She has also put the wheels in motion for a heart scan, kidney scan and metabolic testing, depending on the results of the MRI. And she has a new theory about Grey's secretions. 'Reflux,' she says. 'I wonder if it's reflux.'

It's the first time I've recognised any of the myriad words and conditions that have been thrown around. I have friends with refluxy babies; it's horrid, but not uncommon, and it's manageable.

'His secretions are very thick,' Dr Stewart continues. 'I wonder if it might, in fact, be milk.'

'That would be good?' I'm hesitant; perhaps this is a different kind of reflux. 'Reflux as in the same reflux babies get when they're not in the NICU?'

'Yes.' She smiles. 'I'm not saying definitely, but I do think it would be worth us changing his feeding to bypass his little tummy and see if that makes a difference.'

The staff room is opposite the reception, and this afternoon it's a party venue. A nurse we haven't met is retiring. From conversations we've overheard on the unit, it sounds as though she is very unwell. A couple of Grey's nurses are there, eating pizza, sipping from plastic cups. Seeing them off duty, out of scrubs, out of the NICU, sitting around in a circle, chatting, laughing, reminds me that these wonderful women have their own lives, their own challenges, their own tragedies.

We meet my mum and Finn by the family locker room – Kerry is on her way home as they go to hang up their coats. She's in a sweatshirt and workout leggings (I had her down as an exerciser). 'This must be Finn,' she says, crouching to say hello. She turns to me. 'He's thinking, Who is this weird lady who knows my name? He looks just like you, Georgie!'

Minutes later, Jackie comes past too. 'Doesn't he look like Mike!'

I smile.

Mike carries Finn along the NICU corridor. He looks around, hands flapping in a regal wave to everyone who passes. 'A-LO, a-LO, a-LO ...'

At the door to the NICU we crouch to wash his hands, and then cover them in alcohol rub. He laughs and wiggles his fingers as it dries and cools. Mike scoops him up, carrying him into Grey's nursery. Suddenly, he is quiet, looking around.

'A-lo,' he says to the nurse at the desk, more tentatively than his exuberant corridor greetings.

Mike carries him over to Grey's incubator. 'This is your brother,' he says. 'This is Grey. Can you say "brother"?'

Finn lowers his eyes, looking from Mike to me. Then, 'Ta-ter,' he says gently, extending one finger to point into Grey's incubator. 'Ta-ter ...' He waves at him and grins.

I feel tiny wings unfurl from my soul, lifting my heart, dusting off a little of the anxiety as I watch my boys look at one another.

Mike stands over the incubator so Finn can peer in. His small smooth face looks up, looks around. 'Ta-ter, *shhh* ...' he says, holding one finger purposefully to his lips.

'Yes, your brother is sleeping, you're right—'

Before we have a chance to intercept, he slams his pudgy hand down on top of the incubator with a 'Ta-ter!' and laughs uproariously.

Somehow, Grey sleeps on, unfazed by the crash that reverberates through his little home. Brotherly love.

'Qwack-qwack! Ta-ter, qwack-qwack!' Finn is suddenly animated, shouting and pointing at Grey.

Mike and I are confused. I look down at Grey and back at Finn. Then I notice Grey has kicked down his covers enough for the little gold duck sticker that holds his temperature monitor to show.

'"Quack", he's saying "quack"!' Finn squeezes Mike's arm with pride.

'Duck – you're right, Finny, a mummy duck,' says Mike.

It's a world away from the meeting I've imagined – Grey wrapped snugly into his Moses basket, Finn peering over the edge; or Finn insisting on holding Grey across his lap on the sofa, Mike and I desperately trying to stop his fingers finding a soft spot in his new sibling's eye. But this afternoon has a different kind of magic. All of us together for the first time, a complete family.

Finn seems to sense the gravity of the moment – incubator-thumping aside, he's quieter and more thoughtful than his usual boisterous self, at least for a few minutes. It's a momentary exhale, a gentle sigh amidst the turmoil, the uncertainty, the terror.

Now, whenever Finn picks up the phone for an imaginary conversation, it's always to speak to the same person. 'A-lo,' he says, then pauses, wandering, picking things up and putting them down. 'Ya … ya … ya …'

'Who's on the phone, Finny?' one of us will ask.

'Ta-ter.'

Dr Stewart has warned us that because of waiting lists, even though they're fast-tracking Grey it seems likely the MRI would be at the weekend, so it's a surprise when it's suddenly scheduled for Thursday. Tomorrow, the day after he's met Finn. Eleven days old and having an MRI.

I see a familiar figure by Grey's incubator when I come to sit with him in quiet time.

'Still no news from the genetics, my friends,' Isa says, 'but Grey's MRI is booked for tomorrow.' As he repeats the schedule Dr Stewart has given us, his voice lifts gently, questioning whether this is new information. He rolls the rs gently around his mouth.

He has come to do Grey's gas, so he gently unsticks the little plaster from his heel, pricks it and presses a tiny straw to the puncture, carefully collecting a minute vial of blood.

'He is a strong boy,' he says. 'And you must stay strong for him too. You can do that.'

We nod.

'He will feel your positivity, it is better for him. He must not feel your worry, your sadness. Only love and positivity, my friends.' He smiles his encouragement.

'How's that holiday coming along, Isa?' Mike says.

'My friend, it starts tomorrow. Your influence worked.' He winks. 'I'm back next Wednesday.'

'Big plans?' Mike asks.

'This and that.' He tips his head from side to side.

'I hope you can relax,' I say.

'I will, my friends. I will.'

'Do you miss the Philippines?' Mike asks Nena. The nursery is quiet; we're standing by Grey's incubator. In a little while we'll read him his bedtime story.

'I always miss the idea of it,' she says. 'I love going back to Manila, taking my son, visiting family. It's a wonderful place – wonderful weather.'

'I bet,' Mike says. 'I'd love to visit.'

'But when we are there,' she continues, 'I miss everything about here, all the amazing things about this part of the world. Going back makes me realise this is home now. Kent is home.'

My new phone arrived today, so I'm back in communication with the world. A couple of days of digital space has felt cleansing. On the way home a message pings through from Loula. More wise words: 'I'm going to change the way I live my life because of Grey.'

She's right. I already feel like I have been reshaped. A different version of me is emerging from the day before this little boy was born. Family, friends, health, love. Everything else is background noise, really.

I repeat the words to myself. I hope I will remember them.

13

Eleven days old

In the morning, I open Grey's book. Someone has stuck in the gold duck temperature probe, and added three baby ducks following along behind, with '*My temperature mummy duck probe cover*'. Underneath it is a coil of leads – a heart rate monitor. His has been replaced overnight. It must have been Nena; she was looking after Grey.

Rebekah is on duty today. Mike has discovered her parents are from Trinidad, and they've bonded over Brian Lara.

'Wow, I'd love to go to Trinidad,' I tell her. We feel about as far from a Caribbean beach as it's possible to be.

'My husband is from Mauritius,' she says.

Mike grins. 'Holidays must be pretty rubbish in your family.'

Rebekah laughs. 'If I had to pick one, I'd retire to Mauritius,' she says. 'Mauritius is amazing.'

She has two teenage children. Her daughter was brilliant at the piano, she tells us, but gave it up and now regrets it.

'We all know that feeling,' I say. 'I can remember my parents telling me I'd regret it. I thought, no I won't. I think it's one of those things. I'm sure one day I'll say the same to Grey and Finn ... They won't believe me either, of course.'

'Of course,' she says.

Rebekah's father is a pastor – hence the biblical name. She's brilliantly practical in her approach to the NICU, to looking after Grey. Deft hands and an organised mind, she firmly guides us through his care routine, making sure we're always busy.

Kerry is on duty too. 'It was nice to meet Finn yesterday,' she says, passing Grey's incubator with a box of miniature syringes. 'He's adorable. And he does have quite a big head! I was looking at him, thinking, Gosh, he does have a big head. And it's exactly the same shape as Grey's.'

'He does!' I laugh. 'And it is.'

'I didn't say it in front of him as I thought that would be a bit rude – and in front of your mum; she'd be thinking, Who's this?!'

'She would have laughed too.' I point at my head. 'As Dr Kumar said, it isn't a surprise!'

'Well, I don't look at you and think your head is big.'

'Hopefully the boys will both grow into theirs.'

'Of course they will.' She smiles reassuringly and goes back to what she's doing.

I pump while Mike speaks to Dr Stewart at the ward round. Grey seems more comfortable and his secretions have reduced. She's going to send some for testing. I pray the reflux idea is right.

He's grown, she says, and his lung is looking better. Best of all, he's gagging. Not much, but a little. And his chest looks like his breathing is less laboured. It's all good news. I don't know how to feel. Cautiously optimistic, perhaps. In reality, it's nothing so measured; my mind still ricochets between sheer terror and desperate hope. In preparation for the MRI, he'll be put in a little hat and earmuffs, as well as heel-huggers with warmers inside. Rebekah promises to make sure he's very cosy. His hands will be free.

Everyone comments on Grey's fingers. Though each one is cast in miniature, every detail is there already – the lines, the joints, the perfect whorls of his little prints. They are so expressive. In the absence of cries, of mews, without being able to see his expression through the ventilator, his hands become the principal method of communication. They curl in under his chin when he is relaxed, or asleep; they flutter over his covers, his wires, his tubes as his eyes blink open; they flinch with the prick of a blood gas; clench when his throat, his chest, is suctioned. And when I rest a hand on top of his chest his little fingers curl gently around mine, cocooning me.

Grey's on an afternoon list. I remember the MRI I had the summer before Mike and I got married, to check nothing sinister was happening with my fibroids. I was terrified. I cried through most of it, and I was thirty. And I'm about to put my fragile eleven-day-old baby through the same experience.

'He'll be fine.' Rebekah has read my mind. 'He'll be very gently sedated. Babies cope very well with them, and this guy's made of strong stuff.' She smiles fondly at him. 'It might be a lot of waiting,' she warns. 'I'll go with him, and one or both of you can come too.'

'I think I should stay with Grey,' Mike says, 'and you should go and hang out with Finny.'

I think he's right, but I'm torn. 'Are you sure? Should I stay too? I feel guilty about leaving him.'

'Don't feel guilty, he wouldn't want that. Go and be with Finny, G,' Mike says. 'I'll keep you updated.'

My mum and Finn come to collect me, while Mike stays with Grey.

'Look at my new hat, Mummy.' A message and picture pop through – Grey in a little pale blue knitted hat. 'They had to change his ventilator as the other one had metal in it – obviously not OK for the MRI – so this one is sewn in and now he has this silly hat on.' It looks like a little old-fashioned Victorian bonnet – firmly not Mike's baby-dressing style.

My phone rings and Mike's face flashes up just after I get home to Finn. I answer on the first ring. 'Is he OK? What's happened?'

'G . . .'

I can hear Mike crying.

'What? What is it?' The beginnings of a thousand unvoiced fears start to form in my mind.

'No, it's OK, it's good. The chromosome results came back; he's clear on the trisomies. He doesn't have *any* of them, George.'

I sink back against the pillow. Finally, some good news. 'Oh, thank God, little boy ...'

'We can do this, G. He's so brave,' he whispers. 'I love you, I'll see you soon.'

I fly downstairs. 'Mumma, he doesn't have any of the trisomies!'

Then I type out a message to each of our family WhatsApps. 'Good news today – the trisomies have come back negative. G on his way to the MRI, Mike with him.'

This must be a positive sign?

I let the desperate hope creep in front of the terror.

It feels good.

The MRI is delayed and delayed. Finally, around six, Mike calls to say Grey is back in the NICU. 'Rebekah said he did so well – he was really brave and really good. He's back in his incubator now, but the sedation won't wear off for a while and then he'll be tired; it's been a big day for a small man.'

'Give him my love,' I say. 'Tell him I'll see you later. He's so amazing, MG, he's already been through so much. More than our combined almost seventy years.'

'He'll be an amazing man because of it,' Mike says before he hangs up.

'Surely you wouldn't miss something very, very bad.' We are driving home from the hospital after Grey's bedtime story. 'I mean, on the London ultrasound.'

'Twice,' Mike says.

'Twice?'

'The corpus callosum starts forming before twelve weeks.'

My husband is now a neurological expert. 'So two scans missed it.'

'I know we've already talked about this so many times, but I still need to get my head around it.'

'Also, a missing corpus callosum isn't "very, very" bad, G. It might be nothing very much at all, it's such an unknown.'

'I know, I know. And I know I have to try to be patient. But it's really hard, isn't it?'

'It is. I know, I really do.'

Of course he does.

Mike is looking out of the windscreen, one hand on the wheel, one hand tapping his leg. He's so calm, so rational, so resolute. I wonder at how brilliant he is being, for me, for Grey, for Finn. I know he's terrified too. And yet not for a second does he betray that. He is carrying me, carrying us all.

Friends, doctors, nurses, keep saying it must be so hard being away from home. In fact, I think it's easier. As each day goes by it feels more and more like it was meant to be like this. We have physical space here that we wouldn't have at home, which somehow seems to bring emotional space. We can shuttle between our Airbnb bubble and our hospital bubble with no risk of bumping into anyone.

And much as I love all our friends for saying they'll come, for knowing they will, I'm somehow glad they can't. I'm scared of puncturing the bubble, of letting the outside world in. There's no room for it here. And what is home really? It's so much more than bricks and mortar, than the space where we live.

Mike, Finn and Grey are my home.

So I *am* home.

14

Twelve days old

Nena is on duty overnight. When I call at three, she tells me Grey's temperature has spiked a little, so she's turned down the thermostat in his incubator.

'Do you think it's because of his new hat?' I ask.

'It could be.' She speaks softly, her voice soothing, comforting in the early hours. 'I'll keep a close eye on him. It's gone back down to normal now. I'm with him, you get some more sleep, Georgie. I'll see Mike later.'

I hang up and finish pumping. Most of the time, I try not to think too much about spending all our nights away from Grey. About how unnatural it is. About how lonely middle of the night waking is when I'm feeding two tubes instead of my small son. But tonight I can't push away the missing him. The gap in our room, in my nights. I miss his gentle featherweight body, his long limbs, his tiny hands. Eventually I fall back to sleep.

When Friday starts properly, it's the same as other NICU days – Mike's early-morning visit to the hospital, my early-morning pumping. Mike's mum has finally been cleared by her doctor to come and see Grey. It's a mark of quite how desperate she is to meet her new grandson that by the time Mike is back at a quarter to seven, she's already on her way.

Nena has told Mike that Grey's lungs have cleared and his blood gas is looking good. On the X-ray to check, they spotted

116

a PDA, a small opening between the aorta and pulmonary artery that all babies have in utero, and which usually closes naturally just after birth. It's not unusual for it to be open in preemie babies. Interestingly, she tells us, it closes with ibuprofen – the reason pregnant women can't take the painkiller.

Rebekah has stuck the funny little earmuffs from Grey's MRI into his book, with a note saying how proud she is of him. And Nena has made a collage of pictures overnight, with a handprint in the middle. On the back is a note: *'Thank you Mum, thank you Dad. Three small words, so much to add. For all your love and your support a million words would be too short. The words I love you seem too few to express the love I have for you. Your son, Grey.'*

My breath catches in my throat.

Jackie is on duty, sorting milk as we arrive in the NICU.

'How is he?' I ask.

'He's having trouble regulating his temperature.'

I nod. 'Nena said he was hot in the night; do you think that could be because of the new hat?' I know full-term babies can't regulate their temperature very well in the early days, and wondered if the addition of a woollen bonnet could have warmed him up.

'No, I don't,' Jackie says, not meeting my eye. 'I think it's something mechanical, Georgie.'

I feel a flash of frustration – something inside me clings adamantly to my bonnet theory.

Dr Stewart checks Grey over during the ward round, then says, 'Let's talk later – I know you have the trisomy results, but we should talk through them.'

It seems sensible: I'm not totally clear on what's come back and what we are waiting for. I thank her and go to pump.

As I gather my things and take them into the milk room, I see Jackie moving chairs into the area by the family room. Mike stops to hold open the door for her.

Half an hour later I wash my pump pieces and re-submerge them in the Milton bucket labelled with Grey's name, then carry the bottles of fresh, warm milk to the fridge in his nursery.

'No cots, I'm afraid,' Jackie says. 'I just called. They're still over.'

'I suppose they don't have any idea of when they might have one?' I ask.

'They said definitely not until next week now, with the weekend. I'm afraid, in my experience, cots at London hospitals are rather like hen's teeth.'

Not ideal, but understandable. It's a specialist unit, so very ill babies from all over London, and all over the south-east, are sent there for surgery. Of course they take precedence over a stable baby in an incubator elsewhere.

Dr Stewart is back in the nursery. 'Do you have time for a chat now?' She smiles at Mike and me. We nod. 'Jackie, can you take them to the quiet room?'

Her straight blond hair held back in a low ponytail, Dr Kate follows us down the NICU corridor, back towards the family room. She was last on duty the day after Grey was born.

'Did you have a good break?' I ask. 'Somewhere nice?'

'Just home.' She turns big, slightly earnest eyes on me. 'We all need time out sometimes. A break from all this ...' she stops twirling her pen between her fingers for a moment and waves it in no particular direction '... intensity.'

I can only imagine. She looks about my age, maybe younger.

We chat about the weather – it's grey and drizzly – as they steer us along the hall. The caretaker steaming the floor is making his way slowly towards us. I say hello as we pass; he nods in some form of recognition. A procession of SCBU and HDU nurses emerges from the milk kitchen, clutching bottles.

Jackie guides us into the family section, past the family room. I know there are bedrooms down here, but I haven't been further along the corridor. 'QUIET ROOM', a placard announces. I've noticed it before, wondered what it's for. I thought perhaps a feeding room. She knocks on the door. Satisfied it's empty, she ushers us towards a sofa. 'You can sit here, Mike, Georgie.'

'This room is supposed to have a temperature check every hour.' Dr Kate studies the list on the back of the door.

'Every hour?' I ask. 'Why?'

'Lord knows. I mean, with all the cuts, checking the temperature in the quiet room is pretty low on our list of priorities.' She looks more closely. 'Ah-ha, it hasn't been checked since July 2017.'

We all laugh.

Dr Stewart arrives a couple of minutes later. Her knock seems more staccato. The atmosphere shifts as she sits down opposite us.

She takes a breath. 'I've brought you in here because I've had a look at Grey's MRI with some of the adult brain MRI specialists.'

Not the chromosomes. The bottom falls out of my stomach.

'We don't know very much; we need to wait for the full report. But I wanted to tell you what we can see.' She takes another breath.

I search her face. It's grim. I reach over and grip Mike's hand.

She speaks softly. 'Do you remember Dr Sahu said we couldn't see a fully formed corpus callosum on the ultrasounds?'

We nod.

'Well, it isn't there at all.' She pauses, letting the information sink in. 'Grey is also missing something called a septum pellucidum.'

I understand her expression, her tone, rather than the words, and silent tears slide down my cheeks, drip off my chin into my lap. Jackie hands me a tissue. I swipe at my face, then crumple it in my spare hand.

'This is a membrane which separates the sides of the brain. It's linked to many different systems, including vision.'

Dr Stewart carries on speaking.

'Dr Sahu told you, I think, that the corpus callosum affects the fluid in our brains? Well, in Grey's case, there is too much – a lot too much.'

It's as though my mind has slipped out of my body and is now watching from the wall above my head as she lists the catalogue of things that are wrong with our son's brain – Latin words that mean nothing to me, and then, in plain English, what each one will mean: 'Unlikely to breathe without a ventilator ... speech difficult or impossible ... no sight ... limited hearing ...'

On and on it goes.

Every word reverberates inside my skull. Mike's ashen face crumpling beside me brings my mind back into my body. He curls his head into his chest and begins to sob. I feel my stomach lurch and taste bile in my throat as I watch him listen to her. His pain rips straight through me. I am watching one of the three people I love most in the world try to absorb the very worst possible news. And there is nothing I can do.

I reach for him, put my hand onto his back, hoping the contact might transfer something – strength? Love? But it's useless; it does nothing. I am powerless. I wish with every molecule of my being that I could make this stop. That I could take away his pain. I wish that what she's saying might be wrong. But I am helpless in the face of his agony, our agony.

She can't, surely, be talking about Grey; she can't be talking about our son. That tiny person bravely kicking away in his incubator in the NICU nursery.

'I'm so, so sorry,' she says.

I can see she is fighting back tears. This cheery Scottish doctor having to tell parents the very last things they want to hear.

I take a deep breath and look up at the ceiling, then back at her. Somewhere inside me the image of Grey brings a whispered breath of calm. I focus and take hold of it with both hands. We know the beginnings of what we are dealing with, of how bad the situation is.

'Did I do something? Did I not do something? Did I eat something? Could it be because I sometimes forgot my antenatal vitamins?' I can hear the desperation creeping into my voice.

'Is it my fault?' I ask, finally.

It must be.

'No, no, darling ...' Her voice breaks. 'No, this is not your fault. You must not think that.'

I don't believe her.

'I'm sorry, I don't have more information until we get the full report, but this is *not* because of anything you have done.'

It must be, just must be. Surely there's something I've got wrong? I'm his mother, I'm supposed to protect him, look after him, and I can't, I've let him down all over again. I couldn't keep him safely inside me, and now he's in the world with difficulties so severe I can't even process them.

'We've asked the specialist to hurry the report. We'll let you know as soon as we have it. It will probably be next week now, but sometimes she sends information over the weekend. I'm so sorry. We'll let you know as soon as we have it,' she repeats. 'Do you have any questions?'

Mike asks about the list of issues Grey has and how they are linked. Dr Stewart answers as best she can, but repeats that really they don't know much more than what she has told us.

But what she's told us is enough.

'Thank you,' I hear myself say.

Jackie, Dr Kate and Dr Stewart all look pale. 'Take all the time you need in here,' she says. They walk out, heads bowed. Jackie places a hand on Mike's arm before they leave, pushing the box of tissues gently into his lap. For a minute or two we sit in silence, staring at the wall in front of us.

'Poor little boy; our poor, poor little boy,' Mike whispers.

I have nothing to say. A loop plays in my mind: I've let

Grey down, what have I done, why couldn't I protect him? I can't believe this is happening to my tiny, perfect, utterly defenceless baby.

I look around at this little room. So mundane, and yet I will remember every part of it, the lines of the nondescript furniture etched into my mind. The wall in front of us is covered in large Formica cupboards, padlocked shut. The curtains are layered over net, for privacy I suppose. Behind us on the wall there is a sculpture, of sorts – twisted links connecting domes of beaten metal; it reminds me of an exhibition I once went to in an east London warehouse. It looks angry. Our sofa faces three chairs, a bucket seat and two of the sturdy fake-leather numbers from the NICU. The walls are a cheery yellow, the floor somewhere between brown and purple. The back of the door holds the redundant temperature form that we were laughing about less than an hour ago, slipped into a plastic sleeve.

'I don't know ... I can't ... I don't know what to say ...'

Minutes tick by as we sit in silence, staring straight ahead. I try to clear my mind, to form some response. But what is there?

'Shall we go and get some fresh air?' I ask at last. Mike puts an arm around me, steadying me as we stand.

'A white chocolate and cranberry slice?' he asks, looking at me with bloodshot eyes and a broken smile.

We leave the quiet room, shut the door behind us and walk towards the NICU reception. In the hall, the nurses still come and go, the caretaker with his steam cleaner is still progressing along the corridor, perpetually disinfecting. Vicky and Gemma are still at the reception desk. Nothing has changed, and everything has changed. Our world has been picked up and hurled against the wall, smashed into little tiny razor-sharp shards. There is no possibility of restoring it to the world of an hour ago.

I smile at some passing NICU parents – their baby is on the other side of Grey's nursery, but I don't know their names.

The soft, familiar chitter-chatter of visiting family drifts past my ears.

As we walk out of the NICU towards the hospital Costa I turn to Mike. 'Why did you say "smorgasbord"?'

'What?'

'You said to Dr Stewart, "Grey's smorgasbord of issues".'

'Did I?'

'Yes, and even though everything was awful, for a second all I could think was, Why is he saying "smorgasbord"? Isn't that some kind of Scandinavian sandwich?'

'A Swedish open-sandwich buffet,' he replies with authority. 'Everything on offer.'

'You compared our son's severe brain abnormalities to a Swedish open-sandwich buffet?' I shake my head.

'Well, it works: there is a lot on offer at a smorgasbord ... But, I'll admit, it was perhaps an odd choice of words. Doesn't shock do weird things to your brain? Isn't that a fact?'

'It was weirdly funny,' I say. 'Even though I felt like the world was closing in on me, I suddenly wanted to laugh.'

'It's a relief I can still make you laugh.' He wraps his arm around me.

Thank God for you, I think, for the thousandth time.

I wonder when it will stop. Surely now this is enough testing. He's arrived early, we waited to hold him, we waited for the results, we've tried so hard to stay positive, to be brave for our brave little Grey, for Finny. To make friends, to be civil and kind and polite and reasonable and patient. Mike's been charming and funny and made some signature awkward comments. As Lisa said, we're nice people and we've been really super extra nice. Now someone can come and tell us that it's OK, it was all a test and we've passed and we can take Grey home.

But that's not how life works. That's not the deal.

As we walk to the car, I touch Mike's arm.

'MG ...'

'Yes?'

'Do you think ...' I gulp. 'I don't even know how to say this. Do you think he'll live? I mean, do you think he'll die?'

There's silence.

Then Mike takes a deep breath. 'I think that might be up to us, G.'

PART TWO

THE MEMORY BOX

15

29 November

Twelve days old

'What do you think?' Lisa is holding a fur-trimmed Father Christmas hat. Mike has gone to get a coffee, so I've walked back to the NICU alone. 'For Scarlett? The fur is rabbit, which is a bit creepy, but it's cute, I think. I've decided: if she can't come to Christmas, Christmas will come to her. Starting now.'

'So cute,' I hear myself say. 'She'll look adorable.'

'Well, we're going to get some lunch. I'm hoping for afternoon cuddles.'

She raises crossed fingers as she walks away. I smile and do the same.

Joy, side by side with agony. I wonder if German or Japanese has a single word to encompass this feeling.

Jackie lays down Grey's charts, putting a hand on Mike's shoulder.

'I'm so sorry,' she says. 'I know there's nothing I can say. But we're here, always, whatever you need.'

And they really are. This woman who I've barely known two weeks feels closer to Grey, and to us, than almost anyone else in the world. We sit with Grey for some time, talking to him, stroking him. His hands curl and uncurl as they've always done; his long, elegant fingers grip and release his octopus's tentacles. His legs kick at the bottom of his preemie bed. How can such a tiny perfect body be hiding so much? My darling boy, you've already taught me so much. But I have a feeling the hardest of your lessons are yet to come.

Dr Stewart comes back in the afternoon, to see how we're doing. I'm pumping by Grey's incubator.

'I don't have any news from the MRI specialist,' she says. 'I'm sorry – I must have checked my emails a hundred times already. I'll come and find you as soon as she replies.'

'Thank you,' I say.

She hovers by Grey's cot. 'I've also been thinking about where you could stay. I gather you have to move out of your Airbnb.'

I nod. Mike discussed it with Nena during his early-morning visit.

'The house next door to mine is rented out for short-term lets. It's a little bit further away from here – thirty or forty minutes – but it's lovely, by the sea, very quiet. I think Finn would love it. I know he loves the sea. I can ask my neighbours, if that would help . . .'

'That's so kind,' I say. 'Thank you. I'll speak to Mike; he's been trying to get hold of our Airbnb host, to see if we can stay a bit longer. Until we have a bit of a clearer idea about everything.'

She is nodding.

'I don't feel ready to go back to London now. I don't know if I want to go back.'

We stand side by side. I feel her arm pressing against mine as we look down at Grey. I know she understands.

Mike asks Dr Stewart where in Scotland she's from.

'Edinburgh.'

'I thought so,' he says. 'I love Edinburgh, I was at university there; it's a great city. One of the reasons Grey is called Grey, actually, is that my grandmother, who passed away just before Finn was born, used to tell me the story of Greyfriars Bobby when I was small.'

'Oh, that's a wonderful story.'

'Are you ever tempted to go back?' Mike asks.

'It's funny you should say that. Not to Edinburgh, but a good friend of mine is setting up the NICU services for the Outer Hebrides and asked me if I wanted to go and help. Setting up the air ambulance, working out how you get the tiny babies back to the mainland if they need treatment.'

'Incredible.'

'Incredible ... and full on. I've said no for now, but I wouldn't rule it out for the future.'

Her mind is momentarily elsewhere. Perhaps on a beach in Skye. The white sand, the clear water, the gulls swooping in to the shore.

I wish I could go there too.

Through the course of the morning, Grey's doctors and nurses have closed ranks around us. They are carrying us. Some of the natural barriers, the formality of the relationship, have been broken down. They feel like friends, family, albeit with sophisticated neonatal knowledge. Perfect friends for now.

We promised Finn we'd be home for lunch and we're running late. I watch the fields roll past, stretching out in either direction. The countryside is flat, and there aren't many trees; now and then a house sits right on the road. There is an openness, compared with Somerset – fewer fences or hedges. I can see for miles. I look round. Mike grips the steering wheel. He stares straight ahead. I close my hand over his.

'No matter what,' he says, 'we take the pain. All he is ever going to know in his life is love. Every decision we make, every single one, we have to remember that. If we know he is not going to be in pain, we can take it all. OK, G?'

I nod.

'We take the pain,' I whisper, looking out of the window.

Finny meets us at the door, stamping his feet with excitement – he's been waiting. As he sees me, his eyes light up – Mummy means ...

129

'Dada! Dada!' He flings himself, giggling, at Mike. Sally, Mike's mum, is behind him. She kisses us both. 'This little boy has been very excited to see his daddy.'

'We'll take Finny up for his nap,' Mike says.

They chivvy Finn up the stairs and I follow my mum into the kitchen. I am drawing out each step. Each step before I have to tell her. I wish I didn't have to. I wish I didn't have to tell anyone. This horrible, twisted, shocking thing.

I shake my head as she turns around. I can't stop the tears that pool into my eyes.

'George?' Her brow is furrowed.

'It's so bad, Mumma. So, so bad. His brain, it's not OK, it's not OK at all.' I can't say any more, can't explain the details of what the doctors have told us.

'Oh God, George.' She wraps her arms around me.

'I can't believe it. I can't believe this is happening. I wish I could stop it.'

She squeezes tighter, wrapping me in love.

And we stand. And stand.

My dad is on the way from London. When he arrives, I'm on the sitting-room floor, legs pulled into my chest, chin resting on my knees. He takes his place beside me. We face the wall.

'It's very bad,' I say. 'What they've told us. The results of the MRI. He's so ill, Daddy.' I try to force the emotion out of my voice. It's the only way I can say the words, to tell it like it isn't my son I'm talking about, it's not Grey. I repeat Dr Stewart's words.

He is silent.

'You know I'll do anything, George ...' His voice breaks and he is sobbing, 'I'll do ... anything.'

I know he will. I know. He always has. Every moment of my life has been cushioned by the knowledge that my parents will do anything for me. It is in this moment that I truly real-ise how profoundly lucky I am.

'There's nothing, Dada, there's nothing you can do, nothing we can do. There's nothing anyone can do.'

I have never seen my dad cry like this. Like something inside him is broken. He's not immune to showing his emotions – glistening eyes during carol concerts, movies, beautiful pieces of music. But this is so very different.

I realise I'm tired. Terribly, terribly tired. Speaking these unspeakable words, shattering the hopes that have kept us all going for the last two weeks, and then watching the people I love in desperate pain. I don't want to tell anyone else. But Loula is messaging me about prints for the NICU. I type a message, writing and rewriting it. Finally I hit send. A single message to shatter her heart.

In the afternoon, Mike stays with Finn and Sally, and my mum drives me back to the NICU. We sit in the car, behind the hospital, looking up at the floor-to-ceiling windows of the ITU nurseries. A magpie dances across the grass. I look around for his friend. There isn't another. Of course there isn't another.

'Where's your mother, where's your mother, where's your mother?' I repeat under my breath, thinking how particularly useless the ritual is today. My mum is dialling Lou. I listen to her answer, hear the sobs on the other end of the phone. My heart crumples.

When my mum hangs up she looks straight ahead. 'She's in pieces.' She pauses. 'She asked if maybe his brain could grow.'

We both smile then. My darling Loula, always so full of hope. I tip my head back, close my eyes and then open them again, looking at the roof of the car. How I wish that was even the most distant possibility.

The hospital is a haven. We follow the winding corridors that take us back to the entrance of the NICU and I wonder again whether we were we brought here for some reason. Away from London, away from the hospital where Finny was born safely, away from our life.

Quiet time. My favourite time. It's rare that we can get Grey out; ventilated babies need two nurses free for a decent amount of time, and regular emergencies and new babies often mean that simply isn't possible. So, often at quiet time we sit next to him, talking to him, cradling his head, passing the hours watching the rhythmic rise and fall of his little chest. The nursery is more hushed than it has been for the past couple of days, with Grey's MRI and various emergency arrivals.

'I think Mummy needs a cuddle,' Jackie tells him. She calls to Kerry, and they set us up together, tucking his little body in under my chin. 'Tell Mummy it's OK,' Jackie murmurs.

And he does.

'How's the Greyman?' Mike messages.

I send him a photo. 'How's Finny?'

'We just weed on the carpet and then laughed,' Mike types back.

I laugh too.

Another text pings through seconds later: '*HE.'

'He's pretty excited, my mum brought him an Advent calendar ...' A photo of Finn standing proudly next to a giant felt penguin pops through. It's taller than he is, covered with small numbered pockets and sporting a Father Christmas hat at a jaunty angle. Italic text indicates Mike is still typing.

'... My mum wanted you to know she did NOT choose the penguin, she asked Malcolm to get him one when he went to Switzerland – she meant one of the traditional ones she bought for Elsie last year, but he came back with this. She says she's very sorry.'

My mother-in-law is an artist, with impeccable taste and a very keen eye for detail. I can see that the garish design would not be to her taste; she'd know it may not be to mine either. But the delight on Finn's face makes me feel rather fond of it.

'It's so sweet, please thank her,' I reply.

'Who's on later, do you know?' Mike asks when I get home.

'Nena, I think.'

'It'll be nice to see her.'

The sky is inky black. Grey's incubator is hazily reflected in the window. I turn and lean back against the glass, gazing at my tiny, innocent baby. I try to make sense of it. To rationalise some part of it. When I can't stand any more, I slide down until I'm perching on the wide ledge, a few inches from the floor. I press my palms hard against my cheekbones, and let tears fill the wells they create.

I hear someone sit next to me, then feel a hand brush my shoulder. I open my eyes. Nena holds out a box of tissues.

'Thank you.' I take one.

Mike crouches on the other side of me, his arm touching mine.

Nena turns and looks out into the night. I realise she's crying. Suddenly she reaches for a tissue too, pressing it furiously to her eyes. 'I'm sorry,' she says. 'So sorry. It's so sad. You are wonderful parents and this is so sad. I'm sorry to cry.'

'Please don't apologise,' I say. She tightens her grip on my arm. Her tears show that even here, in the NICU, without our families, we are not going through this alone. The nurses, the doctors, are living this too. They love Grey too.

The worst of times show you the best of people. And the very best people.

I pull up a chair and open the doors of Grey's incubator. He's on his side, one leg out, hooked over the top of his blanket as if he's chosen the cold bit of the duvet. I reach in and place my hand over his tummy, my fingers and thumb pointing up towards his face, spanning his miniature shoulders. One of his hands finds the tip of my index finger, the other finds my thumb, and his fingers curl around them, holding on. 'I've got you, Mummy,' he seems to say.

'I've got you too, Greyman, for ever and ever,' I whisper.

The unknown is always scary. But this unknown, this place we are walking further and further into, is utterly terrifying. One foot in front of the other, one step at a time. There is a way through, somehow. There must be. There always is. He isn't in pain, he isn't in pain. Right now, that is the most important thing. My mum has always told me to do something every day that scares me – allegedly it staves off Alzheimer's, which grasped both of my paternal grandparents and wouldn't let go. But I'm not convinced this level of fear is what she had in mind.

The thought makes me smile.

16

30 November

Thirteen days old

When I wake, I'm momentarily confused. For a split second as I untangle my brain, everything is OK. Then the curtain of sleep is lifted and the axe falls. It's like finding out all over again.

All our siblings are on their way. By the afternoon the house will be pandemonium.

We leave early for the hospital, Mike driving – I still can't because of the C-section. As we take the right turn before the level crossing, there is a couple hurrying along the country lane, backs hunched against the cold, right on the verge. We slow – there isn't really enough room for walkers. As we pass, they both hold up their right thumbs.

I turn to MG. 'I think we should stop. It's freezing today. They look harmless – a little old couple ...'

'You want to pick up hitch-hikers?'

'Why not?' I wonder somewhere in the back of my mind whether good deeds might help Grey. We pull to a halt and they hurry towards us. I wind down my window.

'Town?' the man asks.

'Yes – where are you going?'

'Sainsbury's.'

'We're going to the hospital.'

'Oh yes, it's that way.'

'Jump in,' Mike says. 'We can work out where best to drop you.'

They climb into the back. 'Thank you.' The man blows on his hands and rubs them together. 'It's bleeding cold out.'

He leans in between our seats, his flat cap brushing against the leather, as Mike starts the car.

'So why are you going to the hospital? Visiting?' His eyebrows wiggle up and down as he speaks; the deep lines carved around his mouth mark him out as a big smiler.

'Yes, our son is there.' I pause. 'He's in the neonatal unit – he was born early.'

'I was premature,' the man says. 'And look, I turned out all right.' He points at himself with his thumbs and grins around the car.

'I've got five children, meself,' he adds. 'Five.'

I arrange my face to look suitably impressed. 'Wow.'

'I've got six,' the woman says. She is small, bird-like. She moves her hands as she speaks and I notice she's wearing a pair of fingerless gloves; loose strands of wool suggest they may have been a DIY job.

Their faces are weathered by a lifetime of countryside living; her hair is mid-grey, his covered by his cap. They could be anywhere from their fifties to upwards of eighty. It's impossible to tell.

'Oh, just up here . . .' He points.

I realise we've come to the roundabout at the outskirts of town.

'You'll be going off there.' He points again, this time to the next left turn. 'We're going straight ahead – weekly trip.' He gestures accordingly.

Mike pulls over, into a dead end off the roundabout, and they get out.

'Thank you,' the man says. 'All the best, all the best to your son.'

'The small ones are the tough ones,' the woman says.

'So we keep hearing.' I smile. I wish it could make any difference to Grey.

'I wonder if they would have walked all the way,' Mike says

136

as we watch them potter straight across the roundabout, hand in hand. 'It's pretty far.'

A new nurse is standing by Grey's cot, her back to us as we walk in. She turns to say hello. 'I'm Amy. I'm going to be looking after Grey, and you, this weekend.' She has bobbed blond hair, gentle blue eyes, rosy cheeks and a voice like honey. I'm sure I haven't seen her around before.

Amy says that as well as being a senior nurse, she is in charge of palliative care at the NICU. I wonder if my face falls, because she quickly adds, 'That's not why I'm looking after you and Grey.' She tells us she had friends in a similar position to us, faced with a devastating diagnosis. She doesn't mention the outcome. We don't ask.

Gaby comes over to see how we're doing. 'You know what day it is tomorrow?' She wags her finger at me and grins.

My mind is blank. 'Sunday?' I ask weakly.

'The first of December,' she says. 'And you know what that means?'

Again, I'm silent. She isn't getting much from me today.

'It means Grey needs an Advent calendar.' Her expression turns momentarily serious. 'I'll come and check on Monday that he has one.'

'Finn has two; he can give Grey one. It's covered in glitter that seems to go everywhere. Will that be OK?'

'Of course!' she says. 'We love glitter.'

Amy is back. 'I thought we could take the top off Grey's incubator. Get him dressed, get him out for lots of cuddles, have a really lovely weekend. Do you have any clothes?'

Grey, in clothes. It sounds insane, but the thought hadn't crossed my mind. Amy is looking at me, waiting for an answer. Suddenly I remember Mol's package. She sent a Baby Mori preemie pack – two tiny-weeny baby babygrows with matching vests. 'We do, but not here, and not washed. I didn't expect him to be able to get dressed so soon. Can we get them? Can he wear his own clothes?'

'Of course.'

I call my mum.

'Do you think you can get Grey's babygrows washed in time for us to take them back to the hospital this afternoon?'

Of course she can. An hour later a video pings through to my phone – a string of babygrows poppered to one another, and to the radiator, hairdryer in overdrive. My brilliant mother.

Carla's family is here. Her daughters and one of Dom's stand in a row on a bench in front of Cora's incubator, their noses pressed to the plastic. They're immaculately dressed – matching pinafores, thick tights, zip-up boots, their long hair tied in perfect buns on top of their heads, pink ribbon bows clipped at identical angles. I wonder where on earth she finds the time. Caleb is at the end, on tiptoe. They giggle as they look into the incubator at their sister. I pray she'll get home safely – that by next year Cora will have her own pink bow, that there will be five of them lined up somewhere far from here, waiting for Christmas.

Amy is an angel. Somehow we don't think about Friday, about Grey's prognosis, about what might be coming. My brother Nick comes to meet his brand-new nephew around lunchtime. He leaves his son, Sam, to play with Finn and we meet him and Nat, my sister-in-law, in the hospital Costa that has become our local. Nat quickly assures us that she knows she can't meet Grey. She's come for Nick, and to see us.

Outwardly phlegmatic, with a charming (or irritating, depending on the situation) ability to see the funny side of everything, Nick has been a policeman virtually since he left school thirteen years ago. He's wanted to be a policeman his entire life. When he was much younger, my mum once asked him why and he replied, 'I don't want to get to forty and look back and think that I haven't helped anyone.' That sentence still sums him up. Optimistic, pragmatic, he's fiercely protective of anyone vulnerable.

Mike stays with Nat in the family room and I take Nick to the NICU. At the cot, I unclip the incubator doors and show him how to reach in and cup Grey's head. Even at the highest setting, Nick has to bend to reach into the incubator. His hands amplify Grey's tininess.

'Hello, little man ...' He stares in wonder. 'He seems so much smaller in real life.' He stands quite still, keeping his voice so low even I can't hear what he's saying. It's the first time I've seen my brother cry in my adult life.

This afternoon, Amy helps us lift out Grey for Mike to hold him. 'Do you want to have him skin to skin?' she asks. 'I'm not sure if he'll fit into your T-shirt for kangaroo care.'

'Shall I just take it off?' Mike says.

'Well, it's up to you – would that be best? Will you be cold?'

'It's not me I'm worried about, it's you ... having to see me with no T-shirt on!' He flexes his arms in a mock body-builder pose.

I roll my eyes at Amy. 'Wally.'

She chuckles as Mike settles into the armchair without his T-shirt, then gently curls Grey into his chest.

'As soon as you feel his heartbeat, it makes everything feel OK, doesn't it?' he says.

I nod. The steady thrum of a newborn heartbeat against your chest is spellbinding. The fragility, the innocence, the promise. The magic bound up in new life. With Grey the focus is sharper, every feeling magnified. So there they sit, father and son together, everything feeling so wrong and all OK at the same time.

An hour later we move from the controlled quiet of the NICU to the riot of our Airbnb home. All of the cousins are charging around, Finn trailing Sam and Elsie, with Wilf close behind – football, ball pond, trains. I love watching Finn, relieved that he has no idea why everyone has gathered. That to him today is simply another big adventure with aunties, uncles and grandparents adding to the fun.

Ella greets us at the door, hugging us each tightly. It's the first time she's been able to get here. As a junior criminal barrister, her days are at the whim of her clerks, who send her skittling around the London and Essex court circuit. Eight years younger than me, she's steely ('terrifying', said a friend of Mike's who sat next to her at our wedding), but under that exterior she's softer than any of us, and wiser than I'll ever be. She can't meet Grey because of his limited-visitors rule.

'Daddy's been on the espresso martinis,' she tells me through the chaos, her cheeks dimpling.

'What? When?'

'We went to Pizza Express for lunch and he ordered one, randomly. Then Nat arrived, and they ordered another. I think he had three in the end.'

'I couldn't leave him having espresso martinis alone,' Nat chimes in.

'Wait, I don't understand,' Mike says. 'You went to Pizza Express for espresso martinis?'

'We went to Pizza Express for pizza,' Ella says. 'We were sitting at a table in that weird one in town, and when it came to pudding Daddy asked if they do espresso martinis.'

'And they do!' My dad has joined the conversation. 'They're rather delicious, and very reasonable. Nat joined me in one, didn't you, Natnat? Strictly for medicinal purposes, obviously.'

'Two,' she says.

'I can just imagine it,' Mike laughs. 'I bet you said, "Oh, go on then," didn't you, Nat?'

'Never one to turn down a drink,' she says.

'So you all sat in Pizza Express having espresso martinis at lunch?' I say.

'And crying,' my mum says from the other side of the kitchen.

'Of course.'

'I think they all thought we were completely mad. I imagined the manager saying to the waitress, "I have no idea what's going on at that table, but just give them whatever they want."'

We eat a quick supper and leave Finn squealing with laughter in the bath with all his cousins. The drive allows us a moment of calm after the havoc.

Grey's little corner has been transformed. Amy's taken the lid off his incubator, turning it into a proper cot. At the top end, a jolly printed canopy shades his face from the glare of the fluorescent lights. A wave of love washes over me as we look into his cot – he looks suddenly so much more like a baby. It's an absurd thought. But, dressed in a little white Baby Mori babygrow, he looks so different. I wonder if it's because most of the wires are tucked inside the cotton onesie. But it's more than that – there's something stark, shocking, about Grey's nakedness; his little body isn't ready to be seen, it hasn't had the weeks of fat building, hasn't yet acquired any of the delightful roundness of a term baby. I took huge pleasure in seeing Finn's chunky little thighs and pot belly wriggling around in nothing but a nappy; but it makes my little Grey seem even more vulnerable, exposed, makes me want to gather him up in my arms and insulate him from the world. But clothed he looks like he can hold his own. I know he can.

'I thought I'd get him dressed,' Amy says. 'I got out the bits you left in his drawer – he looks so gorgeous. Everyone has come to see him in his babygrow. The word's gone round that Grey is in his smart clothes.' She's smiling down at him. 'He's stolen all our hearts; he's such a special little boy. Even Dr Sahu said to me, "I really, really like that baby."' Amy looks up at me. 'I've never seen him like that before.'

I can't imagine the stolid consultant betraying his feelings.

We revel in Grey's open cot; it feels so wonderfully normal.

The simple fact of being able to look at the whole of him, rather than the always fragmented view imposed by the incubator. Touching him without navigating the twist and hinge doors, being able to kiss his forehead, his fingers. It's more than just the physical closeness. The thick layer of plastic brings with it a confusing detachment, and that's been taken away.

He looks so cosy, tucked up in his still-too-big babygrow, covered in layers of blankets to keep him warm now that the incubator is no longer controlling his temperature. I kiss him goodnight properly for the first time, bending to press my lips to the downy skin of his forehead, where two tiny dark curls have escaped from his ventilator bonnet. I close my eyes and breathe him in, feeling him wriggle a little at the sensation. 'Goodnight, my darling,' I breathe. 'I love you. I love you.'

We're home. Airbnb home. The cousins have all gone and Finn's asleep. I creep into his room and stand over his cot. He's on his back, Rab clasped in one hand, arms out-flung, Superman-style, towards the top of the cot. I watch his little chest rise and fall. After a few minutes, I creep out and sit on the stairs. I hear my mum come out of her room behind me.

'I keep thinking it must be something I did,' I whisper.

She sits beside me on the top step. 'And I keep thinking it must have been something I did.'

'You?'

'Yes. It's being a mother. I'm your mother, and I'm worried that I did something.'

'But you didn't,' I say.

'And neither did you.'

'But I couldn't protect him from this, this awful, awful thing, and that's what mothers are supposed to do.'

'And I can't protect you, my darling,' she says, 'from this awful, awful thing.'

We sit side by side, our feet sinking into the carpet.

'I wish it was me and not him,' I say after a while.

'I know. And I wish it was me. Believe me, George, all I've thought since you told me yesterday is *me, not him*. I would die today if it could save him.'

'He's so little, so tiny and helpless.'

We are silent, alongside one another, turning this over and over in our minds.

'I've sometimes thought that something bad had to come; that no one gets to be this lucky. Nothing bad has ever happened to me, not in thirty-three years.'

'Life doesn't work like that, my darling.'

'So, occasionally I would think, at the especially good moments, I can't be this happy, things can't stay this good for ever, that wouldn't be fair, no one is allowed that. And year after year, they did. And now the bad thing has happened. And it's happened to Grey, to my baby, to my son. And I'm utterly powerless to do anything to help him.'

17

1 December

Two weeks old

Lou and I are perched on the bar stools in Costa.

'Drinks?' MG asks, as if we're meeting for a regular coffee somewhere.

'Do they have oat milk?' Loula asks.

Mike snorts. 'I might have known. G's already been moaning about the lack of matcha – you Lucas girls do love a complex coffee order.' He gestures towards the tiny stand. 'They do a decent black coffee and a lovely cranberry slice.'

Lou settles for a black coffee.

She is standing over Grey's cot, stroking the blankets that cover his tummy. 'Somewhere inside him he will know how much he is loved,' she says. 'I know it.'

'I hope so, Loula,' I say.

'The most loved boy who ever lived.'

'He is.'

We stand opposite one another, gazing down at the tiny sleeping boy.

Carla's children are in the family room. Today the girls are dressed in matching sweater dresses and thick tights, a different colour from yesterday. Their boots have been swapped for gleaming white trainers; I wonder how on earth they stay so white, and then feel very middle-aged. Today their long hair hangs in perfect plaits; blue bows replace yesterday's pink.

They sit in a row, legs swinging, playing on their tablets. Dom looks up as I come in, then asks the girls to shift so I can sit down and eat my lunch.

'It's all right,' I say, and find a spot between them, on one side of the sofa.

They're discussing their gaming performance. I recognise the hierarchy of a three-sister family. Chloe, the oldest, has the highest score, of course. As they play I notice them glancing up, looking at me. Chloe says, 'Have you played *Subway Surfers*?'

I confess I haven't.

'Shall I show you?' she asks. I wonder if perhaps she thought I looked bored with my rather dry onion bhaji sandwich. She is beside me, her tablet on my lap, before I have time to answer.

'Here, you hold it like this.' She takes my hand and positions it on the edge of the screen. 'And you can control the girl like this.' She swipes a forefinger deftly and the girl is running. 'Then you have to jump the trains.' She swipes up and the girl leaps with her.

'Your turn,' she says. Now Carmen is on my other side, and Dom's daughter, Lizzie, has put down her tablet to watch too.

'Sorry,' Dom mouths over the three small dark heads.

I smile. It's a lovely, welcome distraction.

'Are you ready?' Chloe asks. 'If you are, I'll press start.' She looks at me intently, her little face serious.

'Ready,' I say.

The game starts, I move my finger. Suddenly, out of nowhere, there is a train, I swipe, but it's too late, the train crashes into me, wiping me out on the tracks. Chloe, Carmen and Lizzie look a bit embarrassed.

'Do you want another go?' Chloe asks.

This time I gather a couple of coins before the train takes me out again. Talk about a metaphor for life.

'I'm not very good at it,' I tell Chloe.

'Let's wait for your score,' she says kindly. A big 3 flashes up on the screen.

'Oh dear,' I say. 'That's an awful score, isn't it?'

None of them answer, then Lizzie reaches across and puts her hand on my knee. Her huge eyes stare up at me. 'It wasn't a *high* score, but we play this ALL the time, like every single day.'

I want to cry. The little hand is still gripping my knee.

'Yes, you just need some practice.' Chloe looks like she's willing to relinquish the tablet for the entire afternoon.

'Maybe that's enough, girls,' Dom says as Lou and Mike appear.

'Here's my sister,' I say. 'I think I need to go back in to see my baby.'

'He's in an incubator,' Chloe says with authority.

'Yes, he is.'

'All my sisters and my brother have been in incubators.' She turns back to her tablet and I'm free to go.

A group of nurses are gathered by the NICU window, watching someone in scrubs who seems to be measuring the grass.

'What's happening?' I ask Amy.

'Measuring up for our garden,' she says. 'We've just got approval for it to go ahead. We're going to turn this area' – she points to the stretch outside Grey's window – 'into a peaceful place for parents to sit, or take babies, somewhere away from the clinical environment.'

'That's a wonderful idea,' I say. 'It will make such a huge difference.'

'I'm so pleased you think so,' Amy says. 'The only issue is the smokers.' She waves towards the regular huddle beside the bin. Smoke billows around their heads. One of them holds a drip. It's a painful sight. The ashtray is overflowing with cigarette butts. The bench and its immediate surroundings are rarely unoccupied.

'Hmmm ... It doesn't really make for the most calming ambience, does it?' I say.

'The hospital doesn't help itself, I'm afraid – a massive No Smoking sign right next to a bin with a huge ashtray – mad.

146

Perhaps we can build a giant wall.' Amy is still looking down at the grass. 'We'll work something out,' she says, almost to herself, then turns back to me. 'It's exciting to know it's going ahead.'

Sunday evening and another pizza. We arrive in dribs and drabs – it's impossible to find a parking space here, even on a Sunday. Ella is getting the train straight back to London; she's in court in the morning, and Pizza Express is near the station. Finn is making eyes at the waitress again.

'Finny, stop flirting,' I say.

He giggles, face and hands smeared in tomato. 'Furt, furt,' he repeats. We all laugh.

Mike sits on our bed, Googling.

'It says here, G, that there's an operation they can do to remove fluid from the brain, and then there's a spinal tap. I wonder if that would be a possibility.'

'I think we need to wait for the results ...' Waiting and waiting. I am learning more patience in these weeks than I ever imagined.

Lou messages me: 'I'm reading about a boy who was born with two per cent of his brain and it grew,' she says. 'I still have faith. He's already a little miracle.'

I marvel at them both; their positivity astounds me.

18

2 December

Fifteen days old

We park at the back of the hospital, in the bays, our new route in. The magpie is back, sitting outside the building. He looks at me, cocking his head to one side and springing across the grass. Bounce, bounce, bounce. Taunting me. It's just a bird, Georgie, I repeat to myself.

Grey has a new nurse. Two clips hold back Jen's thick blond hair, which hangs in glossy sheets, cut sharply either side. Her twin daughters were in the same NICU a few years ago. 'I've been on your side,' she says. 'It's *so* hard. Everyone expected me to somehow take it in my stride – I'm a NICU sister, after all. But nothing prepares you for it, not even working here, seeing your tiny babies in incubators, plugged into every piece of machinery. I had to keep reminding people, "Here, now, I'm a mum."'

This week's COW is Dr Chandra. I'm a little afraid of her. With dark hair pulled back from an intense face, she seems a little intimidating. She checks Grey over, thoroughly, but very gently. Her stern expression switches to a soft smile as she looks down at him.

'I have the full MRI report,' she says. 'I know Annabel – Dr Stewart,' she corrects herself, 'went through what she'd seen on Friday. There's nothing very different, but it goes into more detail and has further information. As soon as I've finished the ward round, I'll come and find you.'

*

Dr Chandra goes through each section of the MRI report in the quiet room with Jen and Dr Kate. We sit in silence as she reads out each piece of information, summarising the effects on Grey and his development. She carefully highlights some of the things Grey might face, we might face. The reality that he is unlikely ever to breathe without a ventilator, that he might have seizures, that every aspect of his development will be severely affected.

'I can give you the full report to read, if you'd like,' she says.

'I'd like to read it, properly,' Mike says.

I'm so grateful for his need to know every single detail.

'But can I have a look now?'

She hands it to him. As he turns the pages, I catch the odd line. There is no respite, no good news. Not a single piece. The final page contains a summary of Grey's prognosis. 'Severe end of the spectrum' springs out at me. 'Is that the worst it can be?' I ask. 'Severe?'

Dr Chandra nods.

In every area of development, every area of his life, Grey is going to have the worst problems a medical professional will ever see.

'Now that we have a diagnosis, and some idea of prognosis, we'll create and manage a plan,' Dr Chandra says gently. 'We'll nominate a consultant for Grey, here. And then notify all the different teams who will be involved in his care – occupational therapists, physiotherapists, language therapists ...'

Choosing her words carefully, she explains that if Grey were to come home, we'd need to have an A&E protocol in place, as this is where we would be likely to end up, regularly. The doctors there would automatically work to save him, taking any measures necessary. Without detailed knowledge of Grey's conditions, she explains, this could cause him serious pain.

'We need a DNR, you mean.' It sounds blunter than I meant it to, even to my own ears. My ninety-five-year-old grandmother died earlier in the year; I remember her telling me, in her usual matter-of-fact fashion, about her DNR.

'A plan,' she says, 'but yes, that will need to be considered as part of it.'

'Will we get there?' I ask. 'Will we take him home?'

She looks at me, contemplating my words, thinking carefully before she answers.

'Honestly? At this stage, it's impossible to say.'

A wave of something like clarity washes over me; it brings with it a moment of stillness. I take a deep breath. 'Should we be thinking about whether it's fair on him to put him through all this?' I look her in the eye. 'Should we be considering palliative care?'

I want her to tell me that of course it isn't something that should even cross our minds. To tell me I'm overreacting, that this isn't nearly that bad.

Instead, she holds my gaze.

'That is a brave thing to ask. And I think you are right to ask it.'

But I don't feel brave. I hate myself for asking it, hate myself for thinking it – how can I be thinking that I might want my baby to die? But somewhere inside me, something, someone, is telling me that I need to ask these questions. Somehow, through the blinding fog of pain, we have to work out what is best for Grey. He is what matters most.

'It sounds, from everything you are saying, that Grey won't have really any kind of quality of life.' Mike takes my hand. 'If he can't see, he can't speak, he can't even breathe, how can you put someone you love through that?'

'If that is what's best, how would we make that decision?' Mike says. 'How do we decide if that is the right thing?'

Yes, how?

The word echoes around my mind.

Dr Chandra explains that we should wait for the results of the chromosome testing, to ensure we have a full picture. She is careful to point out that these results will not change

Grey's diagnosis, or prognosis. She'll then speak to the neurological MRI specialist again, and the geneticist, to ensure she has every piece of available information. Then she will sit down with at least one other neonatal consultant, perhaps Dr Stewart, as she's been closely involved in his care, to discuss Grey's case. When the doctors have built a comprehensive picture, we'll all sit down together, as many times as we want, as many times as we need, to come to a decision.

We hold his fragile life in our hands, and the ground feels unsteady beneath my feet.

'I'll speak to Annabel and work out when we can meet,' she says. Dr Stewart is on duty this week, but in paediatrics. Then, softly, 'It's the worst part of our job. This. Having to tell parents this kind of news. I am so sorry.'

'Thank you. Thank you for telling us,' I say. 'We don't want to go back to London.' I glance at Mike, who's nodding in agreement. 'We don't want to have to go through this there. We want to be here, with you, with all of you, who we know, who know Grey. Please can we stay here?'

'Of course,' she says. 'Whatever you want.'

This corner of Kent has become a refuge; the world telescoped. In this strange little bubble, there is only our Airbnb and the NICU village. The nurses are Grey's family, our family; a hospital full of aunts and uncles. If Grey is going to die, he will die here, with his family. Mike has spoken to the owner of our Airbnb, explained a little about what's happening. She's blocked out the house for as long as she can – two more weeks, after which she has a long booking over Christmas – and says we can tell her day to day if we're staying another night.

I wonder at the strange fate that brought us to Whitstable, and then to this hospital. Away from the London hospital where 7lb 8oz of Finn was delivered smoothly at 9.34 a.m. on a Thursday morning. Where we spent a single baking June night; home for supper on Friday evening.

*

It's the afternoon and I'm holding Grey. Opposite me, Carla is holding Cora. We've both stripped down to bras; rugs cover the babies, and some of us – the NICU air conditioning is notoriously patchy.

'I don't really know where to look,' Mike says. 'It feels a bit inappropriate, me being here.'

Carla laughs, and so do I.

'How do you think I feel, mate?' Chris, one of the NICU nurses who hasn't looked after Grey, but is always around, is rearranging the incubator next to Grey's, checking pipes, wires. 'The only male nurse on the NICU ...' His kind eyes crinkle. Mike's do the same.

Finny and his naughty smile light up the unit later in the day. 'Ta-ter, ta-ter,' he says as my mum brings him down the corridor. He stands over Grey's incubator, looking at him. I wonder what he's thinking, whether his developing brain has any concept of what's happening.

'Georgie, I wondered if you'd like to do Finn's footprint, next to Grey's?' Jen says. 'It's a bit messy, but might be nice. To compare the sizes – and we can stick them into Grey's book. Only if you'd like to, though.'

'I think that would be lovely,' I say.

'It's really gentle ink and we can wipe it off with olive oil. I'll get things ready.'

My mum holds Finn while Jen gently sponges ink onto the sole of his foot. 'We're going to tap-tap a little bit of ink onto your foot, to make a footprint, and then we can put it next to your brother's,' she says. 'Tap-tap-tap.'

'Tat-tat,' Finny says, glancing from me to my mum to Jen.

'That's a very old-fashioned look, Finn,' my mum says.

'He thinks we're all barking mad,' Jen says. She presses Finn's sole carefully onto a piece of paper a couple of times, then reaches into Grey's cot and tap-taps his tiny foot with ink.

'Tat-tat, ta-ter,' Finny says, pointing.

'Yes,' I say. 'Tap-tap your brother now.'

Finn squeals with laughter.

Grey's rounded heel is no bigger than half the pad of my finger, the surface of the skin peppered with marks from countless blood gases. Jen stamps his tiny footprint onto the paper. We cut out the best prints and place them next to each other, tucking Grey's foot into the curve of Finn's, the miniature print echoing his big brother's. We stick them into Grey's book, adding the date and their names.

Later, we're sitting at the supper table in the Airbnb.

'I have a confession,' my dad says suddenly. He's just got back from shifting a couple of pieces of furniture intended for Grey's nursery from Somerset to our house in London.

We all look concerned.

'It's nothing awful, no harm done,' he says. 'Well, no real harm.'

Now we all look confused.

'When I picked up the van, I had a little, um, accident . . .'

'*What?*' My mum looks worried again.

'Relax, Min, everything's fine. Really.' He takes out his phone. 'Well, almost everything . . .'

He holds up a photograph. It shows what used to be one of the gateposts on my parents' driveway. The entire top half of the pillar has almost been knocked clean off.

'What on earth . . .?' my mum says.

'I want you to know it's possible to do this without any help from an espresso martini.' He pauses. 'The truth is that when you have a lot on your mind, and you're driving a very, very big van, and it's dark, sometimes you can ever so slightly misjudge a turn.'

'Is the van OK?' I ask.

'The van fared far better than the gatepost, as it happens,' he replies.

We laugh.

'What did you do?'

'I tried to hoist it back into position, but pretty quickly realised I wasn't man enough.'

'Erm, yes,' my mum says; the pillar is about a cubic metre of solid stone.

'Then I had an exceedingly clever idea.' He looks around the table, to make sure we're hanging on his every word.

'You called Rob,' my mum says.

'I called Rob.'

Rob has reassembled most of my parents' seventeenth-century cottage, over the years. He's also one of the nicest men you'll ever meet.

'He was there in ten minutes. He knows what's happening – I told him. And between us, we managed to sort it.'

'Brilliant Rob,' I say.

He nods. 'Brilliant Rob.'

'The thing is, ordinarily I would have found it very stressful. It would have depressed me, as you know.'

We nod. It is a peculiar quirk of my dad's generous, laid-back nature that he is extremely particular about things being pristine. A lack of care and attention for one's possessions is a guaranteed way to incur his wrath.

'But I thought, do you know what, who gives a fuck? Grey's taught me that quite a lot of things simply aren't important.'

He has. He's taught us all. Changed us all.

Later, my hand looped over the side of Grey's incubator, holding his hand, I open his book. Jen has written a note. '*Dearest Grey, It has been an absolute honour looking after you . . .*'

I can't read any more; tears swim in front of my eyes. I run a finger over the footprints next to the note, Finn and Grey, side by side, for ever.

The house is quiet, everyone asleep. I sit on top of our bed, my mind beginning to allow thoughts from the day to swirl, when there is a soft cry. Finn. He rarely wakes in the night, and I'm hyper-aware of his distress, so the sound triggers an alert.

Before I reach his room, I hear him more clearly. 'No, no, no,' he moans.

His door is ajar so I push it open and tiptoe in beside his cot. He is thrashing from side to side, his little brow furrowed, face distressed, as if he's having a bad dream. I lean over and place both hands on his tummy. Almost instantly, his face relaxes, then his arms, in seconds he is lying still. His lips lift with gentle contentment and he reaches for Rab, pulling him close and rolling onto his side. I watch him for a little longer, feeling my breath sync with his, wishing all of today was a bad dream that could be soothed away with reassuring hands.

19

3 December

Sixteen days old

Dr Chandra has the chromosome results. I feel sick. Mike holds my arms above the elbow. 'Remember, G, we've heard the very worst. There can't be anything worse, no matter what the genetics say. They are another part of a picture that we already have.'

'What about Finn?' I ask quietly. I feel guilty for even thinking it. This is about Grey, not Finn.

'This doesn't affect Finn, G. It can't. Finny is fine, really he is.'

We're in the quiet room again with Dr Chandra, Dr Kate and Sofia. Mike makes a joke about it being our second home. We all try to laugh.

Dr Chandra is sitting opposite us, a sheaf of papers in her hand. 'The geneticist has discovered Grey has a chromosome deletion,' she says. 'This is where a section of one of the pieces of DNA on one of his chromosomes has not formed properly, so a chunk of information is missing.' She pauses carefully, then reads out a list of numbers and letters. 'The syndrome doesn't have a name, it's so very rare.' She looks at us, shuffling her stack of papers like a deck of tarot cards.

'Is there any way it could affect Finn?' I ask. Other questions have formed a disorderly queue in my head. If it's genetic, are we carriers? One of us? Both of us? The only thing that could make this worse is if it affected Finn too. 'These notes talk about significant developmental delays. If

Finn is almost eighteen months old and hasn't shown any signs of delayed development, does that mean he doesn't have this?'

Dr Kate tries to reassure me, but no one has any definitive answers. It is too rare, too unknown. 'As soon as I can speak to the geneticist, I will ask,' says Dr Chandra, 'but if Finn is eighteen months old and has had no symptoms, I think it is very unlikely this also affects him.'

'The geneticist has requested samples of both of your blood, along with further blood from Grey, so they can run some more tests. These will be able to tell us if either of you are carriers, and what the chances are of this affecting future pregnancies, future babies.'

That's the last thing on our mind right now.

'I have some information for you.' She hands us the printed pages. 'It's general information at this point, and it's not based on much knowledge or research – I think it really is very rare.'

We flick through the notes; the information is drawn from twenty-three people in the world with this deletion.

I skim the symptoms, the prognosis. Each of the systems of the body is addressed individually; it mentions developmental delays, mobility difficulties, but not the brain structure. And the symptoms of the deletion don't seem to match up with the severe brain diagnosis we discussed yesterday.

'That doesn't make sense, does it?' Mike asks.

'I don't know until I speak to the geneticist ... but we think, I think, maybe the two things aren't linked.'

How can that be? Odds say ninety-nine times out of a hundred placental abruptions don't happen. A missing corpus callosum shouldn't mean brain problems at the severe end of the spectrum. And now a rare chromosome disorder. What are the chances? One in a million? I have a bizarre urge to laugh. There is no rational response.

Dr Chandra is suggesting genetic counselling. I wonder what that is.

'But there's nothing here that is going to change anything. The big problems are in his brain?' I say.

Dr Chandra nods.

'So, really, we still need to think about ...' I trail off, it is so impossible to say the words. 'Palliative care, the palliative route?'

'I would like to adjust his ventilation support, see how he responds. To prepare you, I think everything suggests his brain will not let him breathe alone. But of course we need to give him the chance. We need to try everything.'

'Yes, we do. We need to try everything. Everything, everything ...' I'm torn in two. Half of me wants Grey to prove everyone wrong, to do well without support, to breathe on his own. And half of me wonders what it would achieve. His prognosis is so devastating, his brain problems about so much more than breathing.

My mind flashes back to Grey's birth day, driving to the hospital.

'I can't lose this baby,' I'd said to Mike.

'We're not going to lose the baby, George.' He'd glanced sideways at me and squeezed my hand.

But now I think we are. We are going to lose this baby. We are going to lose our son, our little Grey.

I need to get out. I need to sit somewhere that isn't a hospital room.

'I feel really selfish, it feels so complicated, I'm scared that I'm scared of how much it would impact us, Finn, if he lives.'

'I know,' Mike says. 'I've been thinking the same.'

'But then half of me wants to say no, not palliative, there must be another way. And then I realise that would be selfish too, really. I'd be keeping him here for me. It wouldn't be what's best for him.'

'Fucked either way,' Mike says.

'Completely fucked.'

'No pain, remember.' He puts an arm around my shoulders,

158

pulling me in to him and kissing the top of my head. 'We'll get through it. We'll help each other through it; we'll do the best thing for Grey, for our little boy, G.'

But how will we know?

'We can bend the rules,' Sofia whispers conspiratorially. We are back beside Grey's incubator. 'If you need a coffee in here, bring one in. Snacks? Those too. You do whatever you need, whatever you want, to make anything a tiny bit easier.'

'Can I sit on this staff-only stool?' Mike points at the stool he's already sitting on.

Sofia laughs, then turns to me. 'Now, what can I do for you? Mike needs a coffee; can I fill your water?'

'Fill it with gin,' Jackie says from the other side of the nursery. 'Georgie, you don't need water any more, just fill it with gin.'

'I checked,' she says to Sofia. 'I checked, and apparently these days you can drink whatever you want while you're breastfeeding – there are no set rules, so I reckon neat gin is the answer.'

They both laugh. I smile back.

'Do you think we might be able to get Grey out?' I ask.

Sofia nods. 'We can, of course we can.'

Sofia settles Grey on my chest, his head tucked in under my chin. I look at his incubator, criss-crossed with wires leading to myriad screens. I think of the countless tests, the X-rays, the MRI, the one-to-one nursing. I wonder at how much it must be costing. How amazing that we don't have to pay a penny of it.

We've settled in the chair, Grey tucked under my chin, his arms bent either side of his face, mimicking his brother's sleeping-Superman pose. He wriggles his fingers, tickling my skin; the side of his bonnet brushes my collar bone. I close my hands over him under the thick blanket, holding his back, reassuring myself with his presence. 'Perhaps we can freeze time, stay here for ever, Greyman,' I whisper to him. 'Get Daddy and Finny along here too.'

I look down at his little face. His wise little face. Two weeks and two days old and he seems to hold within himself the wisdom of the ages. I think of my dad and the van. Somehow Grey has brought me, brought us all, a profound sense of what matters, when it comes down to it: health, life, love. The pillars of ourselves.

I'm starting to relax into my reverie when the monitor starts bleeping; slow, deliberate. Sofia looks up, taking note of the numbers, keeping an eye on Grey. In the NICU, my barometer for the seriousness of a situation is the reaction of the nurses. The whirrs, bleeps and alarms are their language; the smallest change communicates vital information. If something bleeps and no one reacts, everything's fine.

The bleep increases. It's a sound I haven't heard before. Sofia looks at Grey, then the nurses spring into calm but deliberate action. The sound is an alarm.

'I'm going to Neopuff him.' Melia is by Sofia's side in a split second as she takes what looks like a small pink plastic whistle connected to a concertina from the instruments behind his incubator. She connects the plastic whistle to the tube in his mouth. Counting in a low voice, she releases and then closes the top of the valve with her thumb. I have no idea what's happening; I stay completely still, barely breathing. His bonnet is still tickling my collarbone. His hands are still curled into me. I daren't move to look at him more closely.

From the other side of the room, Sadie reads out Grey's stats. 'He's coming up, 30, 35, 40 ...'

Sofia is still counting.

'His colour is better,' Melia says.

'45, 50, 55 ... heart rate coming up now, Sofia ... 60, 65, 70, 75, 80, 85, 90 ...'

Sofia releases her thumb, checking his face with Melia. She exhales, looking at the tiny boy under my chin.

'Don't do that, Grey, you made me worry.'

'What just happened?' I ask, remaining completely still.

'He desaturated, but it was quite a big one; did you see his colour? I had to Neopuff him. Sometimes the machines are too sensitive, his colour is the best judge, but he went very grey. He is fine now, look, his colour is good, his numbers are stable. But I think he should go back in his incubator. I'll suction him and resettle him. I don't know why that happened. It might have been his secretions – we'll keep a close eye on him.' Her deep calm has been rattled.

I still don't really know what just happened. I've never seen any of Grey's nurses like this, and these women are not easily flustered. 'Neopuff.' I roll the word around in my head. It sounds like a Pokémon.

Amy the angel finds me in the late afternoon.

'I've been talking to Annabel,' she says. I know Dr Stewart is on call in HDU and SCBU this week. 'We thought that if you'd like, tomorrow, we could take Grey out in the pram—'

'Out, out? Outside?'

'Well, we can set it up to walk around the hospital, and then if it's dry and not too cold, we might be able to wrap him up and go outside. We need to be with you, to monitor Grey, but we can try and find somewhere to give you some space to be just the three of you. Would you like that?'

Out? A pram, some semblance of normality? 'That would be amazing, if we can.' I check myself. 'I mean, I know maybe you'll be too busy.'

'We'll make it happen, Georgie.' She puts her hand on my arm. 'It's important for you. We'll make sure we get it all set up.'

'The only thing, Amy, is that people like to look into prams, don't they? What if someone looks in and coughs or sneezes, or tries to touch him? I'm not normally precious about that kind of thing, all sorts of people prodded their fingertips into Finn's chubby cheeks the summer after he was born, but Grey is a bit different ...'

161

'We'll make sure no one peers into the pram.' She smiles reassuringly. 'We'll try and find you a separate place to be, and you can sit with a coffee and just spend time with him. We'll be with you, so if people come too close we can ask them to give you some space.'

'The royal baby.'

'Only the best for this little man.'

'Has Amy told you about the pram?' Dr Stewart is by Grey's incubator.

I nod. 'She has, thank you.'

'I had an idea I wanted to run by you. There's a little chapel here – have you seen it?'

We haven't. I don't know much of the hospital except A&E and the baby parts.

'I don't know if you are religious … but either way, it's multi-faith and it's very quiet and private. I was thinking I could speak to the hospital chaplain, see if we can maybe borrow it for a little while. Then you can get a coffee and sit in there with Grey – no one will come and look in at him there.'

'That would be really nice.'

Later in the evening, I extract my pump pieces from the bucket of Milton my angel of a mother religiously changes every day, to do my pre-bed pump. As the small bottles fill with milk, I Google 'Neopuff'. 'Infant resuscitation device' pops up instantly. That pale pink plastic tube with such a sweet, innocent name. Grey had been resuscitated. Sofia had saved his life.

I always knew I wouldn't be able to protect my children for ever – an excruciating reality, but the deal you make as a parent. I just didn't expect it to be put to the test so acutely, and so soon.

Mike is asleep by the time I creep downstairs to rinse and re-submerge the pump. I open the freezer and add the bottles to an almost full drawer. When our NICU freezer drawer was full, we had to start bringing it home. Now the drawers here are getting full too. I could, perhaps should, ease up on the pumping, but I seem unable to alter the routine. I close the drawer and get myself a glass of water. When I turn off the tap, the house is silent. So different from London, where there are always sirens, cars, late-night revellers. I climb the stairs, pausing outside Finn's room to hear the reassuring sound of his gentle breathing, then slip under the duvet.

Kind friends keep asking whether I'm managing to get any rest, and somehow, I am. My mind and body seem able to pull together to achieve this one vital task. Each night as my head hits the pillow I fall almost instantly into dreamless sleep, until my 3 a.m. alarm rouses me for more pumping.

20

4 December

Seventeen days old

After a series of dreary, drizzly, overcast days, by some miracle we wake to a clear, bright halcyon winter's morning. The deep blue sky that only appears at this time of year, crisp, fresh air, not a cloud to be seen. Perfect for a walk. The pram, a modern version of an old coach-built design, is navy blue, with a sturdy under-basket, a deep, squishy mattress and an oversized hood. It was a present from parents whose twins had spent several months in the NICU. While it is being set up – no mean feat – Amy and Dr Stewart tell us that we should get Grey ready for the chilly day.

'He'll need *a lot* of layers.'

On Rebekah's instructions, I raid the laundry cupboard for knitwear, rooting through the 3–4lb basket. Its contents look like dolls' clothes that have shrunk in the wash, and this isn't even the smallest size. We cover Grey with extra vests and a double babygrow, adding a little knitted cardi with embroidered teddies, mittens, booties, and a second hat over his woollen bonnet. By chance, I've chosen shades of blue and white – perfect with his pale blue bonnet. He looks like a catalogue winter newborn.

His carriage is wheeled into the nursery with some ceremony.

'Ta-*da*!' Amy announces, jazz hands shimmying. 'It's all ready for him.'

Three oxygen tanks fill the under-basket, with a portable monitor zipped into a heavy-duty oversized buggy bag strapped to the side of the pram. The thick mattress is covered with extra blankets. And Dr Stewart has a heat shield at the ready. Above the hood, a little face peeks out – a felt Christmas elf.

'We thought he could come along for the ride,' Amy says when I spot him. 'Something a bit festive.' She smiles.

They are so kind. So, so kind.

'A stowaway.' I smile too. 'A Christmas stowaway.'

Once the nurses have completed the military transfer operation, and Grey is settled in the pram, we cover him with two blankets, then the heat shield – a half-tube of reinforced plastic – then a thick quilt. Everything firmly tucked in. Alongside the pram, Dr Stewart loads a wheelie case with medical supplies to cater for every possible eventuality. And then there's the entourage: Dr Stewart and two NICU sisters – Amy and Rebekah. It makes Finn's trips to the park seem like a breeze.

We're ready. The NICU team who prepped Grey for his walk wave us off and I tentatively push the heavily laden vehicle out of the nursery, Dr Stewart directing, Amy filming from the front, Rebekah from behind.

'Celebrities,' says Dr Stewart, 'followed by the paparazzi.'

I feel a comforting warmth radiating from somewhere deep inside me.

As we wheel Grey to the lift, Dr Stewart nips forward every few minutes to keep an eye on his stats. 'He's doing beautifully, brilliant numbers – he's so happy,' she says as she pushes open a set of double doors into frosty air and sunshine.

An ambulance stops to wave us past as we loop around the hospital building. I look down at our tiny boy. 'This is the outside world, Greyman. It's a wonderfully sunny day, do you like it?' For the first time in days, the magpie is nowhere to be seen.

'You good boy,' Dr Stewart says. 'Your numbers are perfect – you just wanted to be out and about with Mummy and Daddy, didn't you?'

As we wander along, Dr Stewart tells us about other trips the pram has made. 'We went to the pub once, with a whole extended family – that took a bit of planning! We've been to a café. Sometimes just for a little walk, like this. It's so important for families to feel like they can do something normal with their baby.'

How right she is.

Before now, I would have said the best days centre around universally happy events – Mike's proposal on a sun-soaked April Fool's Day on my favourite block in New York; our wedding in a Brixton warehouse; Finn's birth in the midst of London's 2018 heatwave; beach walks with Grey safely in my tummy on that Whitstable afternoon a hundred years ago. And then suddenly, here, in the midst of everything, is a best day. Somehow, in the face of all the pain, the heart-splintering, breath-stealing pain, the impossible conversations and devastating news, a ray of light. And I realise the very best days are the perfectly imperfect ones.

I look at the women who've made it happen. In burgundy scrubs, bare to the elbow, they are wandering around outside on a freezing December afternoon, knowing the exceptional value of ordinary moments in extraordinary times.

We swing the pram back into the hospital, stopping for a photo in the entrance. The chapel is tucked away to our right. Dr Stewart steers us inside, closing curtained doors against the frenetic hospital hubbub. The quiet in here is magnified by the contrast. The now low winter sun throws shards of coloured light through a stained-glass window onto a simple pine altar decorated with a silver tinsel star. A string of fairy lights runs across the top of it, and along the back wall.

'We made it a little bit Christmassy for you,' Dr Stewart says.

It's toasty warm after the outside chill and we sit in the front row, shedding coats and jumpers as Dr Stewart gently lifts out the heat shield and checks Grey's numbers and gas levels.

Amy appears after a couple of minutes with a Costa tray. 'I hope you like hot chocolate,' she says.

Then they retreat to the back of the chapel, leaving us to sip from the deliciously warming cups. Grey looks so peaceful. I stroke his head, wrapped in his cosy hat, and gaze into his little face. We speak softly to him about his adventure, seeing the outside, feeling the fresh air on his face.

It's a bizarre meld of the extraordinary and the mundane, happiness and heartbreak. I think of all the times I've sat on a bench in our local park with a cup of green tea, a sleeping Finn in the pram next to me. Unremarkable days woven through my memory. I'd never questioned the possibility that I wouldn't have such days with this baby; with Grey. But this might be Grey's only excursion, his only glimpse of the world outside. I stroke his cheek, so soft, so fragile. I sit, and stare, Mike does the same. Committing every little piece of him to our memory.

I've never really understood what people mean when they say they want to freeze time. I'm made for change, always looking forward. My dad often said to me as a little girl, 'Don't wish your life away.' I'm always on to the next thing; the next day, the next weekend, the next holiday. Not because I'm not enjoying the here and now, but because I have a constant need for something new, for whatever's next. Having Finn taught me a lot about trying to be in the moment, not racing him to smile, then sit, then crawl, then walk, then talk. Enjoying what he is doing right here, right now. But it doesn't come naturally. Even before I was pregnant with Grey, at times I was thinking forward to when I might have another baby, when there might be two perfect people sitting in front of me.

Today, I try with every part of me not to look forward, not to imagine the next day, or the day after that, or the week after that. To be here, with Grey, with Mike, in this chapel, in this hospital, with this hot chocolate.

I barely notice that the door has opened. Dr Stewart gets up, murmurs to the man who's just come in.

'. . . chapel closed . . . a ventilated baby . . .'

They exchange a few more words, then he thanks her and rolls out a mat in the corner of the room, in front and to the side of us, and prays silently.

Rolling it up a few minutes later, he thanks Dr Stewart, then gestures towards us.

She nods and turns as the door closes. 'He sends you all of his blessings,' she whispers.

In time, Amy comes over and gently tells us we should probably get Grey back to the unit, and give back the chapel. She and Dr Stewart gather up the fairy lights and the tinsel star.

'I don't know what the chaplain would think of our redecorating,' Dr Stewart says. 'Oh, Georgie – I nearly left him here.' She unloops a knitted bird from a rail that runs along the far side of the room. 'This stork is for Grey. Every baby who goes on a transfer gets one. I know he didn't get to have his ambulance ride, but he's been on a trip – I think he deserves one. You know the nurse, Jen?'

I nod. Jen was the tap-tap nurse who had printed Grey and Finn's footprints.

'Her mum knits them. We should get some more, actually. It would be nice to give them to all the babies who go out in the pram. Well, this one is for Grey.'

'Thank you.' We tuck the stork beside our sleeping baby. It's bigger than he is. 'He's perfect.'

Back at the entrance to the NICU, nurses who didn't see our exit gather to welcome Grey's return. We pose for more pictures by the Christmas tree, with the elf still peeking over the hood.

'He's been such a good boy,' Amy says. 'His numbers have been perfect. He loved being out and about.'

Isa is in the nursery.

'Isa, you're back.' Mike lifts a hand from the pram in greeting, then gestures at his newly cropped hair. 'Nice . . .'

'Thanks, I did it myself.'

'Yourself?'

'Yes, my friend. With the clippers and the razor, in the mirror.' He mimes his styling session.

'Can you have a go at mine?' Mike says. 'It's a bit out of control.'

'Of course.' Isa moves towards him, pretending to shave his head. 'I can bring the clippers, we set up in the family room.'

'Isa's Barbers,' Mike says.

They're both laughing. The nurses are looking confused. I get the feeling that Isa is usually rather quiet. Except, it seems, when my husband is around. They are now play-fighting like teenagers. Isa grabs Mike, looping an arm around his neck in an affectionate headlock and rubbing the top of his head.

'I'll sort it out, my friend,' he says. 'Take it all off, have it looking as sharp as mine.'

He cocks a finger towards Mike, then turns on his heel and is off down the hallway.

Back in the NICU, Rebekah asks if it would be OK for her to take her lunch.

I'm horrified. 'You must be starving! You should have said earlier.'

'I wouldn't have missed Grey's walk for anything. And I'm a late eater, Georgie, don't you worry about me.'

She hands us back to Jen, who suggests we keep Grey out for a cuddle.

Dr Stewart stays with us to check he's happily settled. 'He likes that dry ventilator system,' she says. 'His secretions are much better.'

Her expression becomes more serious. 'I have to go back to my clinic now, but I know we need to meet. I know we need to have a discussion. I think I might not be able to set aside enough time today. Would it be OK to get together tomorrow, with Dr Chandra? It's not a conversation I want to rush.'

I feel my shoulders tense, a shadow cast over the elation

of the morning. Then Dr Stewart is off, leaving us with Jen bustling around Grey.

'Let's transfer him straight to you,' Jen says. Her blond hair falls across her cheeks as she leans forward to check the tanks. She examines each one carefully, her blue eyes animated behind her glasses, then nods to herself and pushes her hair back behind her ears as she straightens up. 'Plenty of oxygen left – Rebekah said there was, but I always like to check myself. We'll put him back in after you've had a cuddle – I don't want to move him around too much.'

I settle myself into the purple chair that has become a faithful part of our corner of the NICU. 'Can I hold him sideways?'

'Sideways?'

'Cradle him, so I can see him? I guess he's so wrapped up he doesn't need to be skin to skin, or cuddled into my chest. I'd just love to be able to hold him and look at him for a bit.'

'Oh yes, of course. I'm sure he'll be very happy like that.' She lifts Grey gently out of the pram, pauses to smile at him before tucking him into my waiting arms and rigging up the usual tape to secure his ventilator over my shoulder. Half mother, half older sister, her presence is a balm.

She turns back to the charts and leaves us to ourselves.

When Finn was first born, I spent hours gazing at him, thinking of very little except his tiny, perfect face. With Grey, it's rare to be able to empty my mind of a million whirring thoughts, to simply be with him, without worry, without the weight of our situation. No time passes without intensity. We don't get to just *be*.

I look down at him now. Togged up in his woollens, his nose slightly snubbed by the ventilator, his blue bonnet covered with a little newborn hat, his eyes closed, relaxing after his busy afternoon. I can't see his little chocolate brown curls, but I know they're there. I examine his hands. Each finger a miniature replica, so small, so exquisitely formed, I almost don't expect them to work, to move – they're like a porcelain doll's. They're long, especially for an early baby. Mike thinks they're my hands; Finn and he share a sturdier design.

It's our after-supper visit to the NICU. Bedtime stories. Grey is tired; it's been a big day. He's peaceful when we arrive. Jackie is on duty. We sit and chat for a while before reading. We tell her about the walk, the pram and the sunshine.

'And you got an elf on the shelf,' she says.

Mike and I look blank.

'Don't tell me you don't know the elf on the shelf? Finn would LOVE it. My grandchildren love it. He only comes out at Advent, and he does naughty things at night. Once he took all the sweets out of the sweet jar, leaving wrappers and an elf with a belly ache. Or he'll wrap everything in the living room in newspaper. The one rule is, children are never allowed to touch him. If they do, he'll lose his powers, and won't be able to do any more funny things.'

'Finn would find that hilarious. Maybe we'll get an elf when he's a bit older. I love new Christmas traditions.'

'Well, keep an eye out tomorrow.' Jackie crinkles an eyebrow. 'See what the elf on the NICU shelf has got up to during the night ...'

In bed, I go through the messages I've missed today. There's one from Sama. She's the only one outside our immediate families who knows everything that's happening.

'I can hear Ed giving Agnes a bath on the monitor. He started talking about Grey, then Blue. Now they are listening to "Higher Love" by Whitney Houston and Ed is singing along; I feel like I'm in a parallel universe.'

I smile, in spite of everything. Parallel universe is right.

And there's a flurry of messages from my book club. The December dinner was tonight. I was supposed to be hosting. I'd chosen the book and then hadn't even had time to order it before Grey arrived. I love book club; we started it two years ago – a group of friends from school, we try to get together every six weeks. It's not a scary, serious affair. Everyone reads the latest choice and we chat about it, but without any pressure to bring notes or say anything especially profound. It's really an excuse to catch up with some of my favourite people, who I don't see enough. And read the piles of books I allow to stack up around our house. 'Your *tsundoku*,' Mol told me once.

I'd looked at her blankly.

'It's a Japanese concept – letting unfinished books pile up around your house. It's not a negative thing, in Japanese culture. I think it's something to do with the magic of the not-yet-discovered stories.'

'Could you tell that to Mike?' I'd said. 'About the magic?'

We'd laughed.

This evening Mol had stepped in seamlessly to host. They've had a good evening. Many bags of Popchips consumed – the book club pre-dinner snack of choice. My selection had been *The House in Paris* by Elizabeth Bowen. We were after something short in the run-up to Christmas – I read it years ago on my dad's recommendation and it seemed perfect. The girls had enjoyed it. 'Beautifully written, lovely story.' 'We missed you, G,' they write. It's reassuring, somehow, a reminder that life carries on, outside our bubble.

Still, they feel very far away. My old life feels very far away.

21

Eighteen days old

We have a new nurse today, Sadie. And hopefully we'll be able to speak to Drs Stewart and Chandra. Hopeful seems an odd word to use, or even think, given what we are going to talk about. The conversation. We chat to Sadie, waiting for Dr Chandra to come round. Overnight Grey's gases weren't very good, and his ventilation support had to come back up.

'He's trying really hard,' Sadie says, looking down at him fondly. 'He's so brave.'

His tiny, struggling system couldn't cope with only marginally less help from the ventilator. It's not a good sign. But it's not a surprise. I realise part of me feels some kind of relief. He's speaking to us, telling us he can't do this.

'Have you spotted the elf?' Sadie asks after a while.

'Oh no, I forgot!'

I look around Grey's incubator, then up at the monitors. There he is, sitting slightly slumped in the gap beside the main screen, with a little box strapped to his front, like a theatre attendant selling ice cream. I walk round Grey's incubator to peer at him more closely.

'What's he got?'

In the box is a small bottle – a plastic medicine bottle, one of the miniature NICU ones. Written across it are three letters: G-I-N.

I laugh out loud. 'Well that explains his posture.'

'Jackie was so proud of it,' Sadie says.

'Jackie and her gin – so funny.'

'So, what are you going as tomorrow night?' Mike asks Sadie.

There's an air of expectancy in the NICU, a kind of bubbling excitement. I realise it's been building all week, without my noticing. The NICU Christmas party, of course; Mike told me about it after one of his early-morning visits. An annual fixture, it's always fancy dress – 80s this year.

'Well, I was going to be quite low key, give a nod to *My Little Pony*. But it's somehow ended up being quite full on.'

'Talk me through it.'

'So, I've got this really long rainbow wig, then a tutu, sparkly earrings, leg warmers ...'

'Very eighties.'

'Exactly.'

'What's everyone else going as?'

'Hmmm, whose costumes do I know?' she ponders. 'Chris is going as Freddie Mercury ... Oh, and Jackie – no one is supposed to know, it's a big secret,' she says in a stage whisper, 'but apparently she's going as Maggie Thatcher.'

'Oh wow,' Mike says. 'That's hilarious, she'll do it brilliantly.'

'Amazing, isn't it?' says Sadie.

As she heads off to sort something for Grey, we chuckle.

'She'll really get in character,' Mike says. 'So good.'

'I called London,' Sadie says. 'Still no cots.'

'I don't think it really matters any more,' I reply.

'It's in his notes to check; it's good to know.'

'I don't want to go anywhere else,' I say. 'Not now.'

We are back in the quiet room. This time with Dr Chandra, Dr Stewart and Sadie. I think I know where this conversation is going to end. The sense of inevitability hangs heavy in the air. But where does it begin? How do you begin to discuss removing life support from your three-week-old baby? It doesn't feel real. It's an A-level philosophy dilemma, not Grey's life.

Dr Stewart speaks first. 'Dr Chandra has taken you through the full MRI, and we've spoken to the geneticist. I think what you're thinking about, palliative care for Grey, is very brave.' She pauses, looks from Mike to me, then, finally, 'I think it's the right thing to be considering.'

'It's horrible,' I say. 'It feels *so* wrong. Every single part of me wants to tell you, keep him alive, keep him here, in the incubator, keep him with us, we can hold him, we can smell him, I can hold his hands. But everything you've said doesn't seem to point to any kind of life, in the long term, for Grey. If you can't breathe, can't see things, can't communicate, can't hear, can't move, is that really a life?'

We discuss the possibilities, *if* Grey were to get home. It's a very, very big if. He'd need a team of nurses – Dr Chandra mentions eight – round the clock, just to be able to breathe. We'd do it, of course we'd do it, somehow, if there were to be any hope of him experiencing any pleasure at any point in the future. But he would be unlikely to even be able to tell us if he were in pain. It's agony. My body aches. I feel sick and hopeless and guilty and then sick all over again. Our baby. Our darling, darling baby.

'You don't need to decide now. And even if you do decide now, you can change your mind. You can take as much time as you need.'

But we do. We do need to decide. I know we both feel it. I want to lie in a dark room somewhere away from here and cry. But what good would that do? What Grey needs now is calm, rational thought.

Parenting is full of decisions. I choose things for Finn every day. Some are small, settled in an instant: do I force him to eat the broccoli he keeps pushing away, will he be warm enough without a second T-shirt, what time should he go to bed? Some are bigger: when will I go back to work? Who will look after him? Mike and I discuss our options, then, each time, we take a leap, hoping that we've done the right thing. Invariably, I worry and then feel guilty, whichever way we jump.

They will get bigger and harder as he gets older, life tumbling us into the more momentous questions: where do we send him to school? Do I let him go travelling on his own? Some are easy, some aren't.

And then there is this one.

Impossible; sickening, stomach-lurching and more painful than anything I could imagine.

I find some steel somewhere inside myself. There is no sense dwelling on the pain of it now; that's for later. Now I must see clearly. I must make the right decision. The best decision. For Grey.

'A huge part of me wants to keep him in that incubator, where he's safe, with all of you, with us. But he can't stay there for ever, can he?'

I glance at Mike.

'If it was me, if I had a horrible accident and this was my prognosis, I'd want Mike to switch off my life support,' I say. 'But it still feels all wrong.'

Silence.

'It is kind,' Dr Stewart says.

In my heart, in both our hearts, we know there is only one thing to do. All the other options bring pain to Grey, immeasurable pain. And we made a promise. So we will tread the only path that keeps that promise. We take the pain.

'What would happen?' I say. 'What would happen, how does it work?'

Dr Stewart takes a breath. 'When you are ready, we would gently take out his breathing tube. We call it a compassionate extubation.'

I take a breath too. We switch off his life support.

She pauses.

'You would need to be prepared that some babies breathe for a little while on their own – that might be minutes, it might be hours. In some cases, it's longer. I think, with Grey, it would be quick, but if it was longer, we have very local hospice facilities.'

She stops.

I digest what she's saying.

'We'll make sure, throughout, that Grey is comfy. We can give him some drugs, if we need to, to make sure that he doesn't feel any pain, to make sure he is not distressed.' Somehow, though the words are brutal, her voice is caressing.

Silence again.

'We have things you can read, about some of the things you might expect to happen. And you can stay with him, as long as you want. We have a suite where you can spend the night with him, you can spend a week with him. We have cold cots that we can put him in. It is all up to you. But there is no rush, you need to take all the time you want.'

Compassionate extubation.

They, we, will withdraw life support and Grey will die. He's three weeks old. I should be deciding how often to feed him, whether he needs a bath. Deciding whether his crying is wind or a dirty nappy, not if we'll need a cold cot for his tiny lifeless body. We should be organising for our friends to come and meet him for first cuddles, not arranging for our families to come and say goodbye.

'And our families? There are only six people on the visitors list ...'

'Those rules don't apply any more. Anyone can come, whenever they want.' Dr Stewart turns to Sadie with a sweep of her hand. 'Sadie, will you make sure everyone knows: take out the list. Grey doesn't have a list any more.'

Daddy and Ella can come; that's nice, I think, they really want to see Grey. For a second I forget why they can come.

'And you can choose your nurses; if there are particular nurses you've got close to, we can arrange for you to have them look after Grey.

'And you can decide if you want to be in the nursery, or we

177

have an isolation room where you can spend some time, or the suite – it is all up to you. You think about it and let us know. And if you have any questions at all, please find one of us, or ask one of the nurses, or the doctors, and they will ask us.'

I feel a strange sense of calm as I realise I'm really listening, I am processing what she's saying.

Mike swallows. 'What about organ donation?' He glances at me. I nod. I hadn't thought of it, but of course he's right to ask.

Sadie answers. 'It's a wonderful thing to ask. I actually did a course in this very recently, so I happen to know all the details. He's too little. Babies have to be at least thirty-four weeks gestation. Grey would actually not be eligible for donation because of his chromosomes, but he is too small anyway.'

The tiny lines around her blue eye deepen a little as she smiles towards us.

'Thank you, though. Thank you for asking, Mike. You let us know when, when you would like to do this. There's no rush, no timeline. Please take all the time you need to decide. Days, weeks. This is your decision. We are here to support you.'

I nod. Mike is nodding too.

Decide Grey's time to die. Where do we begin?

'The other thing we have to ask is, if Grey was to start to desaturate, or if his tube comes out, would you like us to put it back in? Would you want lifesaving measures?' Dr Stewart says.

The questions boggle my mind. On the one hand we are making the decision that he will die, on the other, every part of me wants to say yes to every one of these things, for ever; I want to scream – keep him *alive* . . .

From somewhere, I find a rational response. 'Would that hurt him? We don't want anything that would hurt him. But maybe just for tonight, while we work things out, maybe please do reintubate him? To give us a little bit more time to talk about everything?'

'Yes, of course. I'm sorry we have to ask. I think it's very unlikely, his tube is sewn in.'

'We don't want to hurt him,' Mike says. 'That is the most important thing.'

'Reintubation won't hurt him. I'm on call tonight: I'm going to tell the nurses, if anything happens, if anything changes, for them to call me directly, immediately.'

'And you'll call us?'

'Yes, of course.'

'We can be here in fifteen minutes.'

'I'll call you straight away.'

We sit together, all of us, for a few moments, each thinking our own thoughts. The silence is comforting, it doesn't feel unsettling. Because now, there is simply nothing to say.

'I've never done that before, you know,' Dr Stewart says quietly.

I'm confused.

'I've never spoken to parents about an MRI before having the full results.' She pauses. 'But it was so devastating, what we saw, I couldn't bear for you to wait, hoping, not knowing.' The corners of her eyes are wet with tears.

'Thank you,' Mike says. 'Thank you for telling us.'

'It must have been so hard,' I say. 'I'm so sorry, but thank you, we are so grateful.'

'I'm so ... sorry ...' The words catch in her throat.

Outside the quiet room, the corridor is bright and airy, painted a jolly yellow. I can hear children's voices in the family room – probably Carla's. Something feels a little lighter. Though none of us could say the words out loud, I know the decision has been made and somewhere inside me there is some small liberation in knowing what is going to happen, in knowing that Grey will be free.

22

5 December

Eighteen days old

It's beautifully sunny again. Crisp and cold, with the brightest of blue skies. We put on our coats and get a sandwich from the canteen.

'Where do you want to go, George?' Mike asks.

'Just out; there must be somewhere to sit.'

We walk out of the front entrance.

'Where?' he asks.

'A bench, or something?'

'I think most of the benches are occupied by the smoking contingent.'

He's right. People are nursing cigarettes at every bench outside the hospital.

'What about the back? Behind the NICU?'

'I'm not sure we'll have much luck there either – I think the only bench is by that bin which is always covered in fag-ends.'

We wander round anyway. There is one empty bench, away from the bin, and away from the doors.

We sit and take out our sandwiches, eat in silence. The bench looks up at the NICU windows. We can see the base of Grey's incubator, and scrub-clad legs standing in front of it.

'What do we do, MG? How do we deal with this?'

'Grey dying? I just don't know, G.' He is quiet for a few moments.

'Remember our promise: no pain. Of all the important things, that's the most important.'

'It's there again,' I say. 'One for sorrow ...'

'What?' he asks, looking around.

'The magpie. There's a single magpie, taunting me. Except when we took Grey out in the pram, he hops around outside the NICU every day, has been since last Friday.'

We pass Isa on the way back inside. Mike holds up his hand to wave and the doctor high-fives him.

'When are you going to cut my hair?' Mike calls after him.

'I forgot the clippers,' Isa says, smacking his forehead.

'Remember them tomorrow!'

'Sofia pulled rank on me,' Jackie says as we walk back into the NICU after supper. She is writing notes on the baby in the incubator next to Grey. 'I had to give him up for her.'

'I did,' Sofia says. She's wearing yet another beautiful headscarf. 'We all fight over Grey, but I said, "Tonight, I will have him." She wraps her arms around Grey's incubator.

I smile. 'Lucky boy.'

'Grey and I love our nights together, don't we, Grey?' She has opened the incubator doors and is carefully checking his wires.

'We loved the elf, Jackie,' I say. 'With his gin, genius.'

'Oh, you found him, good. The drunk elf. I told you gin was the answer, didn't I, Georgie? You'll have to keep an eye out tomorrow. He's got something up his sleeve.'

'We certainly will.'

'Ready for the party, Jackie?' Mike asks.

'Sure am,' she says. 'And no one knows what I'm going as.'

'We know,' Mike says.

'No you don't,' Jackie singsongs, not looking up from her charts. 'You might think you do, but no one does.'

'Sadie said that; she said it's a secret, but told us what it is.'

'You don't know-oh,' Jackie says, singsong again.

I really want to find out what she's going as. I hope it's Maggie Thatcher, but then maybe it's something even better.

'What are you going as?' I ask Sofia.

'I'm not going,' she says. 'I'll be here.'

'Oh no, you're missing it ...'

'It's OK, I went last year, and someone has to miss it. Someone has to look after these babies.' She turns to Grey. 'Don't they, Grey? I'd rather hang out with you anyway.'

Sofia pulls up a stool and sits between us. 'How are you both? Today was a tough day for you. Very, very tough.'

I'm so pleased she's on duty.

'You are really brave. You are amazing parents to Grey.'

I'm not sure it's true, but I need to hear it. She looks softly at our little boy. They love him too, I know they do, his wonderful nurses.

'Is there anything I can do? Do you want to talk about anything?' She hesitates. 'I don't know if you've thought about counselling, but we have a counsellor here. I can refer you tonight to see her?'

We say we'll think about it. I'm scared of what a counselling session might unearth, what might come tumbling out if I allow myself to really examine, to face up to, the reality of Grey dying. We talk some more, about how we're feeling, about how we never in a million years imagined we'd ever have the kind of conversations we've had.

Jackie comes over. We discuss some of the logistics. We say we're thinking about Sunday, we don't want to prolong it for him; it feels unfair and there's a symmetry to it being three weeks.

'I think he's helping you to make the decision,' Jackie says. 'He hasn't been doing so well this week, has he?'

She's right – the oxygen desaturations, the Neopuffing, the secretions. Our little boy is struggling.

*

I'm torn. I can't take enough pictures, enough videos. But I also want to experience it all, I want to hold on to every second, every look, every smell, every touch. I want to record in my mind every little movement that he makes. For the long years when I won't have him any more, when all I have is the dream of a smell, the ghost of a hand.

And then there are so many things to think about. When, where, who, do we want a christening, do we want family there? The nurses gently drip-feed us with questions, aware that our frazzled brains can't take on too much at once.

'And how are *you* doing?' Sofia asks me.

'It's quite unfortunate timing,' I say, 'but I think I might have mastitis. My left boob really hurts.'

Within five minutes, Sofia has established that the queue at A&E is about seventy minutes long (the only medical service open in the hospital at this hour) and persuaded a midwife friend of hers on duty on the postnatal ward to come and check me out. The NICU nurses could run the world. In another five minutes, Sofia has buzzed in the midwife and a student, and ushered us into the quiet room.

It's a surreal experience, standing in the room where I heard the worst news of my life, with my top up over my head while a midwife I have never set eyes on before feels my boob to check for blocked ducts. Luckily, she thinks it's unlikely I have an infection and suggests I try a hot shower. And if that doesn't work, fill a nappy with boiled water that has cooled a little, let it cool a little more and then hold it against my skin. Surreal as the timing might be, it's the best engorgement tip I've ever been given.

Amy is at the front desk in sequins and black velvet when I head to our locker for Grey's books. Her rosy cheeks look somehow rosier, her eyes twinkle in the low light.

'You look nice,' I say.

'Oh, my sparkly top. I went for a Christmas lunch; it's a bit OTT.' Her honey voice is instantly soothing.

'It's lovely.'

'I hoped I'd catch you and Mike if I popped in,' she says. 'How are you doing? Today must have been so hard.'

'We're OK,' I say. 'Sort of. It's weird, it doesn't feel real.'

'I'm printing something for you,' she says. 'A booklet I've been working on. About palliative care; I hope it has some things in it which might be helpful to you.'

'That is really kind, Amy. Thank you.'

'I'll come and find you when I've printed it. You go back to Grey.'

Later she brings us the booklet. She explains it's a work in progress. 'Excuse the makeshift design ...' the pages are folded and leafed together with Sellotape '... I wanted you to be able to have it, but it's not really ready yet.'

'We have to let him go, Sama,' I type. 'We've talked it all through and really there is no other way, for Grey. They'll take him off his ventilator and he'll go to be with Blue.'

She replies in minutes. 'That brave little boy has made a bigger impact on this world than many do in the longest lives. I will think about him and love him every day for the rest of my life. This next little bit is going to be unbelievably hard, and I just want to let you know that even when I am not with you, I am thinking of you, and I am with you every step. However dark it gets I will be here, and I promise you will be OK, even if sometimes it may not feel like it. I've had words with Blue and he's under strict instructions to take good care of Grey, they will make mischief in the stars together and watch over us all.'

Just for a moment I feel Sama right there beside me, squeezing my hand. They will, I think, they will.

Back at home, I sit on the enormous L-shaped sofa, the bereaved parents' booklet in my lap. On Sunday, we will be bereaved parents. I wonder if it will ever feel real. My mum, an early to bed, up at six person, is still up. She's knitting.

'I want to finish Grey's blanket,' she says. Her needles click. She looks down, totally absorbed.

'It's late . . .'

'I'm going to finish it tonight,' she says. 'And wash and press it, ready for him tomorrow.'

'It's already eleven o'clock, Mumma.'

'I'm going to finish it tonight, George.'

23

6 December

Nineteen days old

When I come down to collect the bits of my pump first thing, the grey blanket is neatly folded on the kitchen table. I pick it up, feel its soft weight. Elephants are knitted into each square, trunks and tails curled. I've always loved elephants. I remember my granny teaching me the difference between African and Indian elephants' ears when I was small. Grey's are African. I refold and replace it.

When we are getting ready to leave, my mum presses the blanket into my hands. 'This is for Grey,' she says. 'It was never for anyone else, just for him, he has to have it.' Her brow is furrowed, her eyes wide, her teeth gritted. I know she's fighting not to cry; it's taking every bit of control she possesses. And that's a lot.

'It's beautiful, Mumma. He'll love it.' I kiss her on the cheek and she squeezes my arm.

None of the nurses we know are on duty today – of course, it was the NICU Christmas party last night, and the eight-to-eight shift means missing a chunk of the action. Grey's nurse introduces herself as Amina, then goes about her business, not wanting to interrupt us.

We give him his blanket. 'Nana knitted this for you, Greyman,' I say. 'Look how lovely it is, all these elephants, just for you.' I rearrange his bedding, fold the blanket in half and tuck it neatly around him.

'Oh! Where's that elf ...?'

I look up and around, then smile. An old sharps box has been turned into a basket. The elf is perched inside it, legs poking out of one side. Long white ribbons stretch up to a purple balloon (where on earth did Jackie find that?) which is looped over a beam above Grey's cot. 'He's in a hot-air balloon!'

Jackie has propped up one of the elf's arms so it looks like he's waving at us.

At lunchtime, we have to register Grey's birth. How do you register a birth when you know in two days your baby will be dead?

I remember our excitement registering Finn's birth; we wheeled him proudly in his pram, and he slept through the entire appointment. How different today will be. No Instagram 'he's official' posts. Grey won't be coming with us. Another rite of passage, flipped on its head.

'Are you sure you have to go?' my mum asks. 'Can't I do it for you?'

But it's one of those odd sticking points in British law – it has to be one of the parents. So off we go, my mum driving. Although it's quiet time, we leave my sisters holding the NICU fort – Grey's newly extended, open-all-hours guest list.

My mum has brought a package with her. As I open it, I recognise the Jellycat logo. Inside are two corduroy foxes. 'Grey Atticus Fox,' I murmur. I remember Sama asking for our address. A note says, 'Something to hug.' I know it's addressed to Grey, but I find myself tucking the foxes under my own chin.

The civic centre is an ugly, blocky building, all angles and plate glass, too modern for its own good. We're directed upstairs and sit outside the registrar offices. After a few minutes a woman opens the door of the one on the right and walks towards us. She's in a Laura Ashley floral shirt beneath

187

a soft, pinky purple cable-knitted cardigan with a sparkly brooch. Polished black shoes are topped by sensible trousers. She offers a hand and a smile. A badge pinned to her front says 'Margaret'.

Meticulously filling out every part of the form, she asks questions about 'Baby' with a slightly brisk smile. My eyes wander around the room. Signs on the walls advertise chirpy options for novelty birth certificates and warn that false weddings come with a hefty fine.

Then she asks brightly, 'And what name will Baby grow up under?'

She doesn't know. Of course she doesn't know. But it's still like a punch in the stomach. I crumble. Mike puts a hand over mine and tells her Grey's name. I can see she's confused, but I don't have the words to explain to this kind, business-like woman that our baby won't grow up. That in two days he will be dead.

When she's finished, she asks, 'Who'd like to sign?' Her hands are poised over the keyboard.

'You should, if you want to,' Mike says.

'OK.'

She prints a copy of the certificate for us to check. My eyes run down the page. It's all fine.

'All fine,' Mike says.

She slides the document into the printer; two copies land in the tray. I watch her lift and sign each one, the careful looping of the fountain pen, the ink soaking into the paper. I remember reading somewhere that it's special ink, registrar's ink – a chemical reacts with the paper, staining it for ever. Even after the ink has faded, the words remain, etched indelibly.

I watch her cross out 'head' and write 'deputy'. Then she turns the page and pushes it brightly towards me. I sign each sheet. She gathers them up, fills out the registration book, then pulls an early-years folder from the cupboard behind her. I recognise the purple cover.

I also recognise the two books inside. Finn has both of them.

'Are the books all the same?' I ask.

Margaret opens another folder. I can see the top one's different.

'Can I swap?'

'Of course,' she says.

Looking more closely, I see the second title is *This Is Me*, one of Finn's favourites. One evening before bed we read it seven times. I smile. It'll be useful to have a spare copy.

Mike leans across to me and whispers, 'I'm going to ask her about the other appointment; do you want to stay here or wait outside?'

The other appointment.

I thank Margaret and find a chair outside, where I can glimpse her and Mike through the half-closed blinds. I wait. And wait. Finally Mike emerges, holding a folder. 'I ruined poor Margaret's day. Tuesday afternoon,' he says as we walk down the stairs and out to my mum's waiting car. 'One-thirty.'

Four days. In four days we will be back here registering our baby's death.

Back in the NICU, Lou and Ella are laughing about how many nurses thought Lou was me. 'I told at least three people, "I'm not Georgie, I'm not Grey's mum,"' she says.

Amina comes to talk to us about the rota for the weekend. Two nights and two days. Sofia for Friday night, Rebekah for Saturday, Melia on Saturday night and then Nena, our wonderful Nena, is on duty on Sunday. Rebekah will be back on Sunday night, and then Amy on Monday. I don't think we'll get there, but it's nice to know that if we do, Amy will be looking after us, looking after Grey.

My mum arrives, bringing Finn. This time Grey is out of his incubator. It's the first and last time Finn will touch his brother. Mike lifts him up to the arm of my chair and Finny reaches across, delighted. 'Ta-ter, Ta-ter ...' He grins at Mike, at me, and then at Grey.

'Do you want to hold his hands?' I ask.

Finn reaches out, grabs one of Grey's hands.

'Gently,' I say.

Finn relaxes his grip a little. Then, 'Mun more.' He takes Grey's other hand. A deep chuckle rises from his tummy. Sheer delight on his face. 'Ta-ter!' he says.

Amina is taking photos. Family photos. She is trying to take a video; it isn't working, but really, I don't need it, I won't forget this moment for as long as I live. The last time all four of us will be together. For these precious moments, I feel a little bit like the version of me I thought I'd be. Finn and Grey, in my arms, together. For these minutes everything is OK. After days of shuttling between my children, I can finally be a mother to my two boys simultaneously. I wish I could stop time.

Finn is getting tired, and hungry.

'I'll take him to put his coat on and get ready to go home while you sort out Greyman,' Mike says. He scoops him up into his arms, then stands over Grey and me.

Finn is sucking on his knuckle.

'Say goodbye to your ta-ter,' Mike says.

'Seee-ya,' Finn says, waving his hand vigorously. 'Seeya seeya seeya-bo.'

I look up at his huge, innocent eyes. He hasn't said goodbye. Neither of our little boys has any idea that this is the last time they will see each other. It strikes me that is exactly as it should be. Mike turns and they head to the door. I watch them walk away. The NICU feels silent when they're gone.

It's around eight-thirty when we return to the nursery. Sofia is on duty, as she's said she will be, and Nic is also there.

'Any news from the party?' Mike asks. 'Any gossip?'

'I have one or two pics in my WhatsApp,' Sofia says. 'In fact' – she pulls her phone out of her pocket – 'I'll ask for more photos.'

'Do, please,' Mike says. 'We need to see everyone's outfits.'

While Mike chats to Sofia, I talk babies with Nic. I was right, she is pregnant. We find ourselves discussing the joyful moment eighteen-month-olds realise they have some say over what they will, or more accurately won't, eat.

'Ah-ha,' Sofia says. 'I've got pictures.'

We gather round as she holds up her phone. 'Here's Sadie as *My Little Pony*, with Sian – do you know Sian?'

'We might have seen her in the NICU, but it's hard to tell now she has rainbow hair.'

'Here's Judy – you know, our matron – as *Where's Wally?* She went with Shelagh.'

I recognise the Irish nurse who introduced me to the hospital breast pump.

She flicks to the next. 'Ha-ha, it's Anna!'

Anna has looked after Grey a couple of times. In scrubs she is frighteningly competent. Here, she's in a neon visor, chunky chain and blue eyeshadow. It's a close-up selfie, eyebrow raised.

'Brilliant,' Mike says.

Next it's Melia, Nena and Rosa.

'I don't know who they are,' Sofia says. 'I think a pop group.'

'*Charlie's Angels*?' Mike asks. They are all carrying guns.

Sofia frowns. 'I don't think so. They said a pop group, I'm sure. It might come back to me.' She flicks again.

'*Danger Mouse*! Who's that?' The nurse's face is entirely hidden by a giant rodent's head.

'I don't know,' Sofia says.

Mike and I are waiting for Jackie. 'Where's Maggie Thatcher?' he asks.

'There are more. Wait, wait …'

Mike starts laughing as the next shot appears.

'Freddie Mercury – is that really Chris?' The only male nurse in the NICU has donned Freddie's signature yellow biker jacket and holds a blow-up guitar aloft. 'Did he grow that moustache?'

'Yes,' Sofia says. 'Haven't you noticed it this week at work?'

'This is amazing,' Mike says.

Sofia conjures up one more image. 'Are you ready?' she says, before turning the phone around.

'It's got to be Jackie. Maggie Thatcher . . .'

She shakes her head.

It isn't the Iron Lady; it's better. Grey's nurse is dressed in a sharp black suit, a crisp white shirt and black tie, a black fedora and sunglasses. She's even wearing stick-on sideburns. She strikes a perfect Dan Aykroyd pose, complete with inflatable saxophone.

'*Blues Brothers*,' Mike says. 'Absolutely brilliant.'

Another sister we don't know is in the next picture, as John Belushi. They're perfectly in character.

'Sofia, thank you. That has made my evening!'

'How did you manage to get so many pictures?' I ask.

'I messaged our NICU group,' she says. 'I said, Grey's parents are in the NICU, they want pictures. Judy went round the party asking everyone.'

Grey's parents. I like that this is who we are here. He is the focus, he is the centre. Here, even when he's gone, we will always be Grey's parents before anything else.

Sama texts. 'Ed and I are toasting Grey with Baileys – chic.'

I laugh out loud. 'We're looking through snaps of the NICU Christmas party – it's fancy dress.'

'Brilliant,' she replies. 'How epic have they gone on a scale of one to ten?'

Sama and I were champion fancy dressers, all those years ago.

'There are a couple of My Little Ponies you'd be very proud of,' I type.

'Excellent.'

'Enjoy the Baileys x'

24

7 December

Twenty days old

Saturday. The day before the day. It's early, I'm in the kitchen collecting my pumping apparatus, on autopilot. I have to say goodbye, I think. Tomorrow, I have to say goodbye to my baby, and then I have to live for the rest of my life without him. I don't know how to do it.

I drop the bits into the sink, letting my body curl in on itself, letting the sobs come, letting the waves of panic and sadness and horror wash over me.

I howl.

Suddenly, my mum's arms are around me. I sink my head into her shoulder.

'How will I say goodbye, Mumma? How can I ever, ever say goodbye? I don't want to say goodbye. I can't, how will I do it?'

She is silent, stroking my hair, gripping me tightly.

'Because you must,' she says finally. 'You're strong, and you're his mummy.'

The elf on the shelf is riding Grey's stork. I smile, but the more I look at it, the more twisted it feels. Storks are supposed to deliver babies, not take them away.

Rebekah is on duty. Her practical approach is exactly what we need. We undress Grey and do his cares – nappy change, top-to-toe wash. Rebekah gently cleans his eyes, I wipe his mouth with a cotton bud soaked in milk. She suggests not dressing him until the doctors have come round. Dr Sahu is on duty, and so is Isa. Dr Sahu chats to us. 'We won't examine him,' he says, one hand gently cupping Grey's head. He glances at his numbers. 'Everything seems fine.'

He gazes down at him.

We all do.

A sleeping angel, his eyes are gently shut, his chest softly rises and falls to the rhythm of the ventilator, his hand clutches his octopus. Innocent, perfect, completely unaware of the tragedy unfolding around him. I wonder if we're all trying to soak up a little of his calm serenity.

'No, no checks today. I am here if you need me, if you need anything at all.' He shakes our hands, clasping them warmly. Looking us straight in the eye.

Isa nods at us. 'He is a brave boy.'

'There's one thing we wanted to ask,' Mike says. 'Can his ventilator be changed, for tomorrow. Can we go back to the other one, so he doesn't have to wear the bonnet?'

'I will do it myself,' Isa says. 'I have some things to do – some X-rays and gases – but I will do it, I promise.'

We thank him and he walks away.

Mike's parents are here, with Zoë and Jon. I leave them to have some time together while I pump. I'm not sure why I'm still pumping; I don't need to, Grey has enough milk now, far more than enough. But somehow I can't bring myself to drop even one of my sessions. I wonder if it's the control, the connection, the unwillingness to give up the only tangible evidence that Grey needs me.

My sisters, my parents, will come later. Nick has decided not to, decided it would open up too many questions for Sam, my nearly five-year-old nephew. That it might distress him.

As I leave the nursery, I notice a missed call from him. My mum is on her phone in the family room.

'Is that Nick?' I ask.

She nods.

'I just got a missed call from him.'

She hands me the phone.

'Sam is asking about Grey all the time, so I think we're going to explain to him today what's going to happen. I know you're not having anyone else at the hospital this afternoon and I don't want to mess with your plans, but in case Sam asks if he can see him ...'

He swallows before continuing.

'I won't give him the option if it's not a possibility.'

'I think he should meet him if he wants,' I say. 'I need to check with Mike, but I already know he'll say the same thing. This isn't only about us. It is not only our son dying, it's your nephew, it's Sam's cousin. It's important. I'll ask Mike, I'll message you.'

Mike agrees. Of course he agrees.

It's not long before a message pings through from Nick. 'Sam wants to meet Grey, he said it straight away, is that OK?'

'Of course,' I type back.

'We're leaving now,' Nick says.

It's a two-hour drive. They'll message when they're outside.

Lou, Ella and my parents say their last goodbyes. I can't watch. I know each of them will kiss Grey's little head, lay their hands on his tiny body. Somehow fit a lifetime of love, a lifetime of hugs, a lifetime of life into a single touch. And then they'll walk away from him, like we'll all have to. Knowing they'll never see him again.

The thought of it makes me sick to my stomach. I feel such a coward as I try to pretend I can't see the tears in my dad's eyes, the glistening streaks down my sisters' cheeks. I harden my heart to their pain because I can't bear to see that it mirrors my own.

A calm settles over our corner of the NICU when they've gone. Carla has been here with her children, but they've left too. They kept their distance; I think they sensed all was not well. Carla's daughter died here; she knows this pain better than anyone.

Rebekah asks if we'd like to take Grey out.

'You should,' I say to Mike. 'I always hold him first – today you should hold him.' He unbuttons his shirt and Rebekah lays our tiny boy against his chest, carefully draping his blanket over him. Then she goes to get her lunch, asking the other nurses to keep an eye on us, to check on Grey while she's gone.

'He really does make everything OK, doesn't he, G?' Mike says. 'Somehow when he's here, on my chest, the world melts away. It's just us, his heart beating against mine.'

I nod. But what about when he isn't here?

We sit quietly, the blinds drawn, the NICU hushed, the lights low. Peaceful. By some fate there are no other visitors, no other parents, this afternoon. I watch Mike, his eyes gently closed, his hands cupped around our son. Grey's eyes flicker open, looking up at him, then close, relaxing into sleep.

My mind wanders back to our day in Whitstable. Meandering through the eclectic mix of stores – design, art, antiques. A furniture shop with a little armchair that would be perfect for the nursery. A tiny treasure trove on the high street, packed with Christmas decorations. I'd chosen two baubles to add to our slowly growing collection, imagining Finn hanging them on the tree, imagining our last Christmas as a threesome. They were deep grey handblown glass spheres. I had no idea then of the significance of the colour. I wonder where they are – I hope they're safe, they're very fragile, as I'd discovered when one slipped from my hand and shattered on the tiled floor.

The buzz of my phone jolts me back into the present.

Nick, Nat and Sam are here. I meet them at the entrance to the unit. Sam is quiet. Sam is rarely quiet. He's thinking, I can see, taking it all in.

They follow me to the end of the corridor, to outside the ITU.

'We have to wash our hands really, really well, Samjam,' I say. 'To protect Baby Grey.'

'Can you do your best hand-washing, darling?' Nat says.

He scrubs his hands together vigorously, his expression studious, totally focused.

'Now we need some of this ...' I take the alcohol gel out of its holder.

'What's that?' Sam looks suspicious.

'It's magic gel,' I say, 'to make your hands extra clean.'

He holds out his palms and I spray. 'Now rub them together – rub it all over your hands.'

He does. And gives a squeak of laughter.

'I can't feel it!' he says.

'See, I told you it was magic,' I say. 'Do you want to come and meet Baby Grey?'

He nods. We walk into the NICU. Sam clings to Nat's hand, looking around, taking in the lights, the incubators. I imagine seeing it all from his height, how scary it must be. But if Sam feels scared he doesn't betray it for a moment, walking carefully, purposefully into the nursery.

Mike is sitting back in the purple chair, Grey on his chest.

'This is your cousin, Baby Grey,' I say.

Sam stands back, eyes wide, a finger on his chin, an arm on Nat's leg.

'You can say hello to him,' I say.

Nick crouches, in line with Grey, and reaches for his son. 'Come here ... look ... can you see him?'

'He's so little,' Sam says. A beautiful grin spreads across his face, all the way up to the tips of his ears, which go pink with delight. 'Look at his little hands.'

'Do you want to hold his hand?' I ask.

'Yeaaah.' Sam takes Grey's hand in his, giggling with delight. 'He is so small,' he says, suddenly solemn.

We all look at him. 'He is.'

'His eyes!' Sam suddenly squeals, looking at me and pointing. 'Auntie Georgie, he's opening his eyes.'

'He is,' I say. 'He wants to see you, he wants to say hello to his cousin.'

I gather them all together for a photo.

'Cheeeese,' Sam says, teeth bared in a curious school-portrait grimace.

'Do a nice smile, Sam,' Nat says.

I keep snapping. We'll get one. I wish Finn was here. I wish all the boys were here together.

'Sam . . .' Nat crouches. 'Shall we go and see Granny now, darling?' She reaches out; I can see Sam is reluctant to leave.

He puts out a hand to Grey, one last time. 'I-I-I love you, Baby Grey,' he says, his soft 'r'-sound very slightly like a 'w'.

Nat gathers him up in her arms, holding him tightly. He looks over her shoulder at Grey as Nick follows them out. We all stand just outside the ITU, no one knowing quite what to say. There is nothing to say.

'I said goodbye to Grey, Mummy,' Sam whispers.

'Do you remember what we said, Sam? Baby Grey will be in here.' Nick curls his hand around Sam's and places it against his chest. 'Here in your heart, for ever and ever.'

'He'll be your guardian angel,' I say. 'Finn's, and yours, and Elsie's, and Wilf's.' I can hear my voice cracking, feel another piece of my heart twist away.

'And I will tell Baby Finn about him when he gets older.' Sam pauses. 'In case he does not remember.'

'That would be kind, Sam,' I say. 'That would be very kind.'

A not-quite-five-year-old sage.

None of us can speak any more. Nat squeezes Sam closer to her. Nick carefully studies the floor, one giant hand on my shoulder. The air feels heavy. The weight of the moment presses onto all our shoulders.

Then, 'Mummy, you are s-s-quashing my willy.' Sam wriggles loose and our laughter slices straight through the silence.

*

198

'Where are you staying now, my lovelies?' Rebekah asks, just back from her lunch. 'I wanted to say, I know you've been having trouble finding somewhere for very long. I wanted to offer my house. Well, some rooms in my house. I'm out by the coast – it's about a twenty-minute or half-hour drive, but it's right on the sea – it's lovely.'

Her offer is so kind, I want to cry, again.

'My house is quite big and with my daughter at uni . . .' She pauses. 'Well, there's lots of space – we have two spare rooms, so one for Finn.' She has thought it all through. In the midst of night shifts and day shifts and her own life, she has planned out this space for us.

'Thank you, Rebekah,' I whisper. 'I don't know what to say . . . that's so kind . . . I think we're OK for now, our Airbnb lady is letting us stay a bit longer.'

'Well, the offer is always there.' She pauses. 'Any time, actually.'

'We think we'd like to baptise Grey. Can we do that? Not with anyone else, not with our families, just us, but we think it would be nice. We christened Finn; we think we should christen Grey too.'

'Of course,' Rebekah says. 'Leave it with me.'

We would usually have gone home for supper by this time, but neither of us can bring ourselves to walk away.

Without warning, Grey's monitor starts flashing and bleeping, urgently, then his ventilator alarm is sounding. Rebekah is instantly by his head, checking his tubes. A nurse we don't know joins her. In seconds his saturation has dropped. Something is wrong. We watch them working on our son.

Mike is becoming increasingly agitated.

'G, should we let him go?' It comes out of nowhere. 'If he's struggling, should we let him choose?'

I don't know what to say, split between the conversation and watching Rebekah Neopuff Grey. No. I don't think we've reached that stage. I think Rebekah would have told us. I'm not ready. Is that selfish? I don't feel ready for this to be the moment we say goodbye, here, now, in this room.

Then I remember our promise. No pain.

Is he in pain?

Before I have a chance to ask, his numbers are back up.

'He's OK,' Rebekah says.

Mike's head is in his hands.

'Are you two OK?' she asks.

'We don't want to force him to stay alive for us,' I reply.

Rebekah looks puzzled. 'There was a tiny leak in the tube,' she says. 'That was the machinery; it messes with the numbers. He's OK now.'

'Would you tell us?' I ask. 'Would you tell us if it was time, if we needed to let him go?'

'Yes, I would, really. That wasn't the moment, that wasn't what I was thinking. I was trying to work out what was going on with the tube, that's why I had to Neopuff him.'

Mike still looks in agony.

'Mike, what's on your mind?' Rebekah asks softly, looking from him to me.

'That's the first time I felt I was keeping him alive for us,' he says. 'That we selfishly couldn't let him go.'

'I don't think that's what it was, MG,' I say.

'G, you always tell me to say what I'm thinking, and I'm saying it.'

I feel panicked; we have always agreed. With Grey, so far, we've always thought the same thing. We can't fall out now. The stakes are too high.

Mike turns and walks away, shaking his head.

'What in particular is Mike worried about?' Rebekah asks me. 'I've never seen him like that before.'

'He's worried we're putting ourselves first, that we want him to ... to die ... on our terms.'

'Why does he think that?'

'I think he was worried that the desaturation just then was Grey's way of saying it's time for me to go.'

'But that was the ventilator,' she says. 'Really. There was a small leak. It wasn't Grey.'

'I know,' I say. 'It's ... It's a lot to deal with.'

'Of course it is,' she says. 'And you must both be so tired. I think you should go home.'

Mike comes back in. 'I'm sorry,' he says, putting an arm round me. 'This whole thing is so fucked up, it's getting to me.'

'I was saying to Georgina ...' I love that she always calls me by my full name, the quiet authority makes me feel mothered, taken care of '... I think you should both go home. I think ...' She trails off. 'You need to get some rest.'

I nod. So does Mike.

'Tomorrow is going to be a long day.'

So long, I think. So, so long. But not as long as the lifetime after that, that we have to be without Grey.

But she is right. We need some supper. We need to collect ourselves.

'One other thing,' Mike says. 'Rebekah, you know Cora's parents – Carla and Dom – do you think someone could tell them? If we came in and Cora was gone, we'd be really worried. I think it's only fair to let them know what's happening.'

He's right, of course. He's so right. Only Mike would be thinking about other people right now.

She promises to let their nurse know, so they'll be told when they arrive in the morning. I wonder if we'll bump into them. And if we do, what we'll say.

Melia is on duty when we get back.

'How was the party?' Mike asks.

'Your costume was brilliant,' I add. I'm still not entirely clear on the identity of the eighties pop group, but her costume *was* great.

'It was good,' she says. 'We all had a very nice time.'

She is so gentle, so calming. The perfect person to be with Grey tonight.

'Melia,' Mike says, 'has Isa been round? He said he'd

change Grey's ventilator back to the metal one, take off this ... bonnet.' I notice he resists saying 'silly'.

'He did come,' she says. 'This evening has been busy. There's a baby on the other side who is not well – but he promised as soon as he has time, he will do it.'

As if on cue, Isa appears. 'My friends,' he says, clapping a hand on Mike's back.

'Hello, sir,' Mike greets him. 'Have you come to do Grey's ventilator?'

Isa wags a finger. 'I came to tell you that I promise, I will do the ventilator. What time will you be back in the morning?'

'Around six,' Mike replies.

'Well then, I promise that when you come back in the morning, I will have changed the ventilator.' He smiles. 'I promise,' he repeats, reaching for Mike's hand and closing his own around it.

'There are a few other things to arrange,' Melia says. 'You want to be in the isolation room, for tomorrow?'

We nod.

'I have put three radiators in there. It can get cold, but hopefully that will help.'

We thank her.

'The view is—' She breaks off, gesturing out of Grey's window. 'I know this isn't the most beautiful, but the windows in the isolation room look at nothing.' She wrinkles her nose.

'That's fine,' I say. 'Sorry, Greyman, better make the most of this scenery.'

'When would you like to move him?' she asks.

'Well, we'll be in early, can we move him then? I think it would be nice for him to be here overnight, with his dorm mates. I don't want him to be on his own.'

'We need quite a lot of nurses to move him. We can do it at the changeover, is that OK? Just before eight.'

'That's great,' we say. 'Absolutely fine.'

Then we sit and we talk to Grey, telling him things, passing the time, letting him listen to our voices. When we can't talk any more, we read to him. When we can't read, we sit. Sit and look. I don't know how to leave him. I don't know how to get up and walk out knowing this is our last evening with him, his last bedtime story, his last night. Waves of alternating panic and crushing, yawning pain wash over me. Isa's words echo inside my head: 'Don't let him see your pain. Don't let him feel your sorrow . . .'

I swallow.

'G,' Mike says softly, 'I think we should go. He's sleeping. Melia will look after him.' He turns to her. 'You will, won't you?'

'Of course,' she says.

I lean over the cot and kiss his head, kiss his cheeks, press the pad of my forefinger into his hand.

'Sleep well, my darling.'

We thank Melia and walk out.

The corridors are quiet. The caretaker is pushing one of the industrial steam floor cleaners in front of us, whistling. It echoes around the deserted, lino-ed walls. The main entrance is locked; we have to take the long way round, past A&E. My mind flashes back three weeks. I see myself walking in, cradling my bump, telling myself everything is going to be OK. I see the glass-fronted counter where I waited behind an elderly gentleman and a mother with a teenage son.

It's my turn. I step towards the receptionist.

'I'm thirty-one weeks pregnant. I'm bleeding.'

I'm whisked into a side room, the door shut. Somehow two nurses balance gentle with brusque. 'How much are you bleeding? And what colour is the blood?'

'It's bright red.' I fish around on my phone. 'I took a picture, I know that's a bit weird.'

'It's useful, not weird. It's very red. We'll take you to the labour ward.'

'Is your bump always that low?'

'I don't know, I mean, I haven't noticed it changing.' I

haven't really thought about it. 'It looks normal to me . . .' A feeble response. Should I be keeping closer track?

'I think your bump has dropped.'

'What does that mean?'

'It might mean the baby is ready to arrive.'

No. She's wrong. She can't be right because the baby isn't coming for another two months. My C-section date isn't even booked yet. I'll book it in December. The baby will be ready in January; it will come in January.

It feels like a lifetime ago, and like yesterday.

I'm not sure I know that girl with the low bump any more.

We push open the doors and step out into the crisp, cold night. My breath billows instantly in the air around me.

Back at home, in the shower, I look down at my body. My boobs full with milk Grey will never drink. My stomach bulging from my separated muscles, the skin slack, empty. I turn my face towards the water and let the boiling jets wash over me.

I don't know how I will sleep tonight.

25

8 December

Three weeks old

Twenty-one days since Grey was born. Three short weeks, and his whole lifetime.

We wake long before the sunrise. I'm going in with Mike, joining him for his early turn. We shower quickly. No one else is up. We've told them we'll get dressed and leave. We don't want to see anyone. Maybe that's selfish, but we can't carry the weight of their final goodbyes to Grey's cot-side.

As we turn the car around to leave the little cul-de-sac, I notice a figure behind the Venetian blinds, in the still-dark sitting room. My mum. She doesn't move, just watches, a step back from where she and Finny have stood every morning for the last two weeks, waving us off.

I look back to the lane. We turn left on to the main road. Mist floats up, dancing in front of the headlamps. It's cold and crisp. The soft dawn glow beginning to spread from the horizon makes the dusting of frost across the fields sparkle. The roads are wet with the night's rain, a little icy in places. We follow the same route we've always taken.

We arrive at the hospital a little after six-thirty. As we walk along the corridor towards the NICU, I see nurses bustling in and out of the isolation room.

'Don't look yet,' says one I recognise, but whose name I don't know – she hasn't looked after Grey. 'It's not quite ready.' The corners of her mouth lift into the tiniest smile.

True to his word, Isa has changed Grey's sewn-in ventilator for the regular metal one. The bonnet has gone and his face looks less squashed without the padding that framed the whole set-up. His hair has grown darker and curlier. Melia has changed him into a babygrow covered in jolly multicoloured cars.

We sit with him. Foreheads resting against the incubator, hands on his little body. I wonder what it will feel like when the last breath has left his lungs, when his hands can no longer hold ours, when his soft warmth has disappeared, when the reassuring beat of his heart stops.

'I will love you for ever, little boy,' I whisper. 'For ever and ever.'

As we sit, the sun comes up, replacing the darkness with pastel winter light, glimmering through the skeletons of the trees lining the car park.

Gradually the spaces start to fill; staff arriving, patients arriving, visitors arriving.

Just before eight, the day shift nurses are here. Chris is one of the first into the nursery.

'Hi, Freddie,' I say.

'Oh God . . .' He grimaces.

'I can't believe I missed the moustache.'

'It had to go . . . first thing this morning,' he says. 'The wife.'

As Alessia and Nena help Melia get Grey ready to move, Chris shows me pictures of his dogs. We talk about London, Somerset. He tells me that he used to work on the trains before he retrained as a NICU nurse. His daughter is at uni now. They'd like to move to Cornwall; he keeps pestering his wife, but she likes it here.

'She knows her consultants in this hospital, you see; she doesn't want to have to get to know new ones.' He doesn't mention what her consultants are for. I don't feel it would be the right time to ask.

It's time to move out of the nursery.

'Best of luck,' he says. He hugs me, then shakes Mike's

hand. There's a kind of finality about it. I guess we won't see any of the other nurses in the isolation room. It will be us, and Nena. The doctors when we need them.

We follow the incubator down the corridor, turn left into the isolation room. Fairy lights are draped along both walls and a little fully decorated Christmas tree stands on the side table. Melia's radiators have warmed it beautifully.

'Is it OK?' the nurses ask. 'There's not much you can do about things like the lighting.'

'It's perfect: he'll love it, we love it – thank you.'

'You weren't lying about the view, were you,' Mike tells Melia.

The window looks out onto a small concrete courtyard, towards some kind of staff room where a nurse scrolls through her phone, drinking a cup of tea. Taking her morning break as she probably has, day after day, for months, maybe years. A day like any other. Except it isn't, for us. This is the nature of life-changing tragedy, I realise, it occurs quietly, almost unnoticed, alongside the mundane. How many days have gone by in my life without comment, without specific memory, while somewhere, someone's world is breaking.

When everything is plugged back in, the nurses go to leave, hugging us and wishing us well, kissing Grey goodbye.

Melia is the last.

'Thank you,' we say. 'Thank you so much.'

The space feels quiet after the buzz of the ITU.

My mum has packed a big paper bag with bits and pieces for the room. I take them out one by one. I string up the toy soldiers Ella bought for Grey, and tuck one of Finny's rabbits – Rab – in beside him. I prop a framed drawing of Loula's on the wall above the incubator – two wagtails touching the tips of their beaks; she drew it when our granny died, fourteen years after our grandfather. His friends had called him 'the wagtail' because of the way he walked. The two are now finally reunited, wherever they may be. Next is an embroidered cushion, which funnily enough goes perfectly with the purple hospital chair. And a pack of photos – plenty of things for us to tell Grey about. I peg some of them up in the window.

'I need to go and get something,' Nena says. She comes back in with a bunch of flowers and a vase. 'These are for Grey, from me.'

I can't bring myself to hug her. I know I'll cry and I need to keep the tears at bay a little longer, so I squeeze her hand instead. They are beautiful – palest blue, yellow, cream. She must have left early, found them on the way to work. We arrange them in the vase and put them on a small shelf above Grey's incubator. 'And this,' she says: a string of carved wooden letters spells 'Christmas'. We hang it up across some cupboards. It all looks so pretty. Festive and cosy.

Everything seems to be in the sharpest focus, vibrant Technicolor. Every action feels momentous. Am I consciously drawing each second into my memory? Or is my mind doing it automatically? Nena brings baby wash, a big sterile bowl and tons of cotton wool. Grey's hair is a little fusty from days under his blue bonnet, so we're going to give him an incubator bath. He wriggles around as I sweep warm, damp cotton wool over his head and lather his soft curls. He flares his nose. Carefully, methodically, I wash every little part of him. His skin puckers and wrinkles over his arms and legs – so much spare for fat and muscle that will now never cover his bones.

I gently pat him dry with a soft towel and dress him. We've chosen his Baby Mori outfit. It's grey, of course. Grey for our little Grey. A long-sleeved vest and a tiny-weeny onesie, freshly laundered, ready for today. I unfasten and reattach his wires, thread them through the new clothes. When he's ready, we can take the lid off his incubator. He's tucked in, snug, warm. We put on a hat – the same one he wore for his walk – the signature newborn knot at the top.

He's ready now. I will never be.

*

We sit with him, passing the time. Nena comes and goes, quietly checking things. Some of the time we're alone, the three of us, for the very first time. The irony of the first moments alone with Grey marking his last day in the world.

My dad gave us Charlie Mackesy's book. Grey's first Christmas is also the Christmas of this beautiful hardback. *The Boy, the Mole, the Fox and the Horse.* I read it to him, or at least try to read to him, through a mist of tears. Every page is so well observed, so poignant, so uplifting, so perfectly phrased, so completely true.

I have wondered at the promise within my small boy. Who he might be, what he might do. I've looked forward to watching the seedling of a person emerge. A sapling beneath our branches; a little boy, separate to us, with his own likes, dislikes, his own relationships, already, with the people close to him. His own ways of doing things.

But that luxury has been whisked away. We must accept that we'll never have the chance to get to know him. To find out about him. All we have is here and now. Twenty-one days, which should have been the start of something, and will now become the only memories we have. All the thoughts I have of him and Finn racing around after one another, snuffed out. His quiet serenity, his calm, will soon live only in our minds, in our hearts. Together, we have lived a lifetime in three short weeks. Within the pain there can surely be no greater privilege. I remember Loula's words: 'Nothing but love, nothing but love for his whole life.'

We turn to the photos, to show him our favourite places – the seaside, the wild Cornish coastline; we tell him about the freezing waves and the perfectly blue skies. We show him the mountains that we love so much, a dusting of whitest powder coating the peaks. Finn's first time in the snow. The Scottish hills, the lochs, the greenery, the leaves turning to autumn. We tell him about the quiet, the peace, the wind lifting the branches, rippling across the water. The wild flowers in my parents' garden in Somerset, the bees that increase in number each year, their Springador, Inka, sitting, head cocked. So many things that we imagined showing him. I hope, somehow, he'll see them anyway. I promise to take him along with us, everywhere we go.

And then we show him the precious people I have to hope will find him, somehow. My granny, who died in April, who never could have imagined her third great-grandson would be joining her so soon. Mike's granny, who died when I was twelve weeks pregnant with Finn. My grandfather, who died three months before Finn was born. I whisper words to each of them: please look after him, please give our tiny boy all the cuddles that we cannot.

The hospital chaplain arrives at eleven for his blessing. Finn's christening was at eleven, a nice coincidence. I'm not really sure why we've chosen to baptise him. I wasn't especially religious before, more spiritual, I guess, and the last week has made me question everything that religion represents, but it feels like something we might regret not doing, so here we are.

The chaplain wears a light grey shirt; it doesn't have a single crease, even at the arms, where it's tucked; it's entirely smooth. He clasps a Bible to his chest. He shakes us by the hand, softly saying he is sorry for the circumstances. An ornate silver bowl, for the holy water, stands on a small hospital tray, covered with a lace cloth. In the NICU the holy water is a small, sterile pipette, the vicar's thumb a disinfected cotton bud.

Mike and I stand on either side of the open incubator. Nena and another nurse are by the door, with Dr Kate. The ceremony is short. The chaplain reads a few short words from Psalm 139: '*You knitted me together in my mother's womb, before I was formed you knew me.*' Dabbing the cotton bud lightly across Grey's forehead, 'I baptise you Grey Atticus Fox.'

He then blesses our son.

I feel so many things, and nothing at all, the plating of

shock, my newest companion. The chaplain gives us a baptism candle, and a small carved cross made from smooth Bethlehem wood. 'You are all in my thoughts,' he says. 'If I can be of any support at all, please do come and see me.'

His head is bowed as he walks away.

I am suddenly happy we have done this, pleased with the ritual, the calm that the little ceremony has brought with it. Regardless of belief, there is something steadfast, reassuring, in the protocol.

I pump, we read, to Grey, or to each other? Nena comes and goes. She tells us Jackie has called to send her love, to say she is thinking of us. A little later she tells us Sofia has called. She has sent her love to Grey, and to us. She says she will be thinking of us all day.

My family send pictures from the top of the Kent downs. Clear blue skies, not a single cloud, not a breath of wind, long shadows cast across the hills from the low winter sun. They too are thinking of us. If we were in Grey's old incubator spot the sun would be shining in through the window.

Sally and Zoë have taken Finn with Elsie and Wilf to the reindeer centre; pictures ping through of smiling cousins feeding the reindeer, playing, sitting on Father Christmas's lap. I smile at Finn's grin as he holds out feed to an enormous reindeer.

Doctors look in every now and again, they hold Grey's head, or touch his chest, tenderly, carefully, looking at him before looking at us. Dr Sahu is the duty consultant. He explains what will happen.

'When you are ready, and there is no rush – even if you decide you can't do it today, you don't want to do it today, that is fine. But when you are ready, we will carefully take out Grey's ventilator. I think Dr Stewart explained, sometimes babies will breathe for a little bit afterwards. If we think he is experiencing any discomfort, there are some drugs we can give a little of, to relax him, the same drug he had for his MRI. We can make sure he doesn't feel any pain.' He puts a reassuring hand on Mike's arm. 'We are here, for whatever you need.'

'When shall we get him out?' I ask Mike.

'G . . .' He pauses. 'I have this feeling that if we get him out, we shouldn't put him back in.' He means we should cuddle our baby and then let him die.

'How . . . How do we do this? I'm never going to be ready, MG.'

'I know.'

'Who should hold him first?'

'Well, I think . . .' his tone is extraordinarily measured '. . . I think if you want, and you can, you should be the last.'

He thinks it's right that Grey should die in my arms. I think it is too. Except none of this is right.

Mike holds him, tiny Grey snuggled under his chin. He looks so peaceful, his back covered by Mike's hand. The rise and fall of his breathing is almost imperceptible, but it's there, I know it's there.

When we are settled, Nena says she will go to get some lunch. She leaves us with an Irish sister we haven't met before. She stays outside, leaving Mike and Grey and me. We sit, first in silence, then talking quietly to him, telling him we love him, that we'll miss him. That we'll talk about him for ever, that everyone will know him. We tell him we'll look after Finny, that Finny will miss looking after him, that we'll all miss getting to know him, seeing how he grows. Again and again we tell him that we love him, that we will always love him. How do you fit a lifetime of love into three weeks? And then into one day? And then a few hours? And then minutes, then seconds?

Mike says that it's time for me to hold him, so we call the sister, who brings another nurse to help lift and settle him onto me.

Mike's hands stay cupped around Grey's back. 'I love you, I love you,' he whispers, over and over.

As the nurses lift Grey from Mike's chest, his tears fall with deep shuddering gasps. His face contorted. Agony. His body shaking. Each sob reaches deep into my heart and then twists every organ inside me. There is nothing I can do, nothing I can say. Even as I reach towards him, I know I can't save him, save us. I have no way to comfort him.

The nurses reassure Mike that there is no rush, that he doesn't have to do this now. But when will it ever be OK? How can you lift your baby from your chest knowing you will never feel his heart beat there again? He moves from the chair and I sit. They place Grey gently upon me and I gaze down at his serene face. His eyes are closed. He knows nothing of our pain, he will never know this pain. We can give him that; that is all, now, that we can give to him.

A soft knock and Dr Chandra is in the room. Her usually scraped-back hair falls in waves around her face. She wears a printed shirt and jeans tucked into her boots. She isn't on duty.

'I wanted to come,' she says. 'I wanted to come to see Grey, to see you.' She gazes down at his little face. I wonder why I ever found her intimidating. 'Oh Grey . . .' she whispers.

Mike puts an arm around her.

'I should go,' she says, not moving.

I can see she is fighting to stop her tears. She doesn't need to. I want to tell her, you *can* cry, it's OK. We cry for people we love.

She hugs Mike, then turns back to me, to Grey. 'Goodbye,' she says, looking towards me, but not speaking to me. She pulls the door shut behind her.

Once again we are left, the three of us.

The quiet is broken by the alarm on the monitor over my head. Glancing up, I see Grey's oxygen saturation is dropping. Nurses return to the room in seconds; one suctions the secretions from his chest, one monitors his levels. His face twists as the tiny plastic tube sucks the build-up of mucus from his chest. Gradually his numbers come back up. But then minutes later they are down.

'MG,' I say. 'MG, I think he is telling us he's ready. He hates the suction, I don't think we should suction him again, we have to listen to him, we have to let him go. We have to set him free.'

It's as though the words are coming from somewhere else, someone else. As he is suctioned, I whisper that this will be the last time. 'No more, my darling, no more of that. I know it's horrible, we aren't going to do it again. Soon you will be free from all of this.'

When Grey is stable, Mike goes to get Dr Kate, who brings Dr Sahu. They gently explain once more what will happen, and prescribe the sedative that might be needed if Grey is in pain.

Nena is back from her lunch.

I could have waited for a hundred years for the next alarm and it would have been too soon. It's no more than a few minutes before Grey's numbers fall; the increasingly urgent bleeping signals another desaturation.

It's time.

First they unplug all the alerts; they will be able to monitor his numbers, but there will be no more sounds, no more alarms.

Peace, quiet.

Nena calls Dr Kate, who kneels low, by Grey's face, in line with mine.

'Are you sure?' she says.

I nod. 'He hates the suctioning. I'm not doing that to him again.'

One slow, smooth movement and the breathing tube is pulled carefully from his mouth. Nena and Kate work in silence to unplug everything.

'Would you – would you like a picture?' Nena asks.

We nod. She takes the only photo we have of the three of us with no ventilator.

Then, 'We'll be outside if you need us.'

Their eyes are wide, holding back their tears, for Grey, for us.

The sun is shining against the silver frame of the window opposite.

Just the three of us. It's the first time I'm holding him unsupervised, the first time I can see his face without wires and tubes. The first time, and the last time. I look down at our little boy. His little chest is still rising and falling, his hand is curled around my finger. I see his perfect lips for the first time since that momentary glimpse when he was born. They pucker in a little bow as he takes tiny breaths.

'It's OK,' I whisper. 'It's OK.'

Mike crouches over us, absorbing every molecule of him. Grey's fingers begin to go limp, gently releasing mine. The gaps between his breaths have begun to slow. My baby is dying.

Suddenly it is quiet. We listen to the silence. It's broken by a small gasp. I remember the bereavement book. Sometimes in their final moments, babies take small gasps.

Again it is quiet.

'Has he gone, MG? Has he stopped breathing?'

I can't cry.

Mike speaks quietly to Nena, who comes in to check his heartbeat. It's faint, but there.

'Is he in pain?' I ask. 'He can't be in pain.'

'He is peaceful,' she says. 'See his face. But let's give him a little sedative. It will make sure he feels nothing.' She slips it into his mouth. Then leaves.

Each break between gasps, the world seems to stop.

We hold our breath too.

The gaps stretch longer, longer and longer.

'I want to walk around with him,' I say. 'Do you think I can?'

'Of course, G, you can do whatever you want.'

I hold Grey against my shoulder and walk around the

215

room, a little bounce in my step, as if soothing him to sleep. I stroke his little cheeks, then press my finger to his brand-new rosebud mouth. Dark curls poke out from under his hat and his hand rests against my chest.

When Finn was tiny, I would press him to my chest exactly like this, and wish I could keep him like that for ever, wish I could preserve his perfect innocence, protect him from all the bad things, all the pain, all the wrong in the world. In some ways, this is the one thing we can do for Grey. All he has ever known is pure love, for his whole life. Nothing but love.

Time passes. There is silence. I can no longer feel even the faintest murmur of a heartbeat.

'Should we get Nena? I think she needs to check.'

Moments later, Nena slips a stethoscope inside his babygrow. She listens, and listens, and listens.

Then she bows her head and shakes it gently.

'Grey doesn't have a heartbeat.' Then, almost inaudibly, 'My darling . . .'

He has slipped away as quietly as he arrived.

Free.

'He chose, G,' Mike says. 'He chose, not us.'

I know he's right. We sit together, Grey in my arms. I can feel the warmth gently ebbing out of his limbs. I look at his face, examining every part of it. I have a sudden thought: they didn't get it wrong, did they?

'He looks so perfect, MG, they can't have made a mistake . . .? No, they can't.' I answer my own question.

In these precious moments, time feels somehow suspended between life and death. The family montage is more normal than on any of the days of Grey's life. Time is reversed, and suddenly here are the first moments we expected when he was born. Finally, we sit together, alone. Me, in the hospital armchair, Grey cradled in my arms, Mike beside me, his arm around my back, both of us gazing down at our son. At his too-big babygrow and his whole face. Untroubled by strapping, by wires, no longer twisted by the ventilator, no longer pained by the suction. Peaceful. We sit, breathing in the peace.

I feel a strange calm; it's both soothing and unsettling.

I don't know how long we sit like this. Time is no longer measured by normal patterns. Its rhythm is forever disturbed. Three weeks was never a lifetime.

'We should tell our families,' I say. 'They think it's going to be later. I don't want to hear from them before we've told them.'

'Our darling boy has slipped away,' I write. 'He went very peacefully, in my arms, at last free of all his wires and tubes. X'

I hit send. Messages ping back. Support, prayers, love. Oh, the love, the limitless love.

Nick's message is particularly poignant. 'Sweet dreams little Grey,' he writes. 'Just after we received the news we were caught in the biggest wind and rainstorm. Grey saying good-bye, we've all agreed. We all shouted "Goodbye, I love you" at the tops of our voices as he soaked us through. Sammy has told us we don't need to cry. "When the sun comes up it will have Grey's face on it." The most love created in the shortest time.'

How right he is. And Sam, wiser than any of us.

Nena hugs Mike, then me, then both of us. We hug her.

'Thank you, Nena,' Mike says. 'Thank you for being here.'

'It's an honour,' she says.

'You're Grey's family, our family, there's no way we could have done any of this without you,' I say.

'You were there when he was born, and you're here now,' Mike says, 'and so many times in between.'

'You are special parents,' she says, hugging Mike, hugging me.

She picks up a box she's brought with her.

'This is a memory box,' she says. 'We can open it in a

minute, whenever you want, or you don't need to open it at all. It is to hold things for you, for Grey.'

I look at it, not yet quite ready to peek inside, not ready to face the reality that all we have now is memories.

'Should we change his nappy?' Mike asks.

'I think that would be nice,' Nena says. 'We can change him and make sure he is dressed how you would like him to be.'

Mike takes our son from my arms, cradling him for a few minutes in his own. He puts him back down carefully into the incubator and starts to undo the poppers on his babygrow. Nena hands him a new nappy and some cotton wool. I sit in the chair, staring ahead. I can't process everything that is happening. This isn't real.

Suddenly Mike gasps. 'Christ ...'

Nena turns around and my head snaps up.

'Um, he's weeing, is that normal?'

'Yes,' Nena reassures us. 'It is.'

Mike looks at her and then at me.

'A final present for his daddy,' I say.

Mike starts to laugh. I join in, so does Nena.

'Christ, I could have done without that, Greyman. They should put that in the little book of preparation.'

When Grey has a fresh nappy, Mike poppers him back up and hands him gently back to me.

I cradle him, my tiny boy.

There is another soft knock at the door. Dr Kate is back. 'I'm so sorry to interrupt, I need to do some official things.' She crouches beside Grey. 'Little man,' she says. Then, 'Can I take him for a minute, Georgie?'

I present my baby to Dr Kate – until now he has always been presented to me, given to me. I have been the one to ask to hold him, I have stepped back whenever a doctor has approached.

She takes him, so gently, slipping her arms beneath him. Every bit as carefully as she'd handle a living baby. I am so grateful. She lays him gently in the incubator cot, talking softly, reassuringly to him, all the time. 'I'm just going to undo your babygrow, little man. There we are. This is a little cold ...'

She slips the stethoscope onto his chest. She strokes his head as she listens. I count, she listens. Listening to nothing. Checking for nothing. Then she removes the earpieces and carefully refastens his poppers. She scoops him back into her arms and hands him back to me. 'All done,' she says, smoothing a finger over his forehead. Her eyes are unnaturally wide and I can see tears glisten along her lids. We stare at each other.

'He did a wee,' Mike says.

'I'm sorry?' She looks confused.

'Grey did a wee. I just changed his nappy, after he'd died; it frightened the life out of me.'

Kate's face relaxes. The mood has been lifted in one sentence by my darling husband.

'Oh yes, I can see that would give you quite a shock. His systems shutting down.'

It feels so mechanical. So extraordinary. You aren't supposed to learn about bodies shutting down from your three-week-old baby.

When Kate has gone, Nena helps me wrap Grey and Finn's blue Rab in his elephant blanket. He looks like a perfectly swaddled newborn.

The memory box gives us purpose. 'For a lock of baby's hair,' the label on the first little container reads. We snip a lock of Grey's curly hair and slip it inside, cushioned with a tiny square of cotton wool. We take clay mouldings of his minute hands and feet.

We decide what we'll send with him: his Advent calendar, Rab, the elf on the shelf and one of the foxes Sama sent. I look at them, two of them – one tiny comforter, one bigger fox – and I wonder if she knew, I wonder if this is what she had imagined. The comforter going with Grey, the big fox staying with Finn. We pick up his octopus.

'I can't,' I say. 'I need to keep this.'

There's a candle and two little teddies. We decide to keep them both, for Finn – one called Finn and one called Grey. As we gather these treasures I stop once in a while to kiss him, to look at him, to pick him up. I take photos, feeling morbid. And a little video. Somehow the stills make his face look odd – redder than it is, more swollen, emphasising the veins. The video captures his doll-like flawlessness.

The tiny person who has taught me a lifetime of lessons in three short weeks has gone. I will never again see his eyes flicker open when I sing to him. Never again watch those beautiful fingers flex and unflex around mine.

Nena asks if we want to go with him to the mortuary. We don't know. I don't know about anything any more.

'Should we?'

She tells us that sometimes it can be hard, seeing men we don't know coming to take him. Seeing him loaded onto the trolley. That perhaps we would prefer to leave him here.

I realise I need to remember him like this, wrapped in his blanket, tucked into his cot. My last image. She needs to do some paperwork, she says. She leaves us to sort the final things. Then, she says, 'they' will come and get him. Now I am sure I don't want to be here when they do. I want to feel like we are leaving him here, safely in the NICU. With these wonderful doctors and nurses who have become his family, our family. I don't want to watch his little body being wheeled down the corridor to be slipped into a fridge drawer.

Some hours later, I know it is time to say goodbye. I stare down at his tiny body, saving every little part of it. The last time I will touch his rounded cheeks, his button nose, the little cleft beneath his lower lip. I press my lips to his forehead, wrap my hands around him. 'Goodbye, my darling, I love you more than you will ever know.' I stay there as long as I can, telling myself his soul has escaped, telling myself this body is no longer Grey, then turn and walk out of the room, walk away from my baby. Carrying a small bag of things, and two memory boxes.

We bump into Lisa and her boyfriend on the way out.

'Hi!' she says. 'All OK?'

'Yes.' I smile back. 'You?'

'All right today,' she says. 'All right. She's doing OK, she's doing well.'

'That's great.' My voice sounds alien to my ears. 'So great.' I'm glad, they've had a rough ride.

'Bye then,' she says. 'See you.'

'See you,' I echo. They don't need to know. Not now. We empty our locker into the bag and walk out of the NICU, like we've done every afternoon for the last twenty-one days. Except this time we don't leave Grey. He has gone on ahead.

PART THREE
THE GOAT TRACK

26

8 December

In the immediate aftermath, I feel relief. Grey is free. No more wires, no more tubes, no more suction, no more needles.

Then I'm numb.

Everyone has left the house, except my parents and Sally. It is evening. We sit on the huge, squashy L-shaped sofa downstairs and talk about Grey. No part of it seems real. Someone gets a bottle of champagne from the fridge. We raise our glasses.

'Grey Atticus Fox,' Mike says. 'The bravest boy I've ever known.'

I feel lightheaded – champagne, shock, who knows? But suddenly I need to tell people, immediately. Our friends. The people we've been in touch with. I can't face any more well-meaning texts, asking how Grey is doing, asking how we are. They're messages of love. Of course they are. So much love, and so much hope. But here, today, for Grey, there is no place for hope.

Perhaps my mind knows, my heart knows, that now, in the shock of the aftermath, while it still doesn't feel real, this is the safest time to let people know. I draft a message and send it. Replies start to come, slowly at first, and then a deluge. Message after message filled with warmth, with support, with strength. A tower of strength from so many people that we love, that love us.

Mol borrows a line from Don McLean's 'Vincent' – 'the world was never meant for one as beautiful as you'. It's one of our favourites. After a while it's too much, I push my phone away, face down.

*

I need to keep busy. In the NICU, time warped, it turned into a different beast. Hours holding Grey disappeared in seconds, seconds waiting to hear test results lengthened into days. Every single one of them was accounted for. I already feel untethered from the routine. I hadn't realised quite how reassuring the measure of our days had become, divided into segments, each one devoted to a particular task. Now, time seems to stretch out ahead of us.

'How do you feel about his funeral being before Christmas?' I ask Mike.

'And near here?' he says. 'So anyone who wants to from the NICU can join us.'

I've been thinking the same. I want the funeral to be in daylight, I want it to be before Christmas and I want it to be here in Kent. Grey lived his whole life in Kent. He was never a London baby; he chose to arrive by the sea. Here, where I still feel safe.

'Maybe we could go back to Whitstable for a few days,' Mike says. 'Until we can sort everything out. It isn't far, and it would be nice to be by the sea.'

I nod. 'I don't feel ready to go back to London. I want to be here a bit longer. It feels like he's here.'

I think I want his funeral to be before Christmas because it's my favourite time of year. And when the anniversary rolls around, year after year, I want it to be part of the celebration. I want to remember and feel happy. I hate January, I've always hated January, I can't help it, it feels like a month-long hangover.

'I want it to be happy.'

'So do I,' he says.

'I know that sounds mad – how can any of this be happy? But I want it to be a celebration of Grey, of what he taught us, of the lessons we've learnt and how much he brought us.'

'I think exactly the same, G. Exactly the same.'

I want to plan it immediately, to sit and talk through what music we will have, what we'll say and what we'll read. Planning is an anchor; I need an anchor.

'We'll have "Bring Him Home", of course,' Mike says.

'Of course. And would it be OK if I read *You're Here for a Reason*? If I can actually make it to the end. You know, the book we've been reading to Grey.'

He rotates his laptop screen to show me it's already there. 'I thought I might read—'

'"If—".' I almost beat him to it. 'Of course. "You'll be a man, my son." And how about "Vincent"?'

He presses the Spotify icon on his laptop and we listen to Don McLean.

We listen and we cry.

It's the rhythm of the evening.

'I've been thinking ...'

We do this now, a lot of thinking. For two people who never find words in short supply, we do a lot of thinking. Choosing snippets from the reams of footage playing through our minds to share with one another. Selected edits. It works better that way. Apart from anything else, not many of the things I think are fully formed, coherent. 'I quite like the idea of having a nursery rhyme. For Finny, he loves the actions now. And for the cousins. Something that includes them, and might be a little bit of a happy moment?' I carry on. 'I've been thinking about something like "Twinkle, Twinkle"? Finny always does the star bursts with his hands, whenever it plays.'

I wonder if Mike will think this is an odd idea. He is quiet for a minute. 'That would be really nice, G. I wonder if we can find a good version. I don't want one of those weird voices that the Spotify playlists seem to go for.'

I also like the idea of Bob Dylan's 'If Not for You'. 'Maybe it can be sort of my song to you all.'

Mike wants 'Caliban's Dream', which was composed for the opening ceremony of the 2012 Olympics. 'And "Nimrod"?'

'I think so,' I say.

We flick through the options on Spotify, and play the Coldstream Guards' version. 'I love this one,' I say. 'And actually, it's perfect, because I don't think it will make me really, really sad. I always hear David Dimbleby's commentary as they lay the wreaths at the Cenotaph. So sad, but uplifting.'

Mike looks a little baffled, so I demonstrate. 'And here is His Royal Highness The Prince of Wales laying his wreath, with the distinctive plume of ostrich feathers, and a second wreath, on behalf of Her Majesty The Queen . . .'

'Your brain is so weird,' he says.

'I think David will help me keep it together. Remind me this is bigger than us – life, death.' We note down some other ideas, play more music. By the time we head for bed, it feels like we have some kind of a plan. A funeral plan.

I don't expect sleep to come. But it does. Heavy, empty sleep.

'Do you know,' Sally says suddenly, 'I had the most extraordinary experience with Finn on the way back from the reindeer centre yesterday. We were driving along, and he was babbling in the back, the way he does, saying different words that didn't always match. Suddenly he went completely silent, and then said, "Ta-ter, ta-ter, ta-ter," several times. That's what he calls Grey, isn't it?'

We're sitting around the table in the kitchen of the Airbnb.

'It was so extraordinary that I looked at the clock on the dashboard.'

'What time was it?' I ask quietly.

'Five past two.'

I feel a gentle shiver run down my spine. 'That must have been almost exactly when Grey died.'

'Yes,' Mike says. 'Nena checked his pulse at ten to two and he still had a faint heartbeat. Kate pronounced him dead at a quarter past, but he died a little before that, as we'd spent some time with him.'

'I did wonder,' Sally says after a while. 'There was something about the way he said it. Strangely purposeful. Not his usual chattering.'

'Maybe Grey came to say goodbye,' I whisper.

We sit in silence. Wondering whether our tiny baby visited his big brother before he went to his resting place. It's a comforting thought. The minutes they might have had together, just the two of them, in lieu of a lifetime.

27

9 December

Amy hands us Sands booklets – leaflets about baby loss, about what we have to do now. Mid-morning, and we're back in the quiet room. It's our fourth Monday at the hospital. We needed to come. Needed to smell it. Needed to feel the comforting embrace of this little corridor which has been our home for three weeks. And there is admin. Amy asks us how we are. We say fine. It's not the time to unpack what on earth fine means from now on. She recommends a funeral director, tells us they aren't really supposed to, but Lynn is wonderful and will look after us.

Mike pulls a card from his pocket. 'Lynn at Classic Funerals?' Margaret, the registrar, has already recommended her.

'She actually reminds me of *you*, Mike,' Amy says.

'Lucky her.' Mike raises his eyebrows.

'Does she make really awkward jokes?' I ask. 'At really inappropriate moments?'

She shakes her head. 'No,' she says. 'She's efficient, no-nonsense, and really, really kind.'

Mike calls her there and then. She will help, of course, but needs to speak to the crematorium immediately – they get booked up at this time of year. They might be able to fit us in, if we're prepared to have an early morning or late afternoon slot. Can we meet her tomorrow? We can.

She calls back minutes later to say she has three afternoons and one morning slot on hold. It's December and the sun sets at four. I don't want an afternoon slot, I don't want to say goodbye to Grey in the dark. We choose the morning, and confirm it. Grey will be cremated at 9.15 on Wednesday 18 December.

'Georgie, Annabel's grandad was called Grey,' Amy says. 'She never knew, until she told her mum about Grey and discovered it was her grandfather's name.'

'Really?' Mike says. 'She talked to her mum about Grey?'

'Of course. The babies, their families – some in particular – are our family. That doesn't stop at the NICU door.'

'Amy, I don't really know what to do with my milk,' I say a few moments later. 'I really want to donate it – there's a lot in the freezer here and more at home – but Sofia said she doesn't think you can until your baby is six weeks old. Maybe if I can't donate it, I can bring it all here and you could throw it away for me? I'm not sure if I could face it.'

'I don't know the exact guidelines, Georgie,' she says. 'Hearts Milk Bank is the best place to call – they supply all our donor milk; they will know. I'd call them.'

I do. I can donate it. There are some hoops to jump through – forms, blood tests – but when they're done, I can donate all of Grey's supply, as long as I'm accepted less than three months from the date it was pumped. It gives me plenty of time. I'm relieved; it would be horrible to throw it away. And I've seen other mothers here struggle with tiny preemies and no milk. If Grey's milk can make even the slightest bit of difference, can bring someone else hope, that's what I want.

My mum suggests ordering takeaway pizza from the pub tonight.

'Let's eat there,' I hear myself say. Craving some normality? The buzz of other voices to drown out the ones in my head?

We set off into the crisp, cold night, Mike carrying Finn, leaving enough time to see the 18.01 train go through the station. We stand on the bridge and wait for it. I look at my phone – it's delayed.

'Choo-choo, choo-choo,' Finn says as his lips turn blue.

Ten minutes pass. I'm about to say that Finn is cold, that we should perhaps give up, when we hear a low whistle. A speck of light appears in the distance. We watch the engine roll down the track towards us, getting bigger and bigger. Finn squeals in delight as it comes to a halt right underneath us.

We watch the train pull out of the station, then keep walking. The pub we were aiming for is closed. My mum suggests one a little further on.

We make our way along the cobbled pavement of the fairy-lit street. A huge tinselled Christmas tree stands outside the village hall. Spray-on snow adorns the windows of the café on the corner. There's a soft glow and burble of conversation and laughter from within. Through the window, I see women in navy aprons standing alongside tables loaded with greenery and glasses of red wine. Wreath-making, a Christmas ritual for the Etsy generation.

The Queen's Arms is still fairly empty, except for a few festive drinkers at the bar. I ask for a table for five, plus Finn. A friendly waitress finds us one by the fire and brings a highchair.

We order, then sit and chat. By the time Finn's food and our starters arrive, the place is filling up. It's a Monday, but in December Mondays don't really count. My mum takes Finny to wash his hands while his pasta cools. I see tears in her eyes when they return.

'The taps,' she says. 'The taps in the loo are just like the ones in the NICU. I turned them on, and as I was rinsing Finny's hands, he turned his little face up to mine and said, "Ta-ter?" I think he thought we were going to see Grey.'

'Ta-ter, G-ey,' Finn says, clapping.

'We had it all planned out, you know.'

We're back at home, on the sofa, my mum and I. Sally has gone to bed.

'Daddy was going to retire, Lou would take days off from

232

personal training; we were going to make sure you had someone with you, helping to look after Grey, every day.'

She pauses.

'Before we knew ... I mean ... before we knew ... how
bad it was ...'

I hug her. 'Thank you, thank you.' The words aren't
enough, they'll never be enough. 'I wish we could have done
that. I wish it could have been a possibility.'

28

10 December

It's our last day in this house. We're going to find a florist, then register Grey's death, then meet Lynn. We have a funeral director. The thought rolls around my head as if it were someone else's.

Then we'll drive to Whitstable.

The florist is tucked away, off the main road, in a cluster of buildings that also houses a small garden centre and a farm shop. Tinsel and baubles twinkle on the Christmas trees, trestle tables are lined with poinsettias.

It's shut, so we wander aimlessly around the farm shop instead, picking things up – mince pies, mini foil-covered chocolate baubles – adding them to a pile on the checkout desk. Christmas by osmosis.

We get back to town for an early lunch. Pizza Express. We sit at a table near the window. Just after we order, the long table behind Mike fills with women, some wearing lanyards. One hands round glasses of fizz. Here we are, side by side: us, about to register Grey's death; them, enjoying their office party. One of them is talking about a skiing holiday she's planning, another about the wines she's going to serve at her wedding. Their conversations carry the gentle rhythm of normality. Life goes on.

It's time for our appointment. We pay, and leave the Christmas party on their second glasses, retracing our steps to the car park.

This time we bypass the front desk of the civic centre and

head straight up to the first floor. We sit and wait. Margaret opens her office door and walks towards us, wearing a similar ensemble to Friday – another floral shirt and cardigan, today in pale pink. 'Sadder circumstances this time.' She extends a sympathetic hand. 'I'm so sorry.'

I know what she means, but Friday wasn't exactly joy-filled. In fact, as Mike and I agree later, if you want to pit them against each other, registering your son's birth when you know he is going to die is probably more painful than registering your son's death. But there we go.

'Do you have the envelope from the hospital?'

Mike hands it to her.

'I'll come and get you in a minute. There are some formalities, and I may have to call the hospital, which could be distressing for you, so it's better you stay here until that part is done.'

So we sit and wait. I wonder whether she is having to call the hospital, if the form is right. I hope it is. Otherwise we're going to have to change the funeral day, everything will have to be reshuffled. Her door opens again, and she beckons us. We follow her into the same office we sat in five days ago.

'All done, it's all in order,' she says. 'I'm sorry it took a while, I had to Google a few of the causes of death – I didn't want to misspell anything.'

'Of course,' I hear myself say. The smorgasbord.

'There are a lot of different things ... I'm so sorry,' she says, regarding us sympathetically. 'I was so sorry to hear ... what was happening on Friday ... It really affected me ... all afternoon.' Her professionalism falters, then she braces herself. 'Now, I think much of the information ...'

She's back in registrar mode. This must be how she gets through, how she registers death after death, day after day. There is a loud barking outside. She raises her voice a little, '... much of the information is the same as Friday, so to avoid repetition I will fill that out now.'

The barking starts again when she turns back to her computer. Her fingers are poised over the keyboard. 'There shouldn't be a dog in here,' she says.

The barking stops, and her fingers return to the keys. Then it starts again.

'Unless that's a service dog, it really shouldn't be in here,' she mutters.

Mike has got up and moved to the window. 'I wonder what's going on,' he says, relishing the drama.

'I'm so sorry about this,' Margaret says.

'That's all right, Margaret,' Mike replies, still peering through the blind. 'It's not your fault.'

'Can you see if any staff are out there, please?'

Mike looks bemused.

'Oh, of course, you wouldn't know who they are. I'm so, so sorry – if it's OK with you, I'm going to have to pause this for a minute and email the centre manager.'

'No problem,' Mike says, still peering through the blinds. 'You do what you have to do.'

The barking increases; so does the shouting.

'I'm sorry, but I think I ought to go and see what on earth is going on.' She strides towards the door. Before she can grab the handle, someone rushes past outside.

'Ah,' she says, 'Becky's going.'

'Good on Becky,' Mike says.

She sits back down. 'Right, where were we?' She studies the screen, then looks at us, collecting herself.

The barks are now ear-shattering. Margaret is back by the door, inching it open.

'Call an ambulance,' we hear.

She shuts the door abruptly. 'Someone is on the floor,' she says.

It suddenly doesn't feel funny at all.

'What ...?' I ask.

She inches the door open. 'I think he's fine,' she says. She disappears, then returns a few seconds later. 'Everyone is *absolutely* fine. The ambulance is a precaution. Both dogs are detained.'

'Both dogs? I thought—'

'Dogs aren't allowed, no,' she says, disapprovingly. 'Unless—'

'They're service dogs,' Mike concludes.

'Exactly.'

'So do you think the situation is under control?' Mike asks. He's enjoying this a little too much.

We watch and wait. A few minutes later, two paramedics wander up the stairs. Any urgency has dissipated. No barking, no shouting.

'Right.' Margaret turns back to us, and to her computer. 'I really am sorry about that. Not at all good timing, but it seems to be sorted now. Let's finish these things off for you.'

She fills out the rest of the information on Grey's death certificate, then prints a proof for us to check. It's all fine. We ask for two copies.

'Have you spoken to Lynn?' she asks Mike. 'We aren't supposed to recommend funeral directors.'

'Of course,' Mike says, then leans towards her. 'Don't worry, we won't tell.' His tone is conspiratorial.

Margaret looks a little taken aback. 'I might email her after this meeting, actually, if you wouldn't mind, just to let her know everything has been processed OK.'

'You do that, Margaret,' Mike says. 'Make sure you get your kickback.'

I feel my eyes roll upwards. It's his way of dealing with most things, including, it would seem, the death of our son. He says it with warmth, a twinkle in his eye, but Margaret, of course, looks horrified.

'We don't take a cut,' she assures him. 'Everything to do with the funeral of an infant is free.' This poor, kind woman trying to do her job amongst barking dogs and Mike's quips.

'I'm so, so sorry, Margaret,' I say. 'He knows that. He's joking.'

She looks from Mike to me, then back again, utterly perplexed at the idea that anyone could find humour in the circumstances.

Meet my husband.

By the time we leave, there's no sign of the drama outside. Mike is disappointed.

'I wanted to at least see the dogs,' he says.

The episode has somehow managed to completely sideline the purpose of our visit. It's a relief. I wonder if Grey sent the dogs.

We've soon left the outskirts of the town. We drive along winding lanes, through secluded villages, deeper and deeper into the Kent countryside. It feels remote; trees grow over the road and rolling hills and fields stretch away on either side of us. The garden of England. Signs tell us what we can already see – it's an area of outstanding natural beauty. We follow a tiny narrow road down a hill until finally we reach houses. We stop in the middle of the village by a sign that reads 'Classic Funerals'. We're in the right place. Mike presses the buzzer on the gate.

Lynn is tall, with a firm handshake and thick dark hair. She sandwiches my proffered hand between both of hers. 'I am so sorry for your loss.'

She shows us into a cosy, well-heated barn to the left of her house. Bunches of dried flowers are arranged around the room, along with porcelain dolls and teddies. It is strangely soothing. Behind Lynn, heavy brocade curtains are looped back beside a pair of solid oak doors. The chapel of rest. We sit.

'Now, I'm afraid there is quite a lot of admin,' she says. 'Then we can have a talk about the cremation itself. Then I'll get Emma, your celebrant, to come and speak to you – she's great, I'll leave you with her. Then, when you've finished chatting to Emma, we can work out the final points together, before you go. There's no rush with any of this, and we can take a break any time you want. I know that everything about this process is impossibly hard.

'I'm going to address my questions to Mike, if that's OK, Georgie. I tend to find the dad is more on the admin side of things, but please do tell me if that isn't the case here . . .'

Mike has his notebook out, pen poised, papers neatly filed in a transparent folder next to him. I'm clasping a wrinkled, slightly grey tissue. I wonder what gave her that idea.

She has a stack of documents in front of her and begins to ask questions. Cause of death. Place of death. Date of death. Time of death. Death. Death. Death.

Lynn pauses to apologise. 'I know it must be so hard to go over it all again.'

There are a million other questions that can't apply to Grey, but Lynn has to ask them anyway. 'Does anyone object to this cremation? . . . Are there any outstanding investigations into cause of death? . . . Has this body been released for cremation?'

On and on.

'Do you know which coffin you'd like?'

'A wicker one, please,' Mike says.

'The natural wicker one,' I add.

Lynn has the page up on her monitor. We choose the one we've already decided upon. It looks a bit like a Moses basket, with a flat lid instead of a curved hood.

'Now,' she says, 'I'm sorry to have to ask, but do you have any idea how long it will need to be?'

I realise she means the coffin.

How long is Grey's tiny body? I don't know. I'm sure he was never measured. I suddenly remember the cheery GP at Finn's eight-week check. 'We don't measure babies any more.' I cradle my arms across my chest, look down at them, suspended, empty, then up at Lynn. 'I don't know,' I whisper.

I suppose I'll get used to this. Though the thrum of pain has become the soundtrack to everything I do, every waking moment, it is mostly muffled by shock. And then there are moments when, suddenly, it is very acute.

Mike puts a hand on my arm and reaches for his phone.

'I'm sorry,' Lynn says.

He's found a photo.

'OK, leave it with me,' she says. 'Now, would you both like to travel with Grey in the limousine?'

'I think so ...' My voice falters. 'I don't want him to have to arrive on his own. And I think we'd like Finn to come with us too, if he can? You said maybe that would be OK?'

Mike and Lynn discussed some of the preliminary arrangements on the phone.

'Of course,' she says. 'So, we'll meet here, Grey will be here, and then we'll drive to the crematorium. Finn will go on your lap – or you can bring a car seat.'

'We're happy to have him on our laps, if you're happy.'

'We drive very slowly, so that's fine by me. Then, when we arrive at the gates of the crematorium, I usually get out and walk in front of the limousine, if you are happy for me to do this?'

'Walk in front?'

'Yes, it's a tradition – a mark of respect. The limousine will follow me up to the gates of the chapel. Some parents like to carry the coffin inside. Or I can carry it. You don't need to decide now. Or you can decide something now and then change your mind. It is all completely up to you.'

Mike and I look at one another.

'I think I'd like to carry him,' Mike says.

'And would you like everyone following you? Or already seated?'

She looks at each of us in turn.

I turn towards Mike. 'I don't know,' I say. 'Is it easier to have everyone seated?'

'You can do it however you want.' Lynn looks at each of us again. 'But ...' she is choosing her words carefully '... it can be overwhelming. Having everyone already seated, and watching you carry Grey in.'

I suddenly picture all the faces, turned towards us, and feel a little nauseous.

'We can't do that, MG,' I say. 'The last time all those faces were turned to us was at our wedding. I think everyone should walk in behind us.'

Mike nods.

'It is up to you,' Lynn says.

There are so many things to think about. How can there be? We run through more and more logistics – orders of service, flowers, collection.

I remember Sama telling me that planning your baby's funeral is like a sick scavenger hunt – 'All these different quests to complete.'

'Now, when would you like Grey to come here? I can have him here as long as you would like.'

'Can he come as soon as possible?' I ask. The sooner he can be here, in this tranquil home, in this pretty valley, the better. I shudder to think of him in the chill of the hospital mortuary.

'What do we need to do?'

'There are a couple of forms for you to sign to release his body, and then I can collect him and he will be here, with me, in my chapel of rest.'

'Please, please bring him here as soon as you can.'

'And do you have thoughts about whether you'd like to see him?'

'I want to see him,' I say. I have been thinking about it since we said goodbye to him on Sunday. I need to see my baby again. 'I want to see him here, away from the hospital.' I am desperate to see Grey. I want to press him to my chest, see his tiny mouth, his dark curls.

Lynn is silent for a second or two.

'Of course you can see him, if that is what you would like.' I hear her choosing her words carefully again. 'What I have said to parents in your situation in the past, is that I will look at Grey first, I will see how he's doing.'

I'm not sure what she means.

'Bodies can change, sometimes quite quickly, and he might look very different from how you remember him.'

I recoil and then instantly feel a flood of shame. 'Oh no, I hadn't thought of that. I don't think I want to see him if he looks really different.' I have serene memories of Grey wrapped up with his rabbit at the hospital. I don't want to erase them.

I realise that what I really want is to breathe in his smell and feel his fingers curl around mine and watch his eyes flicker open and his legs kick. And I can't have those things. I remind myself that the body Lynn will collect from the hospital, the body which will be here, at rest, the body we will cremate next week, is a shell. The cocoon that housed Grey. He is in the air, in the wind, carried on the rain, his face on the sun as it rises. He is in Finn, in me, in Mike, in every one of our family.

I don't need to see his physical body, I tell myself, because I can see him in my heart whenever I close my eyes.

And I almost believe it.

My body feels heavy, my mind full of cotton wool. All these questions, all these plans.

'Do *you* have any questions? About what we've discussed? Or about anything else?' Lynn asks.

We shake our heads.

'If you think of anything at all, at any point, here, or when you're home, you have my number. Just ask, OK?'

We nod.

'Thank you, Lynn,' Mike says.

'Are you happy for me to go and get Emma? Would either of you like a tea or coffee?'

We decline drinks and say we're ready to meet Emma.

There is a soft knock on the door a few minutes later. It's like a strange sort of speed dating. Our next match. Mike opens the door. I stand.

242

'I'm so sorry for your loss,' Emma says. 'I can't imagine what you've been through, what you're going through.'

Every time someone says that, I want to say, 'It's OK.' It's not OK, it will never be OK, but I don't know what else to say. Is it because we're British? A strange, awkward, automatic reaction.

Emma sits and asks us about Grey, about our time with him, about what he was like. It's lovely to be able to talk about him, to tell someone about him. About his serenity, his deep calm. About his little watchful eyes, his dark curly hair, his gangly legs, his long feet, his expressive hands.

Then she asks if we've thought about the service. We talk her through our music choices, our readings. Together we assemble them into some kind of order, decide how we will say goodbye to this tiny, precious person.

Emma will write her plan for the service, what she is going to say in between our music and readings. She'll send it to us ahead of time for us to read, to check, to edit if we want. Then she buzzes for Lynn.

As we drive away, I think about the next time we'll see them. A week and a day. Our final goodbye.

29

10 December

We drive from Lynn's to Whitstable. It doesn't take long. My mum and Finn are already there; Sally has gone back to London, having kindly transported and unloaded all the miniature bottles of frozen milk.

The new Airbnb is called Heron House. Mike explained why we were coming here to the host and she's been so kind. She has a family coming in for Christmas, but up until then, it's reserved for us. She checked that it was OK for her to put up some decorations, so pretty, rustic arrangements have been draped across the tops of the fireplaces, and we're greeted with mince pies. The combination gives me a little fizz of festivity. It's unexpected, nice.

After the frenzy of the last few days, it feels odd to stop. Stop planning, stop rushing. We walk into the town. The last time we were here was the day before Grey was born. We'd walked along the beach from our Airbnb in Seasalter for fish and chips on the pier. Everything looks the same, except the Christmas fairy has waved her wand.

We want to find somewhere for a lunch after Grey's funeral. Somewhere that isn't too stuffy, and will have space for eighteen in the week before Christmas. I spot an old warehouse right on the seafront that seems to be a restaurant. I press my nose to the glass and peer in. Floorboards, exposed brick, little tables covered with paper cloths. My dream menu on a handwritten blackboard – every kind of fish. I glance up at the sign. 'The Whitstable Oyster Company'.

It's closed, so we can't go in and ask if they have space. Perhaps we'll come back tomorrow.

Tomorrow, which is now today, Wednesday, would have been my granny's ninety-sixth birthday. My mum suggests we have lunch at the Oyster Company. We'll raise a glass to her and see if they have space for next week. As soon as we walk through the door, I know it's perfect. There's a gentle buzz, nothing overwhelming. It's been an overcast morning, but by the time the waitress seats us beside a window overlooking the beach, the sun is bathing the checked tablecloth in light and the sea sparkles under its gaze.

'Hi, Greyman,' I whisper.

We order some starters to share, a kids' fish and chips for Finn and three lobster and chips from the blackboard.

'That's easy,' says the dark-haired waitress, scooping up our menus.

When we've finished eating, Mike heads over to the bar to ask about next week. I see her nod, open the diary, write something down. They must have space.

After lunch we wander the seaside streets. Shops are strung with fairy lights; trees sit in every window. We come across a beautiful florist – steel buckets of cut flowers and greenery spill into the street; the original curved and panelled Victorian windows are filled with arrangements and scented candles.

'This looks perfect, doesn't it, George?'

A bell rings as I push open the door. My mum follows me in, pushing Finn in his buggy. The radio plays 'Driving Home for Christmas'. A dad is showing his son how to carry a posy of flowers. 'For Mummy,' the little boy tells me.

Three women are bustling away behind the counter. 'Can I help you?' one asks brightly. The bell rings as the door closes. The father and son have gone.

'I wanted ...' I falter. 'I wanted to ask about a bouquet of flowers, for a funeral. For my son's funeral.' The women

245

behind the counter stop what they are doing. The shop falls silent. 'I'm sorry,' I say. I'm crying. Chris Rea is still singing. I don't know if I'm imagining it, but I think someone turns down the volume.

'I'm so sorry,' the florist says. 'Of course ... of course we can help.'

I gather myself.

'I want something simple. Nothing too formal. Some wild flowers, some greenery.'

She moves between the buckets, pointing, gently suggesting. 'What size are you thinking?'

'It's for the top of his coffin,' I say. 'It's quite ... small. He was three weeks old.'

She goes pale.

I hold up my hands, palms facing one another; another meagre attempt to demonstrate his size. 'So ... not very big.'

'When is the funeral?' she breathes.

'Next Wednesday,' I say. 'Can we collect them on Tuesday?'

'Of course,' she says.

'The other thing is, I want something, single stems, that people can lay on his coffin. But I don't want roses, they feel too old fashioned. I want something ... lighter ...' I catch sight of the blue irises just as she steps towards them.

'How about the irises?' she asks.

'Perfect,' I say. 'Please can we have twenty-five stems?'

She writes it all down, glancing up at me mutely once in a while. 'That will all be ready for next Tuesday,' she says.

I thank her and we leave.

A snug with a big, cushion-covered velvet sofa, a winged armchair and a wood-burning stove is tucked between the kitchen at the back of the Airbnb and the sitting room at the front. As well as a stack of logs, it's now home to Finn's kitchen, ball pond, octopus and various other little treats he has gathered during our time in Kent. I spend a lot of time here, staring at the flames. Pets are allowed, so my mum's dog was going to join us. Finny adores her. But she's just come into season, so it's all a little too complicated. Right now I miss having her here, on this sofa, her soft head settled in my lap.

A mad idea springs into my mind.

'What do you think about getting a puppy?'

I'm sure Mike's response will be a straight no, so I take his silence before answering as encouragement.

'Do you know, I've been wondering the same thing.'

That's all I need. I go into overdrive and find several possible litters almost immediately. Everyone thinks it's a brilliant idea – but I probably could have suggested a pet elephant and got a similar response. I need something, anything, in our lives to be different, to feel different, when we're home.

It's two days until Grey's funeral. Mike and I are heading to the coffee shop near the crematorium where we plan to have a wake of sorts. Somewhere for a cup of tea and a slice of cake with any of the NICU staff who come along, before we drive back to the sea for lunch. We arrive in the early afternoon.

The place is quintessentially English. Its tables and chairs are a slightly eccentric mix – like they've escaped from an antiques fair – and laid with mismatched tea sets. A dresser holds more porcelain. Oak beams support the low ceiling. It's perfect.

A family sitting in the corner are speaking quite loudly. The sun-kissed couple have flown in from South Africa that morning with their two children. Granny lives nearby. They're cold and didn't bring coats. It's warm in Cape Town. They pour tea through strainers into vintage china cups and eat lemon drizzle cake.

A lady with steely grey hair holds out a hand to greet us, then motions to a table and Mike disappears to the loo. She opens her diary and starts running through the minutiae. So close to the crematorium, they are used to hosting wakes. Behind her, I can hear the Cape Town group running through the list of things they want to do, want to see, on this trip. After they've all bought warm coats.

'How many people will you have?' she asks.

'Um ... we aren't entirely sure. Our families are eighteen – four children – but then there are the hospital staff. Some of our son's doctors and nurses might come.'

'Your son?' She has put down her pen and is looking at me, shocked; she wasn't expecting it. Of course she wasn't expecting it.

'Yes,' I say. 'He was in the NICU. It's his funeral on Wednesday. He was three weeks old.'

Her hand shoots to her mouth. 'Oh my goodness gracious ...' She's moved her other hand to cover mine. 'I'm so sorry ...'

Mike is back.

'Your son ...' She turns to him. 'I'm so sorry, I didn't know, it wasn't mentioned in the diary, I'm so ... sorry.'

'How could you know?' Mike asks gently. 'I didn't tell the person I spoke to; it's a bit of a complicated thing to come out with.'

'Three weeks old ...' She is shaking her head. 'Let me get you a drink. Some cake?'

She brings us enormous wedges of freshly baked coffee and walnut cake and hot chocolate piled with cream and marshmallows.

We finalise the details for Wednesday. When we've finished and approach the counter to pay, she shakes her head.

'I wouldn't dream of taking it,' she says. 'Those are from me.' She searches our faces. 'How are *you* doing?'

'We're OK,' I say. 'Still in shock, I think, but we have another son, he's eighteen months old. He keeps us smiling.'

'They do, don't they?' Something else is on the tip of her tongue. 'When I was thirty-six, my husband, he dropped down dead. I had a three-year-old and a five-year-old. They kept me going. I simply had to get out of bed in the morning.'

She waves away our concern. 'I got through it. I'm still

standing.' She shakes her head. 'Children are a blessing. Losing one ...' She clasps our hands with extraordinary warmth. 'I'll be thinking of you on Wednesday. I won't be here, but I'll think of you.'

She watches us leave. I am not used to this, this new world of shared tragedy. One splintered heart standing side by side with another.

Nick, Nat and Sam are the first to arrive at Heron House, in the afternoon of the day before the funeral. Sam and Finn are going to share a room. Ella and her boyfriend Josh, and Lou and her boyfriend Gus, are round the corner in another Airbnb, but will come over for a bite to eat. Mike's family have found a house at the end of the road. He'll join them for supper. Separate family gatherings. It feels like the night before our wedding.

We eat pasta in the kitchen and try to make small talk, then Finn and Sam have a bath and get ready for bed. Freshly washed, with hair slicked back, Sam brings his monkey to come and find me. He tilts his head. 'Auntie Georgie ...'

'Yes, Sam.'

'Does Baby Grey have a teddy?'

'With him, you mean?'

'Yes, to snuggle.' He clutches his monkey a little more tightly.

'Well, he has a Rab, just like Finny's – a blue one.'

'Good.' He seems satisfied with that, but there's more on his checklist.

'What else does he have?'

'Well, we left him with a cuddly fox, and he's wrapped in a blanket that Granny knitted, like the blankets she knitted for you and for Finn.'

'When I was a baby?'

'Yes.'

'What else does he have?'

I rack my brains. 'He has an Advent calendar, Samjam.'

He grins. 'So he can count down to Christmas, too.' Then suddenly his brow furrows. 'But not a chocolate one?'

'No, not a chocolate one, a paper one. He's a bit little for a chocolate one, isn't he?' The conversation is surreal, but there is shelter in the surreal.

He thinks for a minute. 'Babies can't have chocolate,' he says eventually.

'They can't.'

'If he was to have some chocolate, he might eat it, and then, and then ...'

I can see Nick coming down the corridor as his little boy searches for the right words. It's not like Sam. He normally has them on the tip of his tongue.

'He might die a little bit more,' he says finally, his expression sombre.

Nick shakes his head. I can't work out how to respond, but I think Sam's waiting for some kind of answer. Finally, I nod. He seems satisfied, and pads back down the corridor to his room.

'Sorry,' Nick says. 'I could see the way it was heading, tried to stop it, didn't really know how.'

I laugh. 'Don't stop it. It's so nice that he isn't afraid to talk about it, to talk about Grey. It's amazing, really.'

30

18 December

We wake before it's light. I pump early. I can't stop. I tell myself it's for the milk bank, for other babies, but it's for me. The comfort of the routine I've become so used to, the control I can exercise where there is very little anywhere else. But really, I think, it's my last link to my son, the only physical thing that remains and I'm not ready to let go. So I'm pumping at seven, before his funeral at a quarter past nine.

By the time we're dressed and ready to go, the sun is starting to make its way into the cloudless sky. As I watch, I think of Sam's words, 'When the sun comes up tomorrow, Grey's face will be on it.'

'Hi, buddy,' I whisper. 'Hi, Greyman.'

Finn is jubilant in his car seat, ready for an adventure, still in his pyjamas, next to Grey's flowers, next to my mum. It's about a twenty-minute drive, but we've left plenty of time. Though it's close to Christmas, it's a weekday and the world keeps turning, people keep going to work, clocks and rush-hour traffic won't stop for us. As it happens, it's a smooth run, so we arrive early.

We unload Finn and the flowers, then ring Lynn's bell. Her husband Gareth answers the gate, already dressed in his undertaker outfit. He shakes our hands – a funny mixture of warmth and sympathy playing across his face, in his grasp. 'I'm so sorry for your loss,' he says softly.

We thank him.

He takes us into Lynn's small office for us to dress Finn.

As I check the flowers I realise I've forgotten something.

'Shit! Grey's ribbon ...' It annoys me and then unsettles me, disproportionately. He needs grey ribbon.

Lynn appears, elegant in her tailcoat, cravat impeccably tied, her thick hair tamed by a net, ready for her hat. She says good morning, shaking our hands, then kneels. 'Hello, you must be Finn,' she says. 'Would you like to play with some teddies?' She lifts three from the shelves on the wall.

Finn looks solemn and takes each one carefully. Minutes later they are abandoned on the sofa as he spots a metal sculpture of a dog. 'Woof-woof, woof-woof!' He squats in front of it, pointing and laughing.

Lynn straightens up. 'Beautiful flowers.' She's right, the florist has done a wonderful job – irises, eucalyptus, comfrey, tied simply with twine.

'I'm so annoyed with myself,' I tell her. 'I had some grey velvet ribbon to tie around them, and I've forgotten it. I know it's such a small thing, I just really wanted them to have grey ribbon. But I think they look nice anyway, don't they? Do you think it matters?'

She puts a hand on my arm. 'I have something,' she says.

Seconds later she's back with a length of blue-grey crocheted ribbon. I tie it around the bouquet. It looks perfect, maybe even a better colour than the one I'd forgotten. I hand the flowers to Lynn.

My mum kisses us both, briefly squeezing my hand before turning to go. She is taking our car, meeting us at the crematorium. We dress Finn, slithering twelve kilos of wriggling toddler into navy cords, shirt and chunky grey jumper.

'Soos, soos,' he says, pointing at his new footwear. Mike also took him for his first haircut in Whitstable, so with his new kit and fresh crop he suddenly looks so grown up.

I want to run through my reading before we have to get in the car. I start it, and can't even get to the end of the first line. I refold the paper. That was a bad idea.

Mike tries his, and gets all the way to the end.

Lynn is back. 'We should get going, if you're ready . . .' She hands a children's book to Finn.

Finn's face lights up. 'Book, book!' He likes books almost as much as he likes 'woof-woofs'. He sits on the floor and opens it.

'Thank you,' I say to Lynn, then, turning to Finn, 'Daddy can read it to you in the car.'

Mike lifts him and we follow Lynn outside.

My breath mists in the clear, fresh air. The sky is a perfect blue, barely a whisper of wind or a hint of cloud. A perfectly still, perfectly crisp, winter's morning. I hear Eva Cassidy's 'Songbird' play in my head.

A gleaming black limousine is parked in the driveway. Lynn opens the door and I see the wicker coffin. All the air has left my lungs, someone somewhere has thrust a hand deep into my chest, taking hold of my heart and squeezing. I stand stock still. It's impossibly small. Smaller than the smallest Moses basket I can imagine. The stems of the flowers are longer than the coffin. Grey is inside it. Our baby isn't due for another month; he can't be.

Beside me, Mike has also gone still. 'It's so small. So, so small.' Barely a murmur; it might have been in my head.

I give myself a shake. 'Come on, Finny, let's get into the car.'

We leave the privacy screen open. Lynn and Gareth's low voices are curiously comforting. There's something dependable in their routine, their knowledge of the intricacies of this completely alien process.

While Mike reads to Finny, my eyes barely leave Grey's pale, woven casket, resting on a bed of perfectly pressed lace, all the way to the crematorium.

Gareth stops the car at the gate, and Lynn gets out. For a second I'm confused, then I remember, this is tradition – she'll walk in front of the limousine as we approach the chapel. She does, hands crossed, head bowed. I see our families by their cars, last-minute buttoning and door-opening. They seem to stop, turn, and watch us approaching in slow motion. Their faces are sculpted, white, grim. I can't look any more.

We sweep around the drive that flanks the car park and stop outside the entrance to the chapel. Emma is waiting on the steps. We have only met once, but her expression perfectly encapsulates what is about to happen – mingled sadness, horror, disbelief. I don't know how I am going to get through this. Suddenly my legs won't work. I'm not even going to be able to get out of the car.

'Mama?' Finny takes my hand, offering to lead me back into the world.

'Hello, sweetie, shall we go in?' I bend to help him out of the car.

I smile at Emma, who touches my arm as I try to form a greeting, then turn to look at our families converging on the chapel. I can't meet anyone's eye. If I do, I'll break, I'm sure. I see Amy, Melia, Nena and Rebekah approaching, with Dr Chandra and Dr Kate. My mind can only half grasp how kind it is of them to come.

'Are you ready?' Lynn asks Mike. Then, more quietly, 'There's no rush.' She opens the door of the limousine, reaches in to hold Grey's coffin by its wicker handles, then straightens and lifts him gently out.

She turns towards Mike and pauses. Without saying anything she is reminding him that he doesn't have to do this, he doesn't have to carry our son's tiny coffin into the chapel. She can carry him. Mike nods and she hands Grey to him.

Emma moves an arm towards the open doors and steps back. Mike walks through them. My tears blur the edges of everything.

'Nimrod' begins. David Dimbleby helps me follow, gripping Finn's hand. We make our way slowly down the aisle. Time half stops and half speeds up. Mike places the tiny coffin on the catafalque. His hand rests on top of it for a moment, then we take our places in the front row. I hear Lynn seating everyone else, lining up our families, the nurses, the doctors. I look

254

up at the wicker basket. How can it possibly be that small? A shaft of sunlight shines through the stained-glass window above the altar. Fields and flowers – blue irises echoing the cut stems in Grey's bouquet.

As 'Nimrod' fades, Emma begins her welcome. Her face is grey, her eyes teary. But her voice is strong, full of love, of empathy. She says every word she has planned, every word she has checked and double-checked with us, with such feeling. The next piece of music is 'Bring Him Home'. I have to hold myself together through this; I'm reading afterwards.

'*Bring him peace, bring him joy, bring him home . . .*' All I ever want for Grey, for both my boys, for all my boys. There is such a sense of serenity in this little chapel, in the people who love Grey most in the world. He is home. He has found his way home.

Somehow, I'm at the lectern. I start reading. *You're Here for a Reason* by Nancy Tillman. Grey's book.

The world, our world, *is* different. It has been different for ten days without Grey, and we have a lifetime of different stretching out in front of us. My eyes fill with tears, the printed words start to dissolve in front of me, swimming around the page. One line. I managed one line. At least when I read it to Grey I could get to the last line before the weight of my sadness pulled me under. I swallow, take a breath, think of Grey and somehow keep reading. As I do so, I glance up and see Dr Chandra, Amy, Melia, Nena, Rebekah and Dr Kate sitting in a row, immediately behind Mike's family. I see Finny, driving his train up and down the front pew. Mike, smiling at me through his tears. And then I turn and rest my eyes on the tiny wicker coffin with my baby inside. I stare at it and stare at it and carry on, right to the last line.

I look around the chapel. These words are for Grey, and they are for everyone; everyone here, and everyone not here. Everyone who loves us, who has told us they love us, that they'll be there for us, whenever, however, whatever, no matter what. All the love that Grey has created, has unlocked, has conjured.

And all in twenty-one days. What a legacy.

Twinkle, twinkle little star.

Finn stands in the aisle, facing everyone; a small wooden car is now in his hand. He starts the mime. Then, realising there's something lacking in a one-handed performance, he bends very carefully, places the car on the floor and stands back up. His fingers splay out with the twinkle; he stomps his feet. Elsie and Sam are doing the same. 'Papa!' Finn is beside my dad, thrusting his hands in the air. 'Oo-pa', Mike's dad, is next in his firing line. Everyone is smiling. Smiling and crying. Finn's infectious joy mingles with the dazzling sadness.

Mike reads 'If—' beautifully. The words his sister read at our wedding. The words written in Grey's NICU diary, the words on the wall of Finn's bedroom. The words we have repeated many times. Words to live by. His voice remains unwavering, strong, brave, clear, right until the last lines. 'Yours is the earth and everything that's in it, And ...' he pauses '... which is more ...' he draws a breath '... you'll be a man, my son.' He whispers the last words through tears that catch in his throat. It doesn't matter, we all know that part. I think of Grey's minutes, about as unforgiving as they come. But the distance, the distance is what counts, little man, as Kipling says. And the distance will keep going long after you have gone.

'Vincent' breaks everyone's hearts. It always does. You don't need to be at your son's cremation to cry at those lyrics. And then, before I know it, Emma is telling us it's time to say goodbye.

The end.

I'm not ready.

I wanted it to be over, and now I never want it to end.

The opening notes of 'Caliban's Dream' drift out of the speakers as Lynn hands blue irises to everyone, gently but firmly guiding them out of the pews, towards the catafalque and then the side exit. I watch my sisters lay their flowers on Grey's coffin, bend to kiss it, to whisper a few words into the air. I watch the tears that flow down their cheeks as they walk through the double doors into the memorial garden. I watch my mum carry Finn to the front, watch his rounded hand release a flower onto his brother's coffin. The brother he will never know, never grow up with, never boss around, or fight with, never hug or tell secrets to, or giggle with. I watch my dad's shoulders shake as he lays his flower. I watch Mike's family; his dad, handkerchief in hand, grief etched into the lines around his tear-stained blue eyes; his mum in her grey wool coat, resting her hand for a moment over her iris on top of the little wicker casket; Zoë bowing her head, Jon with Elsie and Wilf. And then I watch Sam. I watch Nick stoop to scoop him up into his arms, carry him forward, lower him to kiss the coffin. I watch Nick put him down; watch him turn, brow furrowed, his eyes filling with tears, one hand pinching them away at the bridge of his nose as he storms back down the aisle. As I watch, I realise he is looking for something. Something to kick. Nick follows him, lifts him gently. Sam lays his head on his dad's shoulder and they follow everyone else outside.

And then it is Mike, and me, and Grey. His body in his wicker box, his presence all around us. I want to sit for longer. I wish time would slow; instead it seems to speed up. Those unforgiving minutes. I force myself to stand. Mike's arm is around my waist, guiding me to the catafalque. I gaze at the blue irises scattered across the top of Grey's coffin. I put a hand to my lips, then rest it on the woven wicker lid.

'Rest well, my boy,' I hear Mike whisper.

'I love you. We love you,' I add.

Lynn steps forward, lifts the bouquet, revealing a plaque engraved with his name, and draws out a single stem. 'We'll leave one with him,' she says. 'The rest you take with you.'

The toll of bells signals that the music is coming to a close. It's time to go.

I can't turn away from him. I slowly back away, unable to wrench my eyes from the wicker, until I am through the doors, out in the sunshine, and I can't see it any more.

We are in a courtyard garden. A pond covered in lily pads is at its centre. Sam and Finn, Elsie and Wilf stand, noses pressed through the railings that border it. Lynn has gathered the extra service sheets, placing them next to the flowers.

The NICU team are waiting for us, faces ashen, eyes red, cheeks flushed from just-dried tears. 'That was very beautiful, Georgie,' Amy says. '"Twinkle, twinkle" . . .' She smiles. 'And your reading – I don't know how you did it.'

'Well, I didn't, really, did I? It was more sniffling and snivelling than reading . . .'

We thank them each for coming, tell them they are welcome for a slice of cake and a cup of tea at the coffee shop. Dr Chandra has to get to the hospital, she is due on shift, and Dr Kate has to go home and sleep; unbelievably, she came straight here from a night shift.

'So many others wanted to come,' Amy says. 'Sofia and Jackie, in particular – they tried to change shifts, to reshuffle, but someone has to run the NICU.'

'It is so kind of you all,' I reply. 'Will you come for a slice of cake?'

'Yes please,' Amy says.

We drive straight to the café; it only takes a couple of minutes. We have to park a little walk away and puddles line the roads. I glance down at my Valentino wedding shoes and velvet trousers.

We fill the homely coffee shop, drinking tea, helping ourselves to thick slices of coffee and walnut cake or lemon drizzle. The mood is cheery, and I don't think it's manufactured. Sam and Elsie dodge between the closely packed tables, persuading their assembled families to let them have far too much cake.

Mike makes a speech to Nena, Amy, Rebekah and Melia. He speaks directly to each of them, so eloquent, picking out precisely why they were so brilliant: Rebekah's mothering practicality; Melia's artwork and gentleness; Amy's encyclopaedic knowledge, her faultless support, gathering us up when our world was crashing in around us; Nena, for being Nena – her quiet kindness carrying us throughout. His words are remarkable, we had no idea who would come, so he's only had seconds to prepare.

Then it's time to drive back to Whitstable. I hug each of the nurses, gripping their arms as I say goodbye.

The Kent countryside flickers past the window, blue skies and bright sunshine rendering the green fields almost luminous. Winter on hold, at least until you step outside. Finn's chattering slows and then stops. I look round to see he's fast asleep, his mouth slightly open.

We walk along the beach to lunch. The tide is out, the pebbly sand shelving away to the water. A couple of dogs potter in and out of the small breaking waves. A wood-burning stove welcomes us inside. We stand by the bar as both families trickle in, ordering drinks. A giant Christmas tree stretches into the rafters. I sit, my body aching. Perhaps I can blame the heels. I remind myself it's only a month since my C-section.

It feels strangely like a wedding morning. Not ours, this time, as we're here too, but someone close. A gathering, drinks at the bar, a bite to eat before the ceremony. As we make our way through the restaurant to our table, the sun pours in through the windows, warming the worn floorboards, twinkling on the red-and-white checked tablecloths, glinting off the wine glasses. Our table is laid along one side of the vast warehouse, doglegging into the corner. The same dark-haired waitress is working, looking after us – Carmen is her name. And the manager, Anna. Between us, we've come here almost every day with someone, so my mum's made friends with them.

The blackboard menu is an A-Z of fish, from here, there and everywhere. Platters of oysters cover the table-top, bottles of wine, baskets full of crusty bread and little dishes of butter crumbled with crisp shards of salt. I look at us all, gathered together. This is what matters. 'Thank you, Grey,' I whisper. 'I wish you were here.' But he is here, I think, in the light that pours through the window, in Finn's grin as he hoovers up fish and chips, in Mike's eyes as he smiles at me down the table, in the tears I can see gathered in the corners of my dad's eyes. He's here.

We eat and eat and drink and drink and talk and talk. The sun moves round and shines in through the glass behind our table, low in the sky, turning scarlet as it sets. Someone has ordered an espresso martini (I wonder who ...). There are calls for more, and then more. Gradually the other customers finish their meals and trickle out, until it is just us, us and Carmen and Anna. I keep asking if they want us to leave, they keep saying we must stay as long as we want. The little ones potter around the floor, looking down through a fenced-off trap door to the sea below, giggling, chasing each other. I wish for their innocence.

Finn and Elsie stand next to the huge window that looks out to the sea. Street lights twinkle, then there is watery blackness. I crouch beside them.

'Tars,' Finn says, pointing out into the night. 'Tars, Mumma, mooon.'

'I think he's saying stars,' Elsie tells me with authority.

'Yes, the stars are out there, aren't they, Finny?'

Elsie has run off. We look out together. 'Your brother's up there somewhere,' I murmur.

'G-ey?' Finn has turned his head, tilted onto his shoulder. 'G-ey?' he repeats more clearly.

'Grey?' I ask him.

He nods, puts a small hand on mine and rests his head

against my shoulder. I wrap my arm around him, feeling his solidness, his here-ness, and together we look out at the stars, the moon and their reflections on the sea.

I realise it's after six, that Finn needs a bath, that he hasn't had a nap, except twenty minutes snatched in the car. That he needs to go to bed. I gather him up, my mum comes with us, and Jon with Elsie and Wilf, Nat with Sam. The rest of them have more espresso martinis in mind. I suggest to Mike that they move to the pub across the cobbled street, let Carmen and Anna close up. He half waves in response.

On our way out I hug Carmen, hug Anna, thank them for a wonderful day, a wonderful celebration of our tiny boy.

'Do chuck them out,' I say. 'Please – there have been far too many espresso martinis for them to make any kind of decision like that themselves – they can go to the pub if they want any more.'

They smile and nod. I know they won't. We retrace our steps along the beach. Sam runs ahead in the dark, waiting once in a while for us to catch up. I carry Finn.

When the children are all in bed, I sit with my mum in the snug, next to the wood-burning stove. The others are still out.

My dad reappears first, swaying slightly but still looking dapper in his black velvet jacket.

He looks slightly bemused. 'I came back via Sainsbury's, and a nice couple asked to take a selfie with me.'

'A selfie?' I ask.

'Yes.'

'Did they say why?'

'I don't think so,' he says. 'Though they may have mentioned Des.'

My mum and I laugh. My dad has more than once been mistaken for Des Lynam – same twinkly eyes, same white, ever-so-slightly-receding hair, same glasses, same generous moustache.

Gradually the rest of the stragglers potter in, until only Mike is left out and about. His phone goes straight to voice-mail. I know he's with Zoë, so I'm not too worried. At last a message pings through: 'Mike with us, all fine, just warming up.' I think very little of it, until my shoeless husband appears on the doorstep about half an hour later, chaperoned by both parents. He's wearing some of Jon's clothes and his hair is wet.

'He went for a swim,' Sally says by way of explana-tion, handing me his sodden shoes. 'He might need some warming up.'

I am alarmed – it's mid-December, night time, freezing.

I crank up the wood-burner and sit Mike right next to it, gradually thawing him out.

'I had to swim, George, I had to. I needed to feel the cold, the sea. I needed it. Zoë was there, I was safe. I just had to.'

I lay a hand on his still-chilled arm. 'I know,' I say.

I go to bed early, leaving Nick, Nat and Mike in the kitchen. An hour or so later, I hear Nat come up. I wake, hours after-wards, confused. My pumping alarm hasn't gone, Mike still isn't in bed. I creep downstairs, assuming he's fallen asleep on the sofa. And hear his and Nick's voices. They're still putting the world to rights.

31

20 December

We drive back to London in near-torrential rain. The motorway from Whitstable looks out across the floodplains, all the way to the sea. It's beautiful, in spite of, or perhaps because of, the deluge. I whisper goodbye to the barely perceptible waves. We're going home. I wonder what that means now.

We arrive in the afternoon and I pause by our front door, Finn in my arms. As he reaches up to repeatedly press the bell, I wonder how the inside will feel. We've unloaded my milk first – the ice-packed bottles at my feet need to go straight into the freezer.

I push open the door and wait for the emptiness to envelop me. The hall is the same, the house is the same. Of course it is. As I round the corner into the sitting room, I stop in my tracks. It looks completely different, painted an inky dark blue that I recognise as a shade we'd mused over several months ago. I see the sofa I'd put on hold when Grey was born, delivered and installed.

'How ...? Who ...?'

Mike has followed me into the room. 'Zo, Jon, Sally,' he says. 'It must be. They asked for the key safe code; I didn't think anything of it at the time, but this is exactly the kind of thing they'd do.'

I had been terrified of the sameness of home. That it would feel too much like nothing had changed when everything has changed. This cosy new sitting room shifts that out of focus, at least momentarily.

As Mike brings in the last bags from the car, our doorbell

rings, properly this time. Mike answers, with Finn on his hip. I'm just behind. It's our neighbour who lives opposite. He's grinning – he's always grinning – and holding up a parcel. 'Did you have a nice break?' he says, then, seeing me over Mike's shoulder, 'And Mum, how's …' He mimes a baby bump.

As Mike moves aside and he registers my lack of bump, I instinctively reach for it and shake my head. His hand flies to his mouth.

None of us speaks.

Then, 'He died,' Mike says. 'That's why we've been away. Finny's little brother. He was three weeks old.'

I just stand there. I'm not sure what else I can do.

His eyes filling with tears, he pushes the parcel at Mike and backs away. 'I'm sorry, I'll leave you. Look after each other.'

I watch the poor man's shell-shocked retreating back. I know this is not going to be the last time we have this kind of exchange, that we shatter someone's unassuming Friday afternoon. What will I do when Mike isn't there to swoop in and save me?

As we unpack, I walk from room to room. We didn't move Finn into his new room, or set up Grey's before he made his early appearance, so there is no nursery, just an empty space. Sama and Ed have done a beautiful job painting it. Later, when we've put Finn to bed, I sit on our new sofa, looking at our dark blue walls. What now, I wonder. What on earth do I do now?

London is the same, but everything is different. Days pass on autopilot. Our Kent bubble now feels like a dream. We start to see friends, to tell them about Grey. Afternoon chats can capture so little of him, of our three weeks together. I'm frustrated that I can't seem to articulate the way in which strands of acute pain and deep anguish are inextricably intertwined with those of the purest joy and the clearest love. I can't explain that though I cry when I talk about him, it also allows a joy to blossom, the seeds of which will always remain deep inside me. I am proud to be his mother.

I've found a litter of Vizsla-Retrievers crosses (Retrizslas, or 'expensive mongrels', as my dad puts it). They live in Cornwall, one of our favourite places. And they'll be eight weeks old on 19 January. Grey's due date. A sign? My mum and Lou are sure it is and, almost more excited than we are, they make the epic drive to meet them.

Videos ping through one after the other as Mike, Finn and I read stories in Finn's bedroom. 'Nena,' Mike says as we watch a tiny fox-coloured pup nestle into my mum's lap and go to sleep. 'Can we call her Nena, G?'

Christmas Eve is the only day I can get an appointment at my GP surgery to have my blood checked for milk donation. The last time I was here, I was pregnant. The thought makes me feel a little queasy. Clutching my bloods pack, I push open the door and give my name to the receptionist, who directs me to the waiting room.

As a healthcare assistant I haven't met before packs up the vials, I start to cry.

'Everything happens for a reason,' she says softly.

I'm sure she feels these words might help, but I find little comfort in them. Right here, right now, on Christmas Eve, two weeks after I said goodbye to Grey, I want to punch her.

I wonder if we can hibernate until Christmas Day is over. Stay at home, go for a walk. Mike persuades me Finn will love to see his cousins. I know he's right, so we drive to his parents' in Chiswick. The roads are quiet. Last year was the first Christmas I spent in London. I loved the buzz of it, the walk along the river, the drinks in the pub, the Christmas Eve trip to Kew Gardens. We always planned to be here this year; it would have been too close to my due date to venture too far away.

I've spent thirty-three years believing Christmas brings joy, love, happiness. I'm a little ashamed that it took my son dying for me to realise it simply acts as a magnifying glass. It brought me joy because I was already joyful. It's a strange mixture, this year – the aching hole left by our tiny boy colours everything. When we arrive, I sit in Sally's studio, looking out of the window, fat tears tumbling into my lap, wondering if anyone would mind if I drove home and crawled into bed.

A sudden screech of laughter reminds me that I can't. Finn. His burbling happiness as he plays with his cousins, opens his presents, laughs at his grandpa, wraps my broken heart in love.

'Silent Night' plays on the radio as we drive home and he drifts off to sleep in the back of the car. *'Sleep in heavenly peace, sleep in heavenly peace.'*

Tears slide silently down my face. It is done. Seventeen days and one Christmas without him.

The time between Christmas and New Year is no man's land at the best of times, and now it feels particularly directionless. Each morning as my mind prepares to haul itself into the world there are those blissful split seconds before reality takes shape. Some days I wonder if staying asleep would fix it.

Physically, at least, I should be healing. But my post-partum bleeding still hasn't stopped. So the day before New Year's Eve I'm back at the GP's office. I cry as she tells me that I should go to the early pregnancy unit, that I need a scan, that while it is rare, retained placenta is possible after a Caesarean. 'Go early,' she says. 'It gets busy, and I want you to be able get this sorted as soon as you can.'

At seven o'clock on New Year's Eve morning, I'm sitting on the floor outside the unit, waiting for the doors to open. The receptionist hands me a form that asks me what gestation I am, or what age my baby is. I whisper through the glass that he is dead, then take a seat.

The doctor says the same thing as the GP – retained placenta is rare after a Caesarean. As she scans me, I see her brow furrow. She whispers to the nurse, who disappears. 'I want the consultant to check something,' she says.

Seconds later there's a knock and a woman with cropped blond hair swaps places with the doctor, taking hold of the pelvic wand and peering at the screen. 'Yup,' she says. 'Retained placenta, about a four-centimetre piece.'

I think I knew, but that doesn't make it any better. The desperate, twisted fact that my uterus has been able to hold on to Grey's placenta long after he is gone.

She rubs my leg, 'Hey, hey, I know it's tough, but it's a simple operation, we'll get you booked in fast. How old is Baby?'

Of course she doesn't know. This poor woman has been hoiked out of some other practice room to check my placenta, and she's a consultant, not a mind-reader. The doctor explains that Grey has died.

'I'm so sorry,' the consultant says. 'And I'm so sorry I didn't know. We're going to sort this out for you. I'm going to do your operation myself. I'll book you in as soon as possible.'

'Do you know how soon?' I ask. 'It's only that we're supposed to be going to Somerset tomorrow for a few days.'

'Not until next week,' she says, then pauses. 'But you're at slightly higher risk of haemorrhage until we remove this. It might be best to stay in London. Just in case. I'm sorry.'

She promises to call as soon as she can book me in.

Two washed and scrubbed babies sit on my lap; Finn on one knee, Agnes on the other.

New Year was always going to be understated. I was supposed to be thirty-seven weeks pregnant and we'd planned dinner with Sama and Ed; they'd come to us for bath time, Agnes would sleep in our travel cot and they'd carry their sleeping bundle home later.

While Sama goes to get milk, I look at the babies looking at each other. There should be four. Two little boys are missing. Half of our children are not here.

After we've read stories, I pick up Finn and Sama picks up Agnes and we stand by the window. The night is clear; the inky black sky, faded by the lights of the city, and dotted with stars. 'Night-night, Blue. Night-night, Grey,' we whisper into the darkness. 'We love you.'

An image of Sama and me dressed as fembots for our friend Will's twenty-first flashes into my mind. We'd made dresses from some high-shine stretch psychedelic fabric we'd found in Leeds market, worn white PVC boots and backcombed our hair. We were so young, so carefree, without the faintest idea of what was ahead. Thank goodness. I still can't fathom how it came to be like this.

Later in the evening, after more than a few New Year's toasts, Sama and I discuss other people's pregnancies. 'I thought it wouldn't bother me at all,' I say. 'I thought because of Finny I was immune, and then yesterday when we were leaving Sainsbury's, I saw a woman about my age, with dark hair, pushing a small blond boy in a trolley. She was pregnant, very pregnant, maybe thirty-seven weeks.'

'The life you should have had,' Sama says.

I nod. 'For a split second, I hated her. And then I couldn't take my eyes off her, Sama.'

'It's fucking hard, George, when it's exactly what you were supposed to have, and somehow, no matter what they're doing, they look like they're taking it for granted.'

I nod again.

'Which you also know is absurd, when you stop to think about it,' she says, 'because you have no idea about their life, no idea what they've gone through. All you see is what you've lost, reflected in her.'

She pulls me in for a bear hug. Sama is very wise. And gives very good hugs.

32

When the newborn Finn slept near me, I often woke a beat before he cried. A magical connection, more profound even than the physical or the emotional, planted deep inside my subconscious. Without Grey's physical presence, it whispers to me. 'Where is your baby?' it asks. '*Where is he?*'

At first, I wonder if I'm going mad. It feels as though I'm being taunted. Then I realise it's simply the atavistic power of the connection. And its questions have no answer.

The first time Mike and Finn leave me alone in our house, the questions become frantic screams. 'Where is Grey? *Where is Grey?*' Over and over again.

It's so loud, I want to go in search of him. To stand by the Moses basket that isn't there. To riffle through cot sheets that we sent back, unopened. To check the bouncer that we long ago lent to Sama. Or find the bassinet that we didn't even have time to bring down from the attic. To scoop up my newborn, my darling Grey, hug him to my chest and tell him it's OK. That I've got him.

Instead, the house is silent. Too silent. I close my eyes, lift my hands to my shoulder and try to conjure him, his smell – milk mingling with ventilator plastic, his tiny fingers fluttering across my chest. For a second it feels so real, I'm sure that when I look down I'll see his tiny navy eyes looking quizzically up at me.

But he's not there. My hands flatten against thin air.

Where are you, Grey? My brave, beautiful, wonderful boy.

8 January

The waiting room is packed, so we find a seat just outside the sliding doors. My ERPC: evacuation of retained products of conception. A rather clinical term for leftover placenta.

My mum has come with me. When my name is called, I go into day surgery alone. I'm ushered into a cubicle. The same blue curtains as the labour ward and the postnatal ward are drawn around me. A folded gown and a pair of compression stockings sit on the end of the bed. The same outfit I wore for Grey's birth.

I've brought a book; they've warned me I might be here a while. I hear a lady two cubicles along ask whether she's first on the list, she's concerned, she has a newborn she needs to get back to. As my tears return, I truly hope they put her before me. Finn is with Lorraine, his childminder. He doesn't need me today. In fact, it's me that needs him, more and more these days.

As the double doors to the anaesthetist's room swing open, the lights blind me, the surgical smell washes over me, and I'm back on 17 November, about to meet Grey. It delivers a strange mixture of shock and comfort. What feels like minutes later, I'm wheeled out. Everything went according to plan. The final piece of Grey's placenta has found its way to a medical waste bin. My uterus is truly empty.

On the recovery ward, the consultant advises me gently that I should stop pumping; I need to let my oestrogen levels normalise, to help my uterus to heal. I know she's right. And not only for my uterus.

Back at home I disinfect all the parts of the plastic machine that has been my constant companion for the last two months. I throw away the tubing, wash and sterilise the pump parts, and add them to the box of Finn's old bottles for the attic. I coil the flex and clip it closed, then sit for a moment with my hands pressed against the plastic casing.

It doesn't hurt as much as I imagined it might.

I remember one of the doctors at the milk bank telling me in the hazy days just after Grey died, 'When the right time comes to stop, you'll know.'

I do know. Now is the right time. To pack this away, to sleep through the night, to let my body register that Grey isn't coming back.

12 January

Before Grey was born, Sunday swimming-pool trips were a father and son ritual. Today they're letting me gate-crash. I wait outside the changing room while Mike gets Finny ready.

'Hello. I haven't seen you for a long while.'

I look up to see the mother of a little boy in Finn's old swimming class. Her hand cradles a bump.

'Hi! And congratulations,' I say. 'How are you?'

'Good,' she says. 'But tired!' She points at the bump.

'When are you due?'

'Three weeks to go. A little girl. I tell you, it's all different the second time round – it's whizzed by!'

It's on the tip of my tongue to say I know.

'And it's even more exhausting when you're running around after a toddler.'

I stop myself from fully engaging. We haven't swum with them since before I was pregnant with Grey. It would beg too many questions. Questions she doesn't need to know the answers to. Instead I hear myself say, 'It must be.'

Her husband and son emerge from the changing room and they load him into his buggy. 'See you soon,' she says as they head off.

'Bye,' I reply. 'Good luck.'

13 January

Time is measured in weeks during the postpartum period – a newborn growing, a mother healing, together, side by side. With Finn, my recovery was inseparable from him. When he was six weeks old, an appointment was made for us, for him to see the GP, me to see the nurse. A feature of early parenthood I took entirely for granted. But what happens now, without Grey? No letter arrives, so I make the appointment myself. A little later than six weeks, on account of Christmas, and anticipating the anguish, I book Finn's MMR booster at the same time. Kill two painful birds with one stone.

I sign us in at the front desk and find a spare plastic chair in the waiting room, where chirpy adverts for healthy eating play on the screen between the ding and flashed-up name that announces appointments. The family next to us have a small boy, older than Finn, and a baby, wrapped in a snowsuit. About eight weeks old; first jabs. I realise I'm staring at her and her cooing mother. She catches my eye, and we smile at each other – a shared parental moment. Then I tear my gaze away.

They're called before we are. 'Got the whole team today,' I hear the father say as the door swings shut and they disappear down the corridor to the nurse's room. It strikes me that I'll never say that, never feel that. A member of our team will always be missing.

The family are back within moments and then off to 'carrots, potatoes and chicken' for tea, instead of the biscuits the little boy is asking for.

'Finley . . .'

The nurse is in the doorway. I smile and wheel the pushchair after him as he totters along the corridor, turning every couple of steps with a 'Mama?' to check I'm still there, or perhaps that I'm OK. I'm so grateful to have him with me.

As we reach her room she says, 'Right, let's do you first, jab last, then if Finley cries you can go straight home.' She flashes us a grin and turns to her computer. In the split second before she asks her next question I realise she doesn't know. Her demeanour is too positive, too natural. There's none of the gentle, faltering awkwardness that has become my normal.

'How old is Baby?' she asks, scanning her screen, maybe searching for the answer.

I pause. 'He died. He only lived for three weeks.'

She is mortified.

'They ... they usually inform us ... oh, I'm so sorry, they should ...'

I'm sure Grey's in my notes, but perhaps she hasn't checked. No one expects babies not to survive; it goes so violently against the natural order of things that 99 per cent of the time it doesn't cross anyone's mind.

She ploughs on. 'Well, what happened?'

'He was born early,' I say. 'He had a brain problem, it was bad—'

'And it didn't show up on the scans?'

I understand why she asks. People want, need, the reassurance that this sort of thing doesn't come out of the blue, that there are warnings – I must have felt something, the doctors must have seen something.

'No.'

'Goodness,' she says. 'I am sorry.'

Neither of us know what to say next. I cling to Finn, who's pointing at the calendar on her desk. It's a modern version of a traditional design, in plastic rather than wood, with buttons to press to change the date.

'Well ...' she gives an awkward half-chuckle '... we'd best get on with the rest of the check.'

She takes my blood pressure, which she has to repeat – I'm not surprised, my heart is racing – then weighs me.

'Well, your weight is good.' She smiles up at me and I smile weakly back. My silver lining?

'Next, contraception.' The awkward chuckle again. 'I suppose you don't really need that right now.'

273

I'm about to say I'd had a coil fitted to help prevent scarring when my retained placenta had been removed and I supposed that would work as contraception if the need arose, when she suddenly hits on something that makes her eyes brighten.

'Have you thought about having another baby?'

She beams at me encouragingly, as though she might have found the answer.

I wonder if she thinks that would fix everything – a simple replacement? Erase the pain, erase Grey.

I start to cry and mumble something about needing to wait, the C-section, not knowing when I'll be ready ...

Finn is looking up at me, wide-eyed. 'Mama? Mama?'

I hate that this tiny person has learnt about my deep sadness before he can even say 'cry'. I clasp his little arms and lift him onto my lap. 'Mumma's OK,' I say. 'Mumma just misses Grey.'

'G-ey, G-ey,' Finn repeats, 'tars, tars,' and we smile at each other.

'What's that?' The nurse is looking puzzled.

'Grey is his brother's name. We say goodnight to him in the stars.'

She looks away.

'Right, injection,' she says. Territory she can navigate.

I will remember this jab more than any of Finn's others. As the needle slides into his little leg he looks straight at me, not even flinching. I look at his face, bracing myself for the delayed scream, but as the nurse depresses the syringe he continues to look at me. She takes it out and covers the little spot of blood with a plaster. Still no reaction, not even a whimper. I know that they can miss a nerve by chance, but right now I feel like it's a message from Grey – no more pain today, Mumma.

Categorising my motherhood is confusing. There is a curious societal need to put people – particularly mothers – into boxes. Working mother, stay-at-home mother, routine mother, baby-led mother, breastfeeding mother, bottle-feeding mother, first-time mother, mother of two, mother of three, twin mother ... The boxes have never seemed much use to me. And without Grey, nothing makes sense. Where do I belong? Which mother am I?

This confusion is the strangest thing I have discovered about grief. The baffling lack of direction. Terms like 'journey' or 'path' imply a sense of purpose, an upwards trajectory. I've pictured it as a tunnel with light at the end. It is dark here, but it will gradually become illuminated; all I need do is walk towards it. In reality, it's a lot messier than that. Topsy-turvy. There is no tunnel, I can't find a path. I wonder if perhaps it's one I'll look back on and see, understand, but it's not marked and there are no maps. The Jungian psychotherapist Dr Robin Royston talks about the goat track, a meandering path to the top of a mountain. It twists and turns, at times it goes backwards, or seems to have no direction; some stretches are treacherous, seemingly impossible to navigate. But the goats trust it.

My mind seesaws and somersaults. Some days I think of all the things Grey will miss and all the things we will. A whole parade that stretches into infinity. Sometimes the grief is so powerful, I can't allow it access to me. I find my inner voice repeating, again and again, the reasons he couldn't stay. As if by converting them into some kind of mantra, I will somehow make sense of it. And then I think of what we had, the twenty-one precious days of him.

33

14 January

Pieces of life are sliding back into place. Our new normal. Mike has gone back to work. Today Finn will go back to Lorraine's full time. I am excited for him, to get back into his routine, to spend time with his friends. And nervous, for me. Scared of the empty days. Or all the empty spaces? Perhaps a little of both. It's the space in my mind that scares me most; the time to think. Though I know it is important to allow myself to sit quietly with my sadness, to let it in, the prospect terrifies me.

I drop Finn and walk home. I am still on maternity leave and I have a vague plan to continue with the novel I started years ago. To use the time Grey has given me to do something I really want to do. The opening door collides with a pile of post. Each day more letters land on the mat; we've never had so many. Sealed-up love from all corners of the world. I think of times I've known someone who's lost someone and felt I should write, then talked myself out of it; it's intrusive, what can I add, what do I say?

Each letter I open and read is a little balm to my soul. Each time I see Grey's name written down I feel my heart leap with his presence. I vow always to write, from now on. I open the first in the stack. It's from an old friend of my mum's. Her only son died tragically in his early twenties. 'Keep all the letters,' she writes. 'I re-read mine all the time; I re-read yours today, before writing.' I know I will, every one. 'Forgive anyone who says an odd thing, they don't mean it.' I mull this over. Because people do say odd things. And with skin several layers thinner now, it hurts. I wonder how many times in my life I will repeat her wise words to myself.

The doorbell rings. It's a cheery man in a high-vis jacket. Of course, my last batch of milk is being collected today. I take him to the freezer and together we transfer the little frozen bottles into his cool bag. They just fit. He fills the top with ice packs as I sign the paperwork, then he hefts the bag onto his shoulder and heads back to his bike. As the lock clicks I feel a mix of emotions wash over me. The last of Grey's milk has gone. And it has gone to help babies like him. Tiny helpless beings, here too soon.

As I leave the house to collect Finn from Lorraine's, my phone rings; it's Jo from Hearts, the milk bank. She thanks me for my final batch.

'One batch has already gone for pasteurising, and there are other bottles waiting.' She pauses. 'Do you know where Grey's milk has gone?'

'I don't,' I reply. 'I'd love to.'

A batch has gone to community mothers – women who've had double mastectomies or may be undergoing cancer treatment, or both. Under data protection she can't share further details of who or where they are, but says they're incredibly grateful. Some of the more recent bottles have been taken that morning to NICUs. She can't tell me which, as usually only one or two babies are on donor milk and I might be able to track them down.

'We cover all of Kent,' she says. Then, 'And, of course, all the London hospitals.'

There's something in her pause that tells me she knows where Grey was born; the drivers collected one of my batches from there, and the bank regularly supplies his NICU with milk. I wonder if some of his milk has gone back there. To a tiny preemie baby in our NICU, in his incubator by the window overlooking the car park where the sun shines through the skeleton trees each morning.

Jo explains that, once pasteurised, the milk is measured into 50ml bottles, and then sent off to NICUs in litre batches. One 50ml bottle will feed a twenty-three- or twenty-four-weeker for about two days. I can picture the little bottles. I hand-expressed colostrum into them in the first days of Grey's life.

'I think you've given us about thirty or forty litres, Georgie,' she says. 'Grey's milk will make a difference to a lot of babies.'

I can see them, curled into incubators, padded with little cocoons printed with hearts, covered with wires. Mums, dads, brothers, sisters, cousins, grannies, grandpas, uncles, aunts, shocked and discombobulated, catapulted into a strange new world. I hope it helps, just a little. My milk, with love, Grey.

As I hang up, I realise I'm going to be late for Finn and speed up.

A man walking towards me points and grins. 'You've forgotten the baby!'

For a split second my stomach lurches and my face falls.

He looks confused and points again. 'Empty buggy ...'

Of course, the empty buggy. Finn's empty buggy. I force a smile as he moves on, looking perplexed.

Finn burbles to me on our way home. He's starting to put words together. I'm looking down at him, so I don't see the approaching buggy until we're almost alongside one another. I look up to see a familiar woman wrapped in a long black Puffa, her blunt blond hair flicking out from under a pale pink beanie. I don't know her name, but she lives on our road and has a daughter a little older than Finny. We were pregnant at the same time; we'd smile at each other as we both carried increasingly unwieldy bumps to the morning drop off. Now her Bugaboo Bee has changed to the bassinet and has a buggy board on the back. Our buggy board is still in its box. It was the first thing I bought when we started rounding up our second-baby kit, celebrating Finny becoming a big brother.

I returned cots, sheets, Moses basket covers, but I didn't

return the buggy board. It was new, I could have done. Except I couldn't. It's the one thing that I can't bring myself to send back. So we put it in the attic. I wonder if it represents a part of my grief that I can't look in the eye. That as well as losing our son, Finn has lost his little brother. Only seventeen months apart, they should have been thick as thieves. One blond head, one dark, bent together, making mischief. Where our first baby was about us, a second baby felt so much about Finn, about the two of them, their relationship. They would outlive us. Their bond, with all the twists and turns of sibling love, would start now and continue long after we're gone. That he's had this snatched away tortures me.

She's gone in seconds, off to collect her daughter, then home for double bath time. I push Finn home to our own bath time. He splashes around, stacking his cups, flipping on to his tummy, relishing every moment as he always does. His laughter is a tonic, but the place where a bath seat should be yawns beside him.

19 January

It's Grey's due date and Nena's homecoming. The two events have become intertwined. All of my family are at my parents' house in Somerset to meet her. As we drove over Bodmin Moor last night, the sun was setting, fiery red. I watched it as the horizon rippled past the window. 'Night-night, Greyman.'

Now we're on our way back, the soft reddish bundle asleep at my feet. We spend the rest of the day in Somerset, then after Finn's bath, pack him and our new addition into the car. Miraculously, they both sleep all the way to London.

We transfer Finn straight to his cot, without a peep. Then turn our attention to Nena. Her puppy crate is set up in the kitchen. We've been warned she will cry in the night. Camps seem to be divided on whether we ignore her, or go to her. 'It's hard to hear the crying,' warns one friend, 'but they all do it for the first few nights. With luck, she'll settle in quickly.'

We set her up with newspaper and puppy pads, stuff socks to lay alongside her in case she misses her brothers and sisters, leave a night light on and the radio down low. Then head up to bed.

She whines when we leave her, but it doesn't last long: exhaustion takes over and she's quiet by the time we've brushed our teeth. When I wake in the night the sound of soft crying takes me by surprise. As I sit up, foggy with sleep, I realise it's Nena. Then I feel a dampness across my pyjama top and look down. The room isn't hot, could I have spilled something?

Milk. It's milk. The crying. Nena's crying. Now I know I can't leave her. I creep downstairs, take her out into the garden for a wee, then stand by her cage in the half-light, cradling the sleek bundle into my neck. Willing her to help soften the edges of the aching hole that I know she can never fill.

The lack of Grey is everywhere – answering the doorbell empty-handed, the solo, hands-free walk back from dropping Finn, uninterrupted dinners. The quiet days, the silent nights. I yearn for the pandemonium that I'm sure comes when you bring a second child home. I ache for my tired eyes to be because I woke too many times in the night to settle Grey. The time I have, now there is no him, echoes in front of me. I try to fill it – with Nena, with yoga, with baking, with writing, with decorating the house. Wonderful things. But things that will never be Grey.

23 January

Unbearable pain sometimes ambushes me without warning. From relative balance, to agony. Today I manage to collect Finn, chat to Lorraine, say hello to the other parents. To bath him, read him a story, snuggle him into his bed with

Rab – and Fox and Octa, the other members of his bedtime trio. To kiss his nose, smooth his little blond mop. While keeping it wrapped up tightly inside me.

Some sadness I can let him see, must let him see, but not this sadness. Sometimes, like today, it is wretched, raw, ugly. I want to throw something, to break something.

When Mike comes home I'm sitting on the sofa, teeth gritted, staring straight ahead, clinging to Grey's book. He prises it gently from my hands and tucks it back into the open memory box. He kneels in front of me, wraps his arms around me. I feel a wall inside me collapse and then I hear screaming.

And realise it's me.

'I don't feel brave,' I scream into his shoulder. 'I don't want to be brave. Or strong. I don't want to have to learn how to cope with this. I don't want this to be our life. I don't want to be the mother whose baby died. I just want him back I want my baby back I just want Grey back.'

The scream turns into a broken sob. 'I want him back. I want him back. I want him back . . .'

'I know, G,' he whispers. 'I know . . . I know . . .' as though he's shushing a very small child gently to sleep.

'I want our baby, MG, why isn't he here? He should be here. We shouldn't have let him go.'

'We had to, G, remember? That was our deal. *We* take the pain.'

I feel some of the anger gradually subside as he rubs my back, leaving in its wake a sadness so deep that no part of me can escape it. I whisper, 'I don't know if I can do this, MG. Sometimes I don't think I can do it.' Sometimes I'm so blinded by the gaping void Grey has left that I can't see any way out.

'You can; we can. We must. We put one foot in front of the other and carry on. There was no other way this could be, G, no other way.'

I know he's right, but it still feels so wrong.

25 January

'Would you like to hold her?'

We are visiting friends with a little girl born a few weeks before Grey. They have a son about Finn's age and a puppy for Nena to meet. As we drove here, I wondered how I'd feel. Now, as I look down at the tiny cherubic face, I know the answer. 'Yes.' I really would.

She cries a little as she's momentarily moved away from her constant source of warmth, comfort, love. As I take her, she wriggles, then gets cosy and looks up at me. Her eyes are that wonderful, innocent combination of quizzical and open; her face breaks into a smile. As I cradle her in my arms, bouncing lightly from one foot to the other, the warmth spreads through me. Minutes later she is asleep.

And when it's time to go home, I realise I am reluctant to relinquish this tiny, warm, sleeping baby.

29 January

Our NICU follow-up has been arranged for the end of January. Mike emails Lynn to ask if we can collect Grey's ashes when we are down to visit the hospital. In the day before she replies, I wonder if there was nothing left of our boy. I remember that when we went through the paperwork for his funeral, there was a form we signed that warned us we may not receive any ashes. In rare cases, it explained, the furnace is so hot and the body so small that nothing is left behind. I wonder if this has happened to Grey. If his little body had evaporated into thin air, leaving no tangible trace.

We ring the bell, and a dark-haired woman who looks not dissimilar to Lynn opens the gate and ushers us in. Lynn's on holiday, but she has Grey. She hands me a glossy white bag with rope handles. Inside is a cardboard carton covered with teddies. I clasp it with both hands, then hold it in my lap as we follow the winding roads back to the hospital.

The car park looks the same as the day he was born. The sky a deep blue; here and there white clouds skim across it. We walk in through the main doors and follow the familiar route. Mike squeezes my arm as we wait for the doors to the maternity department to open. I know we both feel apprehensive back here, in Grey's hospital. We follow the corridor, then buzz outside the NICU. In the seconds that we're waiting for Vicky and Gemma at the front desk to let us in, I wonder if this was a mistake, if we should have met somewhere else. Then the doors swing slowly open. As we walk through them the smell, half clinical, half maternal, washes over me and I'm transported straight back to the days of Grey's life. I realise the NICU still feels strangely like home.

We're meeting Dr Chandra. The corridor looks the same as it always did. The same nurses walking in and out of the different nurseries. Some of them wave, come and say hello, ask how we are. Amongst them we spot a particularly familiar face. 'Rebekah!' Mike calls.

She strides down the corridor and wraps each of us in warm hugs. 'You've lost weight,' she says to me, slightly accusingly, pushing me back from her embrace and looking me up and down. 'I hope you're eating.' She always was our mother hen.

I assure her that I am.

Kerry joins us. We haven't seen her since the week before Grey died; she was on holiday for the last week of his life. 'How are you?' she asks.

'We're doing pretty OK,' I say. I realise it's the first time I've said those words and they've rung true. These are NICU nurses, Grey's nurses, they lived his life with us. They know what OK after the NICU means, the complex web of emotions it covers.

We ask after the other babies. Scarlett has gone home, they say, so has Cora, in the last week or so. 'Do you want to come down to the nursery?' Rebekah asks. 'Grey's side is empty at the moment, we're very quiet.'

My stomach turns over. 'I don't think I can,' I say. 'Part of me wants to imagine that Grey's still there, that he'll always be there, in his incubator, by the window.'

She understands.

I can visit him there whenever I want. I can pull up the purple chair, lift him onto my chest, wrap my arms around him and breathe in his smell. If I saw his incubator empty, the sheets washed and folded inside, I'm worried it would break the spell, and I wouldn't be able to get back to him.

34

3 February

'You have the address.'

'The address?'

'For tonight.'

'Tonight?'

Tonight, we are going to our first Sands meeting. They're held fifteen minutes away, I discover, on the first Monday of each month. I'll meet Mike there. He's coming straight from work.

'The Sands meeting? Minna's babysitting ...'

He still looks blank.

'You don't have to come,' I say. I didn't expect him to want to.

'Oh yes, of course, bereaved parents alone together.'

I roll my eyes at the *About a Boy* reference. 'Mike, you can't say things like that.'

'G, it's a joke, to you. I won't say it there. I won't say it to anyone else. I do want to come, I know it will be good. Sometimes you just have to let me say silly things because it's easier for me to not take things seriously.'

I kiss him goodbye and Finn and I wave from the door.

Minna hugs me tightly when she arrives. My mum and her younger brother, Minna's dad, were inseparable growing up, and we've spent a lot of time together, as cousins go; we're pretty close in spite of a ten-year age gap.

I show her the monitor and her supper, then leave her cooing over Nena and head to the car. The route feels familiar and I realise it's round the corner from where I used to take Finn for swimming lessons. The traffic is awful, I'm going to be late. I pull in and call Mike. He tells me it's at a primary school, in the hall; there's plenty of parking.

I can see lights on when I get there, through partially drawn blinds, people sitting in a circle. In my panic I buzz, not realising the door is open. Someone mimes pushing, and I'm in. There's no sign, so I keep on going. 'Sands?' I ask, then notice Mike on the other side of the circle, with a spare place next to him.

No one is speaking, so I creep round, apologising for being late. I take off my coat and hang it over the back of my chair. Mike's voice breaks the silence. 'Hi, G, we've all just introduced ourselves, and then sung a couple of lines from our favourite song.'

I look around, frozen.

A woman to Mike's right speaks before I can. 'We have done nothing of the sort, thank you, Mike.'

Everyone laughs.

I should have known. How long have I been married to this man for?

'Do sit down, Georgie, it's no problem at all, we haven't started yet.'

'I'm guessing that's not the first awkward comment he's made this evening,' I say, 'while I've been cursing the traffic.'

'I've actually been very well behaved,' Mike says.

The woman introduces herself and explains a little about the meeting, how it works. She is a befriender. Sands is entirely run by bereaved parents; everyone I speak to has lost a baby, everyone, in one way or another, knows how this feels. We are not the odd ones out. The comfort in that knowledge mingles with heartache as I look around me. There are three other couples and several women on their own – all these people have lost babies. So many, too many.

7 March

I'm bathing Finn. We're FaceTiming my mum, the phone propped against the towel rail. Mike came home early and he's taken Nena for a walk. Finny is playing the fool, dancing, piling up his cups and chanting. Roaring with laughter as he trickles water over the floor.

Distracted for seconds by our conversation, I fail to notice that he has turned his attention to the mini basketball hoop attached by suction cups to the side of the bath. As I turn back to him I notice he's gripping it with both hands, realise he is pulling. In the split second it takes me to register and lean towards him, to loosen his grip, the suction suddenly gives way, flinging him backwards, and there's an echoing, sickening thunk as the back of his head hits the enamel.

I reach towards him, whisk him upright, then to his feet, gripping him under his arms. He is silent, his eyes seem to loll in his head, he takes a clumsy step forward.

'George? George . . .?'

My phone has fallen to the floor.

I lift Finn into my arms, gripping him tightly, peering at his face. 'Finny, Finny, are you OK?'

Every part of me vibrates with panic. He looks up at me, dazed.

'Mummy, he's banged his head, he's confused, Mike isn't here, I need to call him, I'll call you back.'

I hang up the phone and immediately dial Mike. By the time he answers I'm hysterical. 'It's Finn . . . he's banged his head . . . he's confused . . . he's not OK, MG.'

'I'm on my way, G, I'm on my way.'

I look back down at Finn. 'Are you OK? Are you OK?'

He gazes up at me lazily, still clasped to my chest.

As I dial 111 my brain scrambles. I remember the time we had to take him to A&E. There was a little girl who'd banged her head in the bath; the doctors were talking about a brain MRI. They were worried.

What if you die? I think as I search his face. *What if you die?*

I'll—

The terrifying thought is cut short by the medic asking for my little boy's name, for my name. He calmly runs through the risk assessment. Finn hasn't been sick, he hasn't lost consciousness. As the checklist continues, Finn feels firmer in my arms; he looks me straight in the eye, his little hand grips my arm. 'Fine,' he says suddenly, as I look down. 'Fine, Mummy.'

I hear the key in the lock and then Mike's feet on the stairs. Finn wriggles off my lap and walks into the hall.

'Daddy . . .'

I follow him, still clutching the phone.

'Our advice is to take him to a primary healthcare centre to be checked,' the voice says, then runs through a list of local hospitals and out-of-hours GPs.

Mike is sitting on the step at the end of the hall, one arm around Finn. 'Look at me, Finny,' he's saying. 'Who am I?'

'Daddy!' Finn squeals.

I thank the man at 111 and hang up. 'We have to take him to hospital, to A&E. He needs to be checked.' I can hear the panic in my voice.

'He seems fine, G,' Mike says softly. 'What happened?'

'He banged his head, he was confused, I thought, I thought . . .' Tears sting my eyes as I lean back against the wall and slide to the floor.

'G, look at him, he's OK.'

'I thought it was really bad, MG. There was a really bad clunk, and that little girl in A&E—'

'She was sick, G. She was being really sick; has he been sick?'

I shake my head.

'I wasn't here, I don't know what happened, but he really seems normal to me, G. But if you think he needs to go to hospital, we will go, now.'

I don't know. 'I was so scared,' I say. 'He went so . . . strange.'

'Well, it would have been a big shock for him, G.'

'And he didn't cry,' I say. 'It's bad to not cry.'

'Maybe the bump sounded worse than it was – that bath is crap. Maybe the clunk was the crappy bath. Why don't I get him ready for bed, read him a story? He can have some water, we'll see how he is then.'

I look at Finn, his little arm wrapped around Mike's neck, his cheeks flushed from the warm bath, his damp hair in spikes. He grins at me. Mike scoops him up and carries him into his bedroom. I stay in the hall, tipping my head back against the wall.

How do I do this? How do I not wrap him in cotton wool? How do I allow him to have a childhood? To play in the bath, climb on the climbing frame, walk along the wall without my hand to guide him? The fear paralyses me.

I can feel so clearly what it might be like to lose him. Sometimes the imagining of it haunts me.

I mustn't allow my fear to control me. The days will go by. He will grow, turn twelve, sixteen, eighteen. He'll leave home, he'll build his own life. The thought simultaneously delights and terrifies me. I have a baffling inability to reconcile that I must let him live, because he can, because he is living, with the fear of the risks that come with living.

I am untethered from my life before Grey. Then, I was being pulled along by my plan, my direction. Our little boy's death has cut the rope, my boat has capsized and I'm adrift. In some ways, it is terrifying – the world is upside down and the waves threaten to pull me under as the currents take me far from where I thought I was going.

But then there are times of deep calm. Sometimes I move backwards, sometimes I move forward. I hope, in time, I will land on beautiful, undiscovered shores. I realise I've always been so intent on my destination. Now I have no choice but to look at the view.

22 March

They've let me doze while the radio plays from an earlier alarm. I hear giggling on the stairs, then Finn trundles into the room, a package clasped in his hands. 'Happy day,' he says to me, plonking the present on the bed. 'Happy *Mother's* Day,' Mike adds, kissing me. I like Finn's version.

'Open IT,' says Finn, stamping up and down, then reaching for the present.

'You come and help me,' I say, lifting him to sit beside me.

We unwrap it together. 'Oh WOW,' Finn says as he opens the package. 'Seaside, *look* Mumma.'

It's Whitstable; the wooden sea defences, the sun shining down on the shale beach, the sea twinkling. I took the picture the day before Grey's funeral. I feel hot tears sting at my eyes as a wave of sadness washes over me. Will it always be like this? I realise I hope it will. I need it to be.

In some ways, my relationship with grief is like my motherhood. The early days with Finn were all-consuming, occupying every waking moment, and most sleeping ones. Like grief, he filled my arms, my mind, my heart, my head, leaving no space for very much else. With time, nurturing, love, tears, he could sit alone for a few moments, then he crawled, then he learnt to walk beside me, hand in hand. And just as he is beginning to loosen his grip on my hand, I know I'll never be ready to let go. That I need him, right here beside me, for always.

Grief doesn't always say sad things or bad things. It's not always screaming that Grey isn't here. Sometimes it whispers that I am, that Finn is, that MG is. That we survived. It tells me to stop and look at the shafts of light emerging from behind the cloud. It reminds me to pause with Finn on the walk home from nursery and look for trains, because really, there is nowhere else I need to be. It shows me butterflies in the rambling Victorian cemetery where we walk Nena, and sun glistening on the spiders' webs that cover the grass on my morning walks over the common.

It tells me to look for light, to look for love and to hold on to it with both hands. I can't count the number of times in a day I tell Finn that I love him. And each night before I go to sleep I creep into his room, lay my hands on his little back and feel the reassuring inhale, exhale of his breath, his life.

A wise friend told my mum when her dad died that grief is the price we pay for love. I have never forgotten it. But now I see it a little differently. Grief doesn't come after love. Grief *is* love. The very deepest love. It is love that has reshaped my world, love that has peeled back the layers of me. It's love in a guise I'd never have chosen, love I will carry with me for all of my life. And love that tells me with absolute certainty that no matter how far I come, I'd go right back to the beginning of Grey's life and I'd live it all again, live every single second of pain as if for the first time, if I could hold him one more time.

Mike wraps an arm around us. 'I wish he was here,' I whisper.

'He is,' Mike says.

35

30 March

The world has changed, and not just for us. We're in the grip of the coronavirus and the whole country has been in lock-down for a week.

An email arrives from our London hospital. I'm momentarily confused. A consultant has reviewed our scans and is wondering if I have time to discuss them. She suggests she calls tomorrow. It's one of the final pieces of the puzzle, in some senses. Checking nothing was missed. It's not something I've pushed for; it's never crossed my mind that the scans will tell us anything – they didn't six months ago.

I type a quick response – I'm around tomorrow, always around these days, in fact, I can speak to her then. I don't think about it much once I've pressed *send*, except to ask Mike if he has any specific questions for her. Twenty-four hours pass, then my phone rings five minutes after I've put Finn down for his afternoon sleep, at precisely the time I've requested.

The consultant introduces herself and explains that she's known about our case for some time, that the delay in calling has been down to an outbreak of coronavirus at the hospital, including her. She is feeling better now, thank you.

'I've reviewed your scans,' she says. 'Let me first explain a bit to you about the brain. It's developing all the time, and there are only certain things we can see on ultrasound. Still, we take a lot of measurements.'

I am murmuring agreement. 'I remember that scan so clearly; it was a morning, Finn had had to come with us. It took hours – they were running a research study and we'd had to see the consultant for something that turned out to be nothing.'

I hear her take a breath.

'The sonographers are often doctors. They spend two years with us to learn sonography very, very carefully. They're often very experienced already, like the doctor you had. A doctor and a sonographer, very experienced.' She pauses. 'I don't know what happened, a bad day ...'

I hear her take another breath, a longer one this time.

'But the fact is, something was missed. A discrepancy in a measurement.'

I feel my whole body lurch. Not once had anything like this crossed my mind.

She continues, choosing her words extremely carefully. 'One of the measurements we take can be an indication of one of the conditions that your baby, your son, suffered. The missing corpus callosum. It should have been noticed. It would have put you on a path for further investigations; you should have had a more detailed brain ultrasound, more checks.'

She pauses, allowing this information to sink in.

'We should have been monitoring you more carefully, seeing how your baby's brain developed.'

She pauses again.

'We missed an opportunity to tell you bad news sooner.'

They made a mistake.

In all my imaginings, in all my attempts to untangle what happened, I didn't expect this.

'Please can I ask ...?' I swallow. 'I'm sorry to cry. But I want to ask, and this isn't about placing any blame, but do you mean that it was a mistake?' I pause. 'I just need to be clear. I understand that people make mistakes. I'm not angry.'

It's true. I realised as soon as she told me. I'm shocked, but I feel no anger. People make mistakes, even doctors.

'Thank you for saying that,' she replies. 'We missed something that should have been seen. It was a mistake.'

I digest her words. I should have had many more scans, she explains, many more investigations; they should have been keeping track of Grey's development week by week. Had this measurement not been missed, that's the path we would have taken.

We talk a little more. She shares a few more details, I ask a few other questions. Then I thank her and hang up.

I sit on the sofa in our sitting room, looking down at the phone in my hand. I feel a kind of stillness. A calm. My tears are drying in the corners of my eyes. I realise they are tears for Grey, rather than for what I have discovered. My overriding emotion is relief.

Would anything have been better, had they found this? I think it would have been worse. Even with extra scans, there wouldn't have been immediate answers. We would have had weeks of worry. Faced impossible decisions with inadequate information. Whichever way you cut this, there was never an easy way. Each path is paved with pain.

In Japanese art, breaks and mends are part of an object's history, lacquered back together with precious metals; *kintsugi*, or golden repair. The cracks are always visible. The object takes on a new kind of beauty. I've always loved the delicate, shimmering web the joins spin across ceramics.

I wonder if a heart is the same. When it shatters into fragments, though broken, light can pour in, and that light becomes the lacquer, helping the pieces re-form into something bigger, stronger. My life is filled with precious lacquer – Finn, Mike, our families, our friends, the rising sun, the sound of the sea. Some pieces can't be replaced: those went with Grey, wrapped all around him. But now, if I were to look closely at the jagged edges of my fragmented heart, I'm sure I'd see that some spaces now shine with gold. And that is what he left for me.

Grey lived. For three weeks.

For twelve days, we lived with hope, with no idea of what

was to come. He felt our love, felt our heartbeats, and we felt his. He saw the sun and felt the fresh air on his cheeks. We held him, felt his little hands clasp ours, saw his eyes flicker open, his legs kick. He met his family, he held his brother's hands.

He was looked after by strangers who became family, and saw more kindness, more love, in twenty-one days than some might see in a lifetime. For his brief moments in this world, he experienced all of the very best things it can offer.

And then he died in the arms of a mother who loves him more than her inadequate words can ever begin to express. In turn, he filled our lives with love, clarity, perspective. We were lucky, we are lucky. I can never regret that. So I see, really, it was the best mistake anyone could ever have made.

Afterword

When I entered my strange stretch of maternity leave, without Grey, in January 2020, I planned to finish the novel I'd begun years ago. Its central theme was motherhood. As I wrote, I found myself unconsciously writing myself, writing Grey, into every character. In a few short days I'd mangled it entirely.

I put aside my laptop and returned to *The Salt Path*. Raynor Winn's quiet, melodic description of her and her husband's epic coastal walk soothed me in the early hours when my broken heart refused to allow my grieving mind to take refuge in sleep.

I heard a voice in the middle of the night. 'Grey's story.'

I needed to write Grey's story. I suddenly knew I wouldn't be able to write anything else until I did.

Mol and Sama were the only friends I told. Both encouraged me to start writing. Then, on the day I sat down at my laptop, a strange thing happened. The letterbox clattered and there was a thud. Heavier than the sound of the wonderful letters we received every day for weeks. I walked into the hall to see a small package lying on the mat. I picked it up and turned it over in my hands. An Australian postage stamp, writing I didn't recognise. Inside was a book. An old friend of my dad's lost her son, Freddie, to cot death when he was ten weeks old, almost thirty years ago. The book was their story. 'It helped me,' she wrote on the title page, 'to roll around in my grief.'

I began to write.

First, I wrote anything and everything that came into my mind. I kept those early drafts, jumbled thoughts; missing him, loving him, life without him, all the things he would know if he were here – how much his brother has grown, how he's now chatting, and running, and turning into a little boy. The pain in those early notes is so fresh, I can hardly bear to reread them. But Grey is fresh too. Back then I could still conjure his smell in a split second. So for all the agony in my words, I envy that version of me, because I was still so close to him.

I remembered every single second of our life together. I could replay every moment to myself. Gradually I transferred those memories into these pages. Because, even when we will them not to, memories fade. I don't think I'll ever forget his face, or how it felt to clutch his tiny body against mine. But already the vividness of his smell is fading. And there's no way for me to hold on to it – you can't write a smell.

I am lucky to have grown up knowing the priceless value of language. That words are more precious than a prized gemstone. But it was not until I wrote Grey's story that I truly understood their power and their magic. Every time I reread these words, Grey's story, our story – our life – I will the outcome to be different. I wish I could rewrite the quiet room meetings. Change the diagnosis, the prognosis, write Grey back into the world. I know I can't. But, as I read, he returns to me.

A few months after Grey died, I discovered that in pregnancy, cells from the fetus cross the placenta into the mother's body, where they can become part of her tissue. So I carry my son with me for ever.

In attempting to describe the months after Grey died I have condensed hours, days, months, into these pages of text. I could never write all the conversations with Mike, with our families, our friends, my therapist, the wonderful women I have met, the never-ending support and love and the hours of thinking, crying, shouting, reading, which allowed me to arrive at some of the thoughts I have articulated within these pages.

My narrative draws to a close after my call with the

consultant who reviewed our twenty-week scan. The real story, of course, will never end. There will never be a day when I wake up and it is done. I will love him, grieve for him and celebrate his life for the whole of mine.

On the first anniversary of Grey's death, 8 December 2020, Mike planned a Kent marathon, running to the beach in Whitstable. The first, he hoped, of many. Covid lockdown rules intervened, and instead he plotted a route through London. Finn and I met him on the freezing finish line in a park near our home in south-east London.

Later that evening, as I lifted Finn to kiss him goodnight, he turned to me and said softly, 'Daddy ran with Grey, Mummy.'

'He did, he ran for Grey – you're right, Finny.'

He thought for a minute.

'I miss Grey,' he said, curling a strand of my hair around his forefinger.

'So do I, Finny, so do I.'

He was quiet again.

'But one day I will run too, with Grey. And you and Nena and Daddy.'

He looked up at me.

'One day we will all run with Grey,' he finished, his huge, innocent eyes utterly unaware of the poignancy and wisdom in his words.

I swallowed the tears that caught in the back of my throat.

'We will, Finny, you're right. One day we will all run with Grey.'

I loved the boy with the utmost love of which my soul is capable, and he is taken from me – yet in the agony of my spirit in surrendering such a treasure I feel a thousand times richer than if I had never possessed it.

William Wordsworth

Acknowledgements

If not for many people, this book would not exist.

Richard Beswick, my brilliant and intuitive editor, who believed in my words and turned Grey's story into a book. Zoë Gullen – surely the most exacting copy editor, I am in awe of what you do and endlessly grateful you worked your magic on *If Not for You*. Laura Sherlock, my sensitive, lovely, inimitable publicist, the brilliant Emily Moran, Duncan Spilling for the most beautiful cover, and the rest of the fantastic Little, Brown team.

Alice, my excellent agent, for your endless optimism and sage advice. Niamh, and everyone at the Soho Agency, supporting me behind the scenes. My astonishingly distinguished early readers, thank you for sharing your collective wealth of incredible insight. Hannah, thank you for your expert medical eye.

My wonderful physio, Emma @thephysiomum, who put me back together again, mentally as well as physically, after Grey died. Janet, my kind, funny, wise, miracle midwife who held my hand through my third pregnancy and delivered Finn and Grey's little brother, Bear, safely into the world. Mr Dooley, for the huge role you played in bringing me my three little boys. My therapist, for the many hours of support.

Grey's medical team, who are truly heroes. Having a baby in the NICU is like going through hell, in heaven – and that is because of you. Thank you will never come close to being enough.

Mol and Sama, for believing in this book before I wrote a single word, for reading early drafts, always being on the end of the phone, and, of course, for everything else. My

303

brilliant book club girls for your perceptive thoughts on titles and covers. My – our – other dear, dear friends, how very fortunate we are that there are too many to name each of you here, but you know who you are, we are so lucky to have you. I love you very much.

The women I have met who walk through life without their babies. I wish we'd never had to find each other but I'm so grateful that we did. To everyone who has told me their story since writing this book, it is a privilege to know about your precious children.

Sally, Malcolm, Zo, Jon, Elsie and Wilf, the very best in-laws I could hope for. My brilliant siblings, Nick, Loula, Ella, I have not a clue what I'd do without you. Wonderful Nat, Gus and Josh – what a line-up. And superstar Sam, your wisdom is so far beyond your years.

My parents, who have filled every second of my life with love. My truly exceptional mumma, who is always there – even if it's a step back from a shadowy window – you are a wonder, I hope when I grow up I'll be even half the mother you are; and my darling daddy, who I've always known will do anything for me.

GV, my amazing grandmother, I miss you and wish I could have told you about this book – I know what you'd have said: 'Here's tae us.' Here's to you – look after my boy.

Finn, Grey and Bear, for the incredible privilege of being your mother.

And last, but never least – MG – if not for you, my sky would truly fall.

We have launched the Love Grey Foundation in Grey's memory: lovegrey.org

Charities offering support to families affected by prematurity, baby loss and rare diagnoses – this is by no means a complete list.

Aching Arms
achingarms.co.uk
Supports those who have suffered the loss of a baby during pregnancy, at birth or soon after.

Arc
arc-uk.org
Helps parents and healthcare professionals through antenatal screening and its consequences.

Bliss
bliss.org.uk
Aims to give every baby born premature or sick the best chance of survival and quality of life.

Borne
borne.org.uk
Researches the causes of premature birth in order to save lives.

Child Bereavement UK
childbereavementuk.org
Supports families and educates professionals when a baby

or child of any age dies or is dying, or when a child is facing bereavement.

Group B Strep Support
gbss.org.uk
Provides information and support to families, including parents suffering what can be devastating consequences of GBS infection.

The Lullaby Trust
lullabytrust.org.uk
Provides information and research into safer sleep for babies, supports families.

Mama Academy
mamaacademy.org.uk
Empowers all maternity professionals and expectant parents on stillbirth prevention methods to help more babies arrive safely.

The Mariposa Trust
mariposatrust.org
Supports those affected by baby loss and bereavement.

The Miscarriage Association
miscarriageassociation.org.uk
Supports those affected by miscarriage, molar pregnancy or ectopic pregnancy.

Our Missing Peace
ourmissingpeace.org
Helps all who have been affected by the death of a child.

Petals
petalscharity.org
Provides specialist counselling after baby loss.

Sands
sands.org.uk
Provides support for anyone affected by the death of a baby,
improves the care bereaved parents receive, works to create a
world where fewer babies die.

Saying Goodbye
sayinggoodbye.org
Provides comprehensive information, advice, support to
anyone who has suffered the loss of a baby, at any stage of
pregnancy.

Teddy's Wish
teddyswish.org
Funds research into the causes of baby loss and provides hope
for grieving families.

Tommy's
tommys.org
Provides support and funds research into stillbirth, premature
birth and miscarriage.

Unique
rarechromo.org
Supports and informs families living with a Rare
Chromosome Disorder.

Credits